The Aquarian Message

The Aquarian Message

Gnostic Kabbalah, Tantra, and Tarot in the Revelation of St. John

Samael Aun Weor

GLORIAN
2008

PUBLISHERS NOTE: When seen in this book, the symbol † indicates additional information available in the Glossary. A more extensive glossary is online at *gnosticteachings.org*

The Aquarian Message
A Glorian Book / 2008

Originally published as "El Mensaje de Acuario," 1960.

This Edition © 2008 Glorian Publishing

ISBN 978-1-934206-31-7

Glorian Publishing (formerly Thelema Press) is a non-profit organization delivering to humanity the teachings of Samael Aun Weor. All proceeds go to further the distribution of these books. For more information, visit our website.

gnosticbooks.org
gnosticteachings.org
gnosticradio.org
gnosticschool.org
gnosticstore.org
gnosticvideos.org

Contents

Prologue 1
Preface 23
Introduction 25

Part One: The Son of Man

Chapter 1: The Son of Man 33
Chapter 2: The First Begotten of the Dead 39
Chapter 3: The Seven Churches 43
Chapter 4: The Serpent of Metal 49
Chapter 5: Internal Meditation 53
Chapter 6: The Church of Ephesus 57
Chapter 7: The Church of Smyrna 59
Chapter 8: The Church of Pergamos 63
Chapter 9: The Church of Thyatira 67
Chapter 10: The Church of Sardis 75
Chapter 11: The Church of Philadelphia 83
Chapter 12: The Church of Laodicea 87
Chapter 13: The Jinn States 93
    Practice 95
The Aquarian Message 101

Part Two: The Sealed Book 101

Chapter 14: The Throne in Heaven 103
Chapter 15: The Sealed Book 107
Chapter 16: The Seven Seals 113
Chapter 17: The Four Angels 119
Chapter 18: The Seventh Seal 129
Chapter 19: The Fifth Angel 137
Chapter 20: The Sixth Trumpet 141

Chapter 21: The Seventh Trumpet 145
Chapter 22: The Two Witnesses 151
Chapter 23: The Woman and the Dragon 159
Chapter 24: The Two Beasts 169
Chapter 25: The Lamb in Sion 177
Chapter 26: The Seven Angels with the Seven Vials 185
Chapter 27: The Seven Vials Are Poured 189
Chapter 28: The Whore and the Beast 203
Chapter 29: Babylon is Fallen 207
Chapter 30: The Maitreya Buddha 213
Chapter 31: The Millennium and the Judgement 229

Part Three: The New Jerusalem

Chapter 32: The New Jerusalem 235
Chapter 33: The Pure River of the Waters of Life 253
    Practices for the Imagination 253
    Practice 255
Epilogue: About Alcyone 263
Glossary 279
Index 297

Prologue

The sidereal year exists as well as the terrestrial year. We understand the terrestrial year as being the movement of the earth around the sun during a period of 365 days. The terrestrial year has four seasons: spring, summer, autumn, and winter. The sidereal year also exists, lasting for approximately 25,968 terrestrial years.

Our solar system travels around the zodiacal belt and during its voyage many unusual things happen. The solar system returns to its original point of departure after completing its voyage around the zodiacal belt, thus concluding the sidereal year.

The sidereal year also has its four seasons: spring, summer, autumn, and winter. Spring is the Age of Gold, summer is the Age of Silver, autumn is the Age of Copper, and winter is the Age of Iron.

Each Root Race endures a complete voyage of the solar system around the zodiacal belt.

Our present Root Race, the Aryan Race† that populates the five continents of the world, was born after the universal flood† and will last throughout the era of Aquarius, which we are presently in. The voyage of our solar system began in Aquarius and will end in Aquarius.

Before this present voyage, our solar system completed another voyage. Another Root Race existed during that previous voyage, that is to say, during that previous sidereal year. I would like to emphatically refer to the Root Race that inhabited the lost continent of Atlantis.

The Atlanteans, who had bodies that were three meters in stature, created a very powerful civilization. The Atlantean continent was immense; it extended from the south to the north, from the austral region to the septentrional. This Atlantean Root Race had its four seasons, or ages.

During their spring or Golden Age, borders and passports were unnecessary. Frontiers did not exist, and everywhere there was love among humanity. Innocence reigned upon the face of the Earth. One who knew how to play the lyre could shake the universe with its melodies. At that time, the lyre had yet to be smashed into pieces by falling upon the floor of the temple. This was because the Solar Dynasties were still governing.

As the Age of Silver arrived, everything from the Golden Age diminished. However, human beings were still in communication with the ineffable beings who are known in Christianity as Angels, Archangels, Principates, Thrones, etc.

When the Age of Copper arrived, the radiant splendors of the Golden and Silver Ages became dark. The same splendors of the past did not exist. People started to establish frontiers, wars were begun, hatred was born, as well as selfishness, envy, greed, etc.

Finally the Age of Iron, the Black Age, arrived.

Obviously, the Age of Copper was the autumn, and the Age of Iron was the winter of the Atlantean Root Race.

During the Age of Iron, the Atlanteans developed a very powerful, materialistic science. They built atomic rockets in order to travel to the moon. In fact, these Atlantean ships were so powerful that they were able to travel to Mercury, Venus, Mars, and generally to all of the planets of our solar system.

Atlantean medical science went far beyond our modern medical science. The Atlanteans were experts in transplants. They transplanted not only visceras like hearts, kidneys, pancreas, etc., but furthermore, they could transplant brains.

The transplanting of brains was the breaking point of the science of transplants. As a result of this science, a person could remain alive for many centuries and through many bodies without interruption, simply by transplanting their brain from one organism to another.

The Atlantean science was indeed formidable. Presently, in the Himalayas, there are many hidden caverns containing certain mechanical apparatuses that are being preserved in order to telepathically transmit knowledge that can help human beings. From this we can see that the Atlanteans did not need to be bookworms in order to receive knowledge.

The lighting system used in Atlantean structures was atomic. Those hidden caverns of the Himalayas and others in Asia are lit with the atomic lamps of the Atlanteans. The Atlanteans utilized solar energy as well.

The Atlanteans were not just scientists, they were also magicians. Sadly, many of them developed their magical powers purely for the purpose of evil.

The Atlanteans were clairvoyant and it is obvious that through this sixth sense they could see not only the third dimension, but furthermore, they could see into the fourth dimension, the fifth, sixth, and even the seventh.

The Atlanteans knew very well that the elementals of fire, water, air, and earth were sentient beings of nature. They were just like human beings, yet unlike them because of their complete innocence. These elementals of nature, known as salamanders, sylphs, fairies and gnomes in children tales, were for them a tremendous reality.

Therefore, with this knowledge, they were able to create a mechanical robot and endow it with an immortal and intelligent elemental. Thus, this is how these robots were in fact converted into intelligent androids whose purpose was to serve their masters, simply by taking possession of those creatures which are invisible to the ordinary senses.

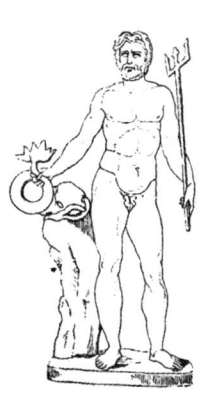

The most powerful rite of Atlantis was the rite of the God Neptune. This rite endured for many centuries. However, when the Atlanteans ignored the laws of the God Neptune, their society began to degenerate.

During the age of Kali Yuga,† the Atlanteans possessed tremendous powers. I remember the story of Jezebel, "Queen of Woeful Destinies." Jezebel was an extraordinary queen who made herself immortal.

When this queen found that her glands were becoming old or sick, she would then have her doctors immediately extract the atrophied glands and replace them with others.

Therefore, the Atlanteans easily handled the endocrine system, and they furthermore knew that these glands of internal secretion are related with the Tattvas, that is to say, they are related with the subtle forces of nature. The Atlantean physicians understood the vibrations of the Tattvas; they knew how to use them. In this way, Jezebel of the Woeful Destinies lived for thousands of years.

Disgracefully, Jezebel established anthropophagi (cannabalism) in Atlantis. Young women and children were immolated to the potencies of darkness for their religious cults. However, after these people were sacrificed, they were brought into the laboratory in order fot their heart and glands to be extracted for the service of Jezebel. Afterwards, the multitudes threw themselves upon the corpse in order to devour the flesh.

The Atlanteans had degenerated a great deal, and had now started using their awesome powers for evil and anthropophagi. Their magical science became black, and with these changes came horrible devices.

The Atlanteans could now create a mental monster that could crystallize into existence through their willpower. This monster needed blood as food to stay alive.

The last days of Atlantis were both frightening and apocalyptic. Their beautiful cities were destroyed by their atomic wars, and finally the solar system had completed its voyage around the zodiacal belt. When this happened, there was a great disturbance in the axis of the earth. The oceans were completely displaced through the changing of their beds.

The cold points of the Earth that we refer to as the poles were converted into the equator, and the equator into the poles. Millions of people perished, and all of the powerful cities of Atlantis submerged within the ocean that now bears its name.

This reminds me of the story of a multitude who invaded a certain temple during a time of earthquakes, whilst everything was inundated with fire and water. The desperate people cried out unto Mu, the great priest of Ra-mu, saying, "Mu, save us!"

Mu appeared before the multitude saying, "The truth was predicted many times, and now it is too late. You will perish with your women, your slaves, and your children, and if the future race follows your example, they shall perish as well." Tradition states that the last words of Mu were suffocated by smoke and flames.

Three great earthquakes sank the Atlantean continent within the boisterous waves of the ocean that bears its name. When that incredible catastrophe finally concluded, the new Root Race began.

Obviously, there was a group of people that escaped from within the multitudes before this catastrophic event took place. It has been traditionally stated that a great master named Vaivasvata, the biblical Noah,† undoubtedly called the people together in order to tell them what was going to happen. But, of course, the people did not believe him. They mocked him and laughed in his face.

The evening before the great catastrophe, people were eating and drinking, marrying and giving in marriage. Never did they suspect that the very next day they would be beneath the sea in an oceanic grave.

The Holy Beings who direct the destiny of humanity warned the Master Vaivasvata Manu† of the coming destruction. This was in order that he might be able to save his brothers and sisters before the Atlantean continent submerged within the ocean. The great Manu knew what to do in order to escape in time. They escaped during the night.

However, during these times, the Lords with the Tenebrous Countenance, who were owners of the very powerful androids which we spoke of earlier, were also owners of supersonic planes for the purpose of space travel. Therefore, the leaders of the select people, lead by the Master Vaivasvata Manu, took possession of some of these planes during the night and destroyed the rest.

THE UNIVERSAL FLOOD. ENGRAVING BY GUSTAVE DORÉ.

> The deep's great license
> Has buried all the hills, and new waves thunder
> Against the mountain-tops. The flood has taken
> All things, or nearly all, and those whom water,
> By chance, has spared, starvation slowly conquers.
> - Ovid, *The Metamorphosis*

Thus, when the perverse dwellers of that land awoke from their dreams the next day, they noticed with extreme astonishment that the waters of the ocean were invading their land. So, they ran to their spaceships, but they could not find them anywhere. Many of them suddenly understood what was happening and went in search of the followers of the Manu.

Only a few of the followers were left to be killed by the crazed multitudes who, momentarily, would be killed themselves by the crushing waves of the ocean.

At present, if properly explored, we can find marvellous cities, magnificent palaces on the bottom of the Atlantic Ocean. In aforetime, these existed with many people walking within their splendid halls. Now, only sharks and fish swim within the dark ruins.

Our solar system started another voyage around the zodiacal belt after the submergence of Atlantis. This catastrophic event finished off the fourth Root Race. Those few who were saved emigrated to the high plateau which is situated in the central table land of Asia, presently known to us as the small country Tibet.

It was there in Tibet that the survivors were mixed with the Hyperboreans and with the Nordics in order to originate the new Root Race, the present Aryan Root Race.

Our present Aryan Root Race was born after the deluge. Obviously, each Root Race has seven subraces. The first subrace was formed on the central plateau of Asia; in those times it was known as Hasha.

The second subrace flourished in India and China.

The emigrations carried humanity to the lands of Persia, Chaldea, Egypt, Jerusalem, where the third subrace of the great Aryan Root Race flourished.

The fourth subrace was formed by the Greeks and the Romans.

The fifth was formed by the Germans, English, French (Anglo-Saxon and Teutons).

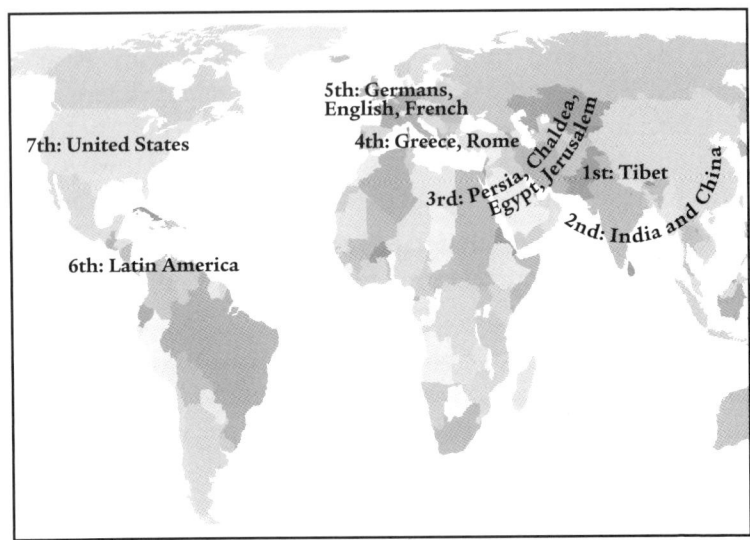

THE SEVEN SUBRACES OF THE ARYAN ROOT RACE.

The sixth was formed in Latin America. We know very well that many survivors of Atlantis came to Mexico: the Nahuas, the Zapotecs, the Toltecs, etc., all the original ancestors of America, as well as the Mayans who were living in Yucatan, Honduras and in Central America. However, the Aztecs, also known as the Nahuas, advanced throughout the land of Central America because they were warriors, finally arriving into the land of Panama.

Also in South America, the Incas and their powerful civilization existed. There is no doubt that the most powerful pre-Hispanic civilizations were the Mayans, Incas, and Nahuas.

I do not want to say that the Chibchas, Araucans, etc., did not have beautiful cultures; the strongest civilizations, however, were the Nahuas of ancient Mexico, the Mayans of Yucatan and Central America, and the Incas in Peru who lived in the mountains of Cusco.

When the Spaniards arrived in the Mexican land after they invaded all the land of Central and South America, they then mixed themselves with the autochthonous races. Out of this mixture the Latin Americans were born. They are the ones who form the sixth subrace of this Aryan Root Race.

The seventh subrace is in the process of being formed in the United States of North America; this subrace exists right now. It is the result of the mixture of all of the races of the world.

We have stated that a Root Race lasts as long as the voyage of the sun lasts in its travel around the zodiacal belt.

Our Aryan Root Race was born under the constellation of Aquarius, during the Era of the Water Carrier, immediately after the universal flood.

Now the end of this Aryan Root Race is at hand because the voyage of our solar system has finished. It has returned after many years to its original point of departure due to the fact that in this precise moment we are in the Era of Aquarius again.

This Era of Aquarius started again on the fourth of February of 1962 between two and three in the afternoon. At that moment, all the astronomers of the world could see with their telescopes the heavenly transit rush under the constellation of the Water Carrier.

What we are asserting is perfectly documented. We are not affirming anything that does not have proper documentation.

If someone states that the Age of Aquarius has not yet began, or affirms that it started sometime earlier than the date already mentioned, what does it matter to science or to us? The plain reality is that the Age of Aquarius started on the date already mentioned and that this phenomena was seen in all of the countries of the world by all of the scientists, astronomers, astrologers, etc.

This scientific cosmic event is a concrete, official, and irrefutable fact. On that date, there was a solar and a lunar eclipse that some of you might remember. Therefore, cosmically speaking, only a few degrees are needed in order for the solar system, which is presently in Aquarius, to arrive exactly at the original point of its initial departure.

The poles of the Earth are shifting during the voyage of the solar system around the zodiacal belt. If right now, guided exclusively by the magnetic needle of a compass, we were to take a plane to the North Pole and if we descend vertically to land,

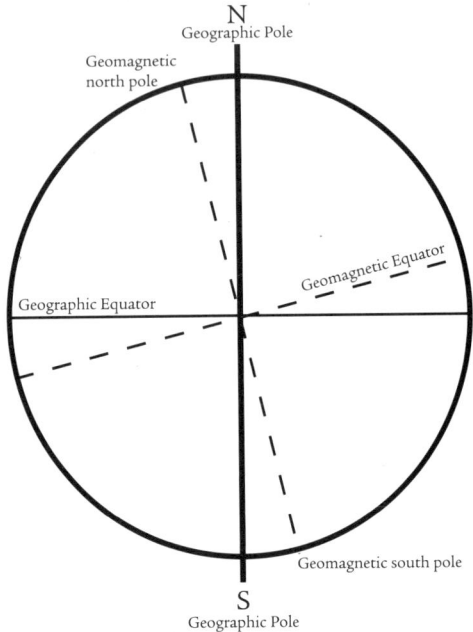

THE MAGNETIC AND GEOGRAPHIC POLES OF THE EARTH

we will see that the pole is no longer there; in other words, the geographic pole does not coincide with the magnetic pole. The poles of the Earth are being shifted.

Eventually, the poles will convert themselves into the equator, and the equator into the poles. This will occur when our solar system concludes its defined voyage around the zodiacal belt.

Therefore, when the solar system arrives to the exact degree of original departure, the continents of the planet Earth will submerge themselves into the bottom of the ocean.

An unusual event is going to accelerate this process of swift change to the axis of the planet Earth. I am referring to the planet Hercolubus. This planet is six times bigger than the planet Jupiter. The planet Hercolubus belongs to the distant solar system of Tylo. The solar system of Tylo is rapidly approaching our solar system, and Hercolubus is rapidly approaching Earth.

Modern astronomers have before their sight the planet Hercolubus, or, as it is known by modern science, the Barnard star.

This planet is a powerful giant that will pass through our solar system at an angle. When this happens, the revolution of the axis of the planet Earth will accelerate violently. Then the final catastrophe will occur.

Some scientists believe that they will be able to push this monstrous planet away with nuclear explosions, but this will be useless. It will be impossible to push this tremendous mass of a planet out of the way with mere nuclear bombs.

This same planet brought Atlantis to an end. Before Atlantis existed, it annihilated the existence of another continent. We know very well that the continent of Mu or Lemuria sank within the waters of the boisterous Pacific Ocean after 10,000 years of earthquakes and incessant volcanic eruptions.

When Hercolubus passed at an angle through our solar system during the end of the Kali Yuga of the Atlantean continent, then the universal flood occurred causing displacement of all the seabeds. It was the end of Atlantis.

Easter Island, off the coast of Chile, and Australia are remnants of the Lemurian continent. The Caribbean Islands are remnants of Atlantis.

When Hercolubus once again passes through an angle of our solar system, you can be absolutely sure that another great catastrophe will occur. This indicates that the destruction that is approaching is not the first, nor will it be the last.

If we very carefully study the Solar Stone, or the Aztec Calendar, we will find extraordinary wisdom there. In relation to this calendar, the Nahuas (Aztec Masters) say that the Children of the First Sun were devoured by tigers. The Children of the Second Sun were cleared away by strong hurricanes and converted themselves into apes or monkeys. The Children of the Third Sun perished by fire and great earthquakes and they transformed into birds. The say that the Children of the

THE AZTEC CALENDAR

Fourth Sun were swallowed by the waters and they converted themselves into fish.

They do not say anything about how the Children of the Fifth Sun perished, because we are the Children of the Fifth Sun. Yet, when they speak of the future, they indicate how we will most certainly perish.

These wise men who wrote of the destinies of the races of the past in this calendar also prophesied about the future. They say that the Children of the Fifth Sun will perish by fire and earthquakes. They also affirmed that in the Epoch of the Fifth Sun, the Gods will be dead. The meaning of this prophecy, "the Gods will be dead" is that the worship of the Solar Gods will be abandoned. This prophecy has already been fulfilled.

The Nahuas (Aztecs Masters) made an emphasis when they said in their Aztec Calendar that in the epoch of the Sixth Sun the Gods will resurrect. They also said that in the epoch of the Seventh Sun everything will be divine.

Let us talk about the Children of the First Sun. These people of the First Sun (the first Root Race) were people who lived on a primordial land, more than 300 million years ago, on the protoplasmic† continent. The Nahuas stated that they were "devoured by tigers"; in other words, that they were children who were devoured by **wisdom**.

The Children of the First Sun were the Protoplasmic Root Race. This referral to protoplasmic people seems to clash with Hegel's theory that refers to that bit of salt named protoplasm. These protoplasmic people had gelatinous bodies; they were ductile, elastic, very flexible. They could assume a gigantic stature or reduce their bodies down to a mathematical point. They were also androgynous,† and reproduced themselves as the cells of our organism do; that is to say by **cellular division**.

Today, this phenomena of reproduction remains in our blood; thus, this is how one cell is reproduced into two, and the two into four, etc. This is called **mitosis** (reproduction of the cells).

The Protoplasmic Root Race was devoured by tigers; in other words, they were devoured by wisdom.

When the Nahuas mentioned the Children of the Second Sun, they said that they were "cleared away by strong hurricanes"; this is an esoteric statement. They now refer to the Hyperboreans.

The Hyperborean Root Race had androgynous bodies as well, but much less gelatinous and more gaseous. The Nahuas stated that they were "transformed into apes"; in other words, that some of them came to degenerate themselves and therefore they perished.

It is also stated in this calendar from the culture of our ancestors of America, the Nahuas, about the Children of the Third Sun, the Lemurian Root Race.

The Lemurians were gigantic hermaphrodites.† We can see their representation in those sculptures which are in Tula, Mexico. The Lemurians were oviparous.†

The Children of the Second Sun reproduced themselves by budding, but the Children of the Third Sun reproduced themselves in an oviparous way. It is clear that the hermaphroditic body of Lemurians ovulated, and that the ovum that escaped from their ovaries was already fecundated.

The Lemurians were male-female (hermaphrodites), as the Bible states:

> *In the day that God created man, in the likeness of God made he him; Male and Female created he them, and blessed them and called their name Adam, in the day when they were created.*
> -Genesis 5:1-2

Therefore, it is stated that within a determined period the egg within the womb of the hermaphroditic Lemurian body was open and a child was born from it. This child was then nourished from the breasts of the father-mother.

When we state that the Lemurians were hermaphrodites, it invites us to explore the modern physical body. Certainly, the nipples on the male body are nothing but atrophied mammary glands, and the clitoris on the female body is an atrophied masculine phallus that has withdrawn with nervous ligaments. So in the human organism we have the evidence that in the past, the human body was hermaphroditic.

Still in these times we find people with both sexual organs. Therefore, this is proof or testimony for the persons who deny this fact, so that they cannot obstinately deny or ignore these truths which are unknown to so many people.

The Lemurians were divided into opposite sexes over the years through the process of evolution. Then, children were born with one sexual organ more developed than the other. Finally the day arrived in which the children appeared unisexual (with one sexual organ).

Therefore, when the sexes were divided, sexual cooperation was needed in order to create. During the epoch of Lemuria, the sexual act was still considered to be very sacred. The sexual act was only performed as a sacrament within the great temples of mysteries. This was a different age in which humanity had not degenerated.

The Nahuas stated that the Lemurians converted themselves into birds. I can tell you as a testimony of this that in Bolivia, South America, people discovered a small race of what we would call Lilliputians.

These Lilliputians were only 10 or 20 centimeters in stature, tiny men and women who inhabited a small town. This town resembled a toy town. These tiny beings disappeared one night by placing themselves into the fourth dimension and transporting themselves to another, safer place. They had to escape, as they were afraid of becoming a public "freak" show.

Many people were trying to get into the place in order to see these tiny beings before their escape, but now only the tiny town remains very well guarded by the natives of that area. Thus, this is how we understand that it is very true that the Children of the Third Sun were converted into birds.

The Nahuas stated that the Children of the Fourth Sun would perish by the waters, and that they would transform themselves into fish. Thus, this is true of public knowledge, according to history, that Atlantis was devoured by the ocean.

As for us, the Children of the Fifth Sun, they said that we will perish by fire and earthquakes. Obviously, the earthquakes are intensifying from instant to instant, from moment to moment.

Why so many earthquakes in this epoch? What is happening? The fact of the matter is that the ocean floor is cracking more and more all of the time.

A series of faults exist at the bottom of the Atlantic and Pacific Oceans. Many of those faults are so deep that the ocean water is already in contact with the magma (liquid fire) of the interior of the Earth, thus causing steam and creating immense pressure within the fault lines so as to increase the movement of the continents. This is the secret cause of so many earthquakes that are currently destroying so many cities of the world and filling people of all nations with tears, pain, and mourning.

Therefore, that theory which states that the earthquakes are due to the simple shift of the continents or some geological layers does not convince anyone.

The crude reality of this matter is that soon the trembling in one country will be the trembling in another. The earthquakes are going to become more frequent and intense over time.

We can add to all of this calamity the tremendous nuclear explosions that the scientists are performing within the interior of this planet Earth. It is a very clear fact that a great catastrophe will occur, and should not surprise us when it does.

It is really sad that this planet is submitting itself to a long agony. The fish of the ocean are dying because we have contaminated the waters. There is no doubt that the oceans have become huge garbage cans.

The nuclear waste could cause, at any moment, a catastrophic event, since the containers that are used to house the nuclear waste are, in reality, completely useless. Therefore, at any moment, I repeat, this nuclear waste could provoke a frightful disgrace for our world.

The chemical fertilizers which many people have been using are, in reality, sterilizing the soil.

The forests are being cut, finished, destroyed.

The cities are full of pollution. There are many scientists which will affirm that, in the direction we are headed, within forty years humanity will perish from the smog alone.

We can see then how this current humanity has degenerated itself, the oceans, rivers, lakes, the atmosphere. Everything has been contaminated.

The organic life that exists on the flesh of the Earth: trees, animals, people, etc., are necessary for the life of the planet Earth. The trees attract particular types and subtypes of cosmic energy that they transform and project to the interior layers of the Earth. The most insignificant insect attracts specific modalities of energy that it transforms and projects in the same format previously described.

Each one of us attracts particular types and subtypes of energy that are transformed and soon retransmitted into the interior layers of the Earth. The organic life of all animal, plant, mineral, and human kingdoms are necessary to sustain the life of the planet. Therefore, without the organic life of all creatures of nature, the Earth would convert itself into a great desert.

Everything is being disgracefully altered. Hunters are finishing off so many species of animals. Thus, this is why large game reservations have been set up in Africa. This is done so that they will not finish off all the creatures of nature.

The fruits of the Earth are being adulterated by the "know-it-all" scoundrels. Thus, this is why it is very difficult to find pure, unaltered apples today.

Any tree that has not been grafted or adulterated attracts, as a logical fact, the energy that is related to it. This energy is then transformed and retransmitted into the interior layers of the Earth.

Nonetheless, the trees that have been grafted can no longer accomplish their precious mission. They no longer charge their fruits with the vital principles that are inherent in all natural functioning organisms. In this day and age, we see in all parts of the world very beautiful fruits that are a pleasure to the eye, but disgracefully these fruits do not produce in the organism the same effects of the fruits whose trees have not been altered by grafts, or crossbred, etc.

Because of our present actions, the Earth is being submitted to a tremendous agony, and this must come to an end.

Nostradamus, the great astrologist who lived in the Middle Ages, asserted that in the year 1999 Hercolubus will pass close to the Earth, and he clarified this in his prophecies when he said, "Then we will see like two suns." He emphasized that the consequence of this will be the end of the present Aryan Root Race. It is obvious that this Root Race must come to an end.

In our past there have been two world wars: the war of 1914 to 1918, and the war of 1939 to 1945; but a Third World War is coming that will be more devastating than the first or the second.

As far as human beings are concerned, they are full of hatred. Therefore, as long as people carry within their interior the factors that produce wars, there will always be wars.

The words of Daniel the prophet come to my memory at the very moment of writing this:

The four winds of the heavens strove upon the great sea.

And four beasts came up from the sea and they were diverse one from the other.

The first beast was like a lion, and had eagles's wings: I beheld till the wings thereof were plucked, and it was lifted up from the earth, and made stand upon the feet as a man, and a man's heart was given to it.

And behold another beast, a second like to a bear, and it raised up itself on one side, and it had three ribs in the mouth of it between the teeth of it: and they said thus unto it, Arise , devour much flesh.

After this I beheld, and lo another like a leopard, which had upon the back of it four wings of a fowl; the beast had also four heads; and dominion was given unto it.

After this I saw in the night visions, and the fourth beast, dreadful and terrible and strong exceedingly, and It had great iron teeth and everything that the beast devoured broke into pieces and it stamped the residue of the pieces with its feet. It was diverse from all of the other beasts that were before it, and it had ten horns.

...And shall devour the whole Earth, and shall wear it down and break it into pieces. And he shall wear out the saints of the most high, but when judgement takes its seat, the judge will take away his dominion and the kingdom will be delivered unto the kingdom of the saints.

The kingdom will be delivered unto the saints with the arrival of the new Golden Age. Obviously, the four beasts that Daniel saw in his vision are a reference to our four ages: the Age of Gold, the Age of Silver, the Age of Copper, and the Age of Iron, which is our present age.

In the Iron Age, humanity always arrives in the state in which it is presently. Thus, this is how this fourth beast (Iron Age) has been as dreadful and terrible as Daniel said, diverse from all of the other beasts (other ages), but his end will come from night to morning. As it is written, the day of the Lord will come when it is not expected. He will come "as a thief in the night."

Therefore, in these precise moments, we are in the beginning of the end. The Apocalypse tells us of the beginning of the end, and we are precisely in the end of our era, that is to say, the end of Kali Yuga, the end of this fourth beast (humanity).

You will see within a very short time how the cities of the world will fall. Everything will be reduced to ashes, the earthquakes will intensify frightfully, they will be each time more and more powerful.

Therefore, you will be witnesses within a very short time, in your bodies of bones and flesh, of the events which will occur between the years of 1982 and 1992. You will remember by yourselves and then you will remember what we have written here. Alas, it is necessary for us to pay attention to these times, for the end is at hand.

With solar mechanics we can demonstrate that the solar system is arriving at the end of a great voyage. Truthfully, I say unto you that every voyage of the solar system around the zodiacal belt has always finished in a great catastrophe for our planet.

As for this humanity, the scripture states, "For her sins have reached unto heaven, and God hath remembered her iniquities." Therefore, "Babylon the great (this present humanity), the mother of harlots and abominations of the earth" will be destroyed, and from this perverse civilization of vipers, none will remain, not even one stone upon the other.

The Apostle Peter, when prophesying, said, "The heavens shall pass away with a great noise and the elements shall melt with fervent heat, the Earth also and the works therein shall be burned up." Certainly, the fire will be the first element to enter into action with the approaching of Hercolubus.

The magnetism of this planet Hercolubus is so great that the magma (liquid fire) from within the interior of the Earth will start to surface. Then many volcanoes will start to emerge everywhere, and a great bonfire will be propagated from the north to the south poles.

Nevertheless, before these events come to pass, the Antichrist will perform true marvels. The Antichrist, or the false science, will perform miracles. He will make atomic rockets that will be able to travel to any planet of our solar system. Frightening weapons will be invented, and all the people will kneel to the ground worshipping the great beast and saying, "There is nothing like this official science, there is no one likened unto the beast, there is no one like the Antichrist."

Few will be those who will hear the words of Christ. Within a short period of time, people will not listen to this doctrine. People say in these times, "I want demonstrations, I have to see it in order to believe it, I only believe in what my physical senses inform me. Those mystical matters from the roof above no longer concern me. There is no one like the beast," they say.

Therefore, all of you who read this message in these very moments, let it be known that the times of the end have arrived.

Nevertheless, if, as in the case of Atlantis, there were a select few that knew to leave with Vaivasvata Manu towards the central plain of Asia, then there must as well in these times be a select group that will survive the impeding doom. These people will be taken away from the fire and the smoke before the great catastrophe.

Who are the ones that will be chosen to survive? These will be people who have chosen to explore themselves internally, those who eliminate their psychological defects, those who are finished with the cult of their **EGO**, the cult of their **MYSELF**, or **ITSELF**.

These chosen people will be formed by women and men of good will who in reality are able to transform themselves radically. These select people will be taken to a specific place in the Pacific Ocean. These chosen few will live during the end in a place for two centuries, where they will be able to see the struggle between the fire and the water in a battle to the death.

Therefore, when a double rainbow appears upon the clouds (a sign of a new alliance of God with human beings), these chosen people will abide in the new lands and new heavens, then the Golden Age will dawn.

This is why Virgil, the poet from Mantua said, "The Golden Age has arrived, and a new progeny commands."

Samael Aun Weor

Guadalajara, Mexico 1976

Engraving by Albrecht Dürer.

Preface

In the name of the truth, we, the brothers and sisters of the temple, give infinite thanks to our brother Manuel S. Sanches and to all the brotherhood of the Sanctuary of Barquisimeto for making possible the printing of the first Spanish edition of this book. That sanctuary will be named from now on "Sanctuary Maitreya" because of the services given to the Cosmic Christ, as well as the service given to this great suffering humanity. This Sanctuary Maitreya is accomplishing a gigantic world mission.

We also give thanks to our brother Ramon Flores Derma for his technical Biblical work, and in general to all those who in one way or another were concerned with the triumph of this work.

We called all religions, schools, sects, orders, lodges, etc., in order to form the worldly salvation army.

We invite all people of good will to enlarge the columns of AGLA. We are not against anyone, neither against the religion or school of anyone. We consider all religions, schools, and sects as precious pearls linked in the golden thread of divinity.

We do not attack anyone, we do not hate anyone, we do not combat anyone.

We explain the secret doctrine of our adorable Savior. We intensely love this poor suffering humanity. We warn this humanity of the planet Earth about the apocalyptic hour in which we are.

We disclose the veil of the book of Apocalypse. This is a terribly divine book. The human beings will have to define themselves as Angels or demons, eagles or reptiles, with this book.

The times of the end have arrived and we are in them. Those who suppose that the times of the end are in a very remote future are very mistaken.

Events are speaking by themselves. The dreadful cataclysms that recently struck Chile and that caused terrible harm to

Japan, as well as the terrible earthquakes that are occurring in different parts of the world, and all the unknown sicknesses that are appearing that medical science cannot cure, deadly hatred, atomic bombs, etc., are showing us in an evident way that the times of the end have arrived.

The world's Gnostic movements, the South American Liberation Action, and Sivananda Aryabarta Ahsrama are standing, fighting for the new Aquarian Age. So, the triangle ALAS - Gnosis - Sivananda Aryabarta Ahsrama fights for the new age.

The terrible hour has arrived and we cannot remain indifferent.

Soon the atomic war will explode and terrible events will occur in all of the corners of the earth.

The apocalyptic hour has arrived. Woe! Woe! Woe to the dwellers of the earth!

August 17, 1960

Mexico City

Introduction

The Age of Aquarius began on February 4th of 1962 between 2:00 and 3:00 pm. Many schools await the new era. This book is the message of the new era of Aquarius.

Many esoteric students will be amazed because we predict frightful cataclysms for the new era of Aquarius.

The "I," the "myself," the reincarnating ego, certainly wants comfortable situations. It longs for an era of security and an era that offers many unharmful things, safe surroundings, a sensual comfortable era, without war, hatred, or problems.

It is urgent to know that life has begun its return towards the great Light. This signifies catastrophe.

The Earth will experience a process of planetary disintegration and reintegration. Aquarius brings terrible cataclysms.

All that is written in the book of Apocalypse is for the times of the end. We must inform humanity that the times of the end are at hand. The Apocalypse is the message of the new era.

We have studied the verses of the book of Revelation (Apocalypse) in the Superior Worlds. We give the result of our investigations in this book.

Much has been said and written about the Apocalypse. However, only intellectual speculations have been made and the words of various authorities have been repeated.

The present work is the result of tremendous esoteric investigations that were patiently performed by us in the Superior Worlds.

We have found the Apocalypse to be divided into three parts: the first we have entitled "The Son of Man," the second "The Sealed Book" and the third "The New Jerusalem."

The first part teaches the Path of the Razor's Edge.

The second is related with the times of the end.

The third tells us of the future Earth.

This is a book of practical Christification. This is a book of transcendental esoterism, and it is absolutely practical.

We do not theorize in this book. This work is one hundred percent practical.

Many students long for their Christification, but they do not know where to begin. They do not know the code, the secret.

In this book we give away to every student the code, the secret, the key. Here you have the key, you who thirst, lovers of the truth. Now, let us practice.

You are not alone. We profoundly love you, and when you are walking on the path of the razor's edge you will be assisted by the brothers and sisters of the temple.

AGLA (American Gnostic Liberation Action) is constituted by the triangle ALAS-Gnosis-Sivananda Aryabarta Ashrama.

These are three powerful, united movements that propagate Gnosis. Throughout the world, they teach the Gnostic esoterism of our adorable Savior of the world.

If after reading this book you wish to enter AGLA, you must write to us. Not a single letter will remain without answer. AGLA is formed by millions of people in the west, as well as in the east. AGLA is forming the world salvation army.

The supreme chief of AGLA is Jesus Christ. Let it be known, beloved brothers and sisters, that Jesus the Christ is alive.

Jesus Christ resurrected on the third day with his body of flesh and bone, and he still lives with this same body in Shamballa.

The secret country of Shamballa is in the Orient, in Tibet. The Master Jesus has a temple there. Other Masters live with him who have also resurrected and who have kept their bodies over the many ages of time.

The adorable Master Jesus the Christ has been very active and has worked intensely by helping this poor, suffering humanity. He is the chief of the Gnostic Movement. He is the supreme Hierarch of AGLA.

Although it seems incredible, the adorable Savior of the world worked as a nurse in the fields of battle during the First and Second World Wars.

Let us transcribe the touching story of a wounded soldier written by Mr. Mario Roso de Luna, the ingenious Theosophical writer. This story is found in "The Book That Kills Death," or "The Book of the Jinn," which is a fine piece of work by Mr. de Luna. The story is as follows:

"Strange news came to us when we were in the ditch at war.... certain rumors were spreading along the stretch from Switzerland to the sea, yet their origin or authenticity were unknown. Word came and went quickly and I remember the moment in which my partner George Casay looked at me strAngely with his blue eyes and asked me if I had seen the friend of the wounded ones. He then told me what he knew in respect to the rumor that was circulating. He told me that after many violent battles, a man dressed in white had been seen bending over the wounded soldiers as bullets were fired all around him and grenades fell at his feet. However, nothing had the power to harm him. He was a hero superior to all heroes or something greater still.

"This mysterious person whom the French call 'the comrade dressed in white' seemed to be everywhere at the same time. In Nancy, Argona, in Soissons, in Ypres, and everywhere, all men spoke of him with their voices lowered. However, some of them smiled and said that the ditch was affecting their nerves.

"I was frequently being careless with my words and I exclaimed that I must see in order to believe, and that I needed the German knife to wound me so that I may fall to the ground.

"The following day, we were at battle at the front; the cannons were roaring from morning till night and began again the following day. At midday we received the command to move in and take the front, which was two hundred yards from our position. As we were advancing we realized that our cannons had failed to fire at the moment of attack. We needed hearts of steel in order to march on. None of us thought, we only acted, and we continued to march on.

"We had advanced 150 yards when we realized that we had acted poorly. Our captain commanded us to take cover, and precisely at that moment both of my legs were wounded and by divine mercy I fell into a hole. I must have fainted because when I opened my eyes I was alone. The pain was excruciating, however I remained motionless for I was in fear that the Germans would see me, being only 50 yards away from them. I was hoping that someone would have pity on me. Soon I realized that there were men nearby that would have considered themselves in danger within the obscurity of the night if they had known that a comrade was still alive.

"I felt relieved as nightfall grew nearer. The night fell and I suddenly heard footsteps that were not weak but firm and strong, as if neither obscurity nor death could have altered their movement. I never would have guessed who was approaching. Even having seen the clarity of the white cloth within the obscurity, I assumed that it was a farmer wearing a shirt, and it even occurred to me to be an insane woman. But suddenly, with amazement - whether of happiness or terror, I do not know - I realized that he was the comrade dressed in white and at that precise moment the German rifles began to fire. The bullets could not have missed such a target because he raised his arms begging them to stop. He then retracted his arms and remained in the form of a cross, as the crosses that are frequently seen along side the roads of France. He then spoke. His words were very familiar. I remember only the beginning of his words, 'If you have known', and the end, 'But now they are hidden to your eyes.' Then he bent over and took me into his arms, I, the heaviest man of my group. He carried me as if I were a child. I suppose that I fell asleep because when I awoke that childlike feeling was gone. I was a man wishing to know what I could do in order to serve and help my friend.

"He was looking towards the stream holding his hands together as if he were praying. I then saw that he too was wounded. I believe that I saw a deep wound on his hand and as he prayed a drop of blood fell from his wound to the ground. I screamed without control because the wound appeared to me to be more terrifying than any of the wounds that I had seen throughout that bitter war.

"'You are also wounded,' I said with humbleness. I do not know whether he heard me or whether he saw it in my expression, but he answered with gentleness, 'This is an ancient wound, but it has been bothering me lately.' I then noticed that the same cruel mark appeared on his feet.

"Amazingly enough, I did not realize who he was until I saw his feet. I then recognized him as the living Christ. I had heard the chaplain speak of Him a few weeks before, but now I understood that He had come towards me, towards I who had removed Him from my life in the ardent fever of my youth. I wished to speak with Him and give Him thanks, but I could not find the words. He then stood and said, 'Remain close to the water today and I will come for you tomorrow; I have a duty for you to do for me.' Moments later He was gone.

"As I waited for Him I wrote this in order not to forget this experience. I feel weak and lonely and my pain increases but I have His promise and I know that He will come for me tomorrow."

This is the story of the soldier written by Mr. Mario Roso de Luna in his book "The Book That Kills Death." This concrete fact infallibly demonstrates that Jesus still lives with the same physical body the He used in the Holy Land.

Here in this book we have delivered the key for the resurrection. We have removed the veil of the centuries; we have delivered the secret doctrine of the Adorable One with seven seals in the book of Revelation (Apocalypse) to the poor and suffering humanity.

The Aquarian Message is a book of terribly divine powers. Here we find all of the secrets; here we find all of the keys of the Christification. Here is written the doctrine that the Adorable One taught in secret to His humble disciples.

The Adorable One will remain with us even unto the end of the world and evermore.

This is His doctrine. Here you have it. Study and practice it.

Inverencial peace,

Samael Aun Weor

Maitreya Buddha
Avatar Kalki of the new Aquarian Age

Part One

The Son of Man

Nos autem gloriari oportet
In cruce domini nostri Jesu-Christi

Adoration of the Shephards by Juan Bautista Maíno.

Chapter 1
The Son of Man

> *Blessed is he that readeth, and they that hear the words of this prophesy, and keep those things which are written therein: for the time is at hand.* - Revelation 1:3

Son of Man, reveal to us the hidden. Each delicious symphony of the ineffable cosmos, each note, each tender melody hidden within the very pure enchantment of the exquisite fragrant roses of the gardens of Nirvana, is the living incarnation of the Word.

The times of the end have arrived!

> *Behold, he cometh with clouds; and every eye shall see him, and they also which pierced him: and all kindreds of the earth shall wail because of him. Even so, Amen.* - Revelation 1:7

Behold, the Adorable One is at hand! He who has bled so much for us... Behold, the Blessed One is at hand; He comes as an anguished mother in search of her little children...

Listen, you men and Gods: within the mystery of each profound wave, the Adorable One is at hand... He who makes us kings and priests unto God and his Father.

At times, the morning breeze brings us sweet melodies like the murmur of a mother, yet other times is so severe like the lightning that terribly flashes within the catastrophic tempest of the furious, apocalyptic ocean.

Within the delicious and ineffable profundities of the sanctuary, the Beloved One speaks with a paradisiacal voice and says sublime things:

> *I am Alpha and Omega, the beginning and the ending, saith the Lord, which is, and which was, and which is to come, the Almighty.* - Revelation 1:8

A terrible lightning flashes within the blue velvet of the starry night... He is the Son of Man! The Innermost emanates from this divine Ray.

The choir of the Saints resounds, and tenderly the Virgins of Nirvana sing. These Virgins are deeply moved when this Ray penetrates the soul of a Holy Man.

The ineffable Ray (Christ) penetrates the Soul and transforms into Her. He transforms himself into Her and She (the Soul) transforms herself into Him. The Divine becomes human and the human becomes Divine.

These are the eternal weddings of the soul with the Pascal Lamb.

That which we call the Son of Man is the result of these alchemical weddings, of this mixture of love and peace. He is the resplendent and luminous **I AM**, our resplendent Dragon of Wisdom. He is the richest treasure that the Adorable One has brought to us.

He is the Man-Sun, Ormus, Osiris, Vishnu, Chur, the Lamb, also the man of time and of the river sung of by Daniel, the prophet.

He is the alpha and the omega, the first and the last, which is, which was, and which is to come. He is the Eternal Beloved, the Elder of Days.

The Lord of all adoration wants to dwell within the depths of each soul. He is the oil of the myrrh and the fragrance of the incense; **He is** the Adorable One and the Adorer.

The phrase "I am" must be translated as "I am the Being." In reality, the Beloved One is the Being of our Being, that is, was, and is to come. We possess a precious tabernacle (the physical body), an anguished soul, and a Spirit (the Innermost). This human triad emanated from that terribly divine Ray (Christ), who strikes His bell in the infinite space when we come into the world.

Each person has his own particular Ray that resplendently shines with the power of its glory in the world of the ineffable Gods. This Ray of dawn is the Being of our Being, the Inner Christ of each human being. This is the Sephirotic Crown of the Kabbalists, the Crown of Life.

Be thou faithful unto death, and I will give thee a crown of life.
- Revelation 2:10

Whosoever knows, the Word gives power to. No one has uttered it, no one will utter it, except the one who has incarnated it (the Word, the Christ).

The guests participate at the banquet feast of the Pascal Lamb. Those who have incarnated Him shine with glory at the table of the Angels. The countenance of the Beloved One is like lightning.

Christ is the Army of the Voice.† Christ is the Word. The personality does not exist within the world of the eternal Beloved One, neither individuality, nor the "I." We all are one within the Lord of supreme adoration.

When the Beloved One becomes transformed into the soul, and when the soul becomes transformed into the Beloved One, that which we call the **Son of Man** is born from this ineffable, divine, and human mixture.

The great Lord of Light, being the Son of the living God, becomes the Son of Man when he transform himself into the Human Soul. The Sun-Man is the result of all our purifications and bitterness. The Sun-Man is divine and human.

The Son of Man is the final outcome of the human being. He is the child of our sufferings, the solemn mystery of the transubstantiation.

Christ is the Solar Logos (multiple, perfect unity). Christ is the eternal, great Breath, profound, immeasurable, which emanates from the ineffable bosom of the Absolute.

Christ is our eternal, incessant Breath, profoundly unknown to himself. He is our divine Augoeides.

Christ is the purest, ineffable, and terribly divine Ray that shone as lightning on the face of Moses, there... within the solemn mystery of Mount Nebo.

Christ is not the Monad.† Christ is not the Theosophical septenary.†

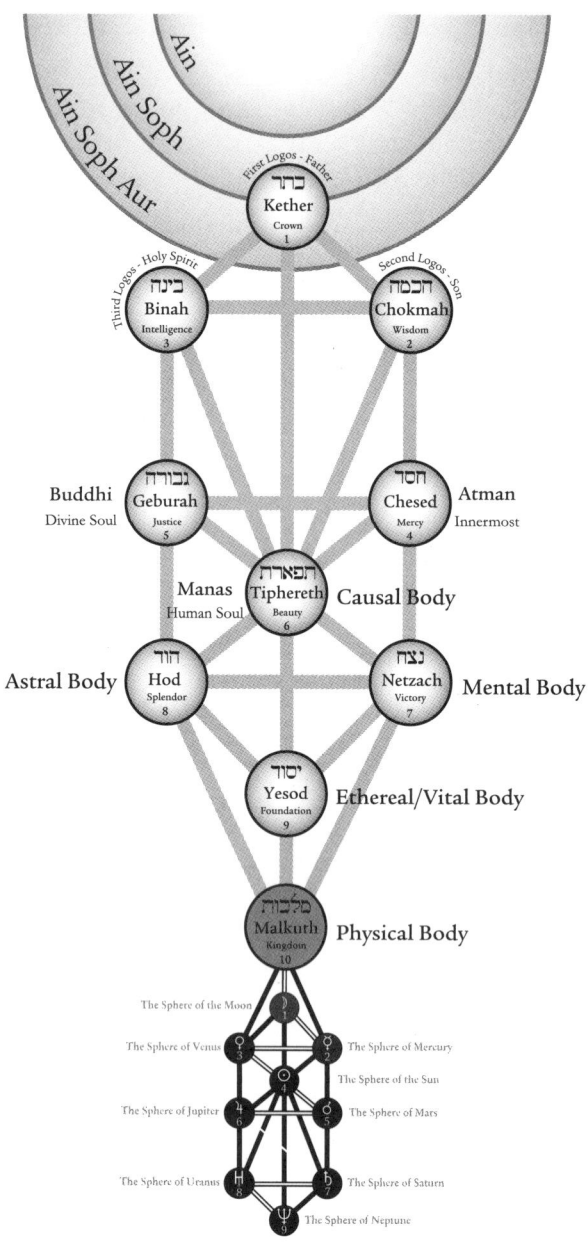

THE TREE OF LIFE: THE KABBALAH
Christ is the Solar Logos (Kether Chokmah, Binah).

Christ is not the Jivan-Atman. Christ is the ray that unites us to the Absolute. Christ is the central Sun.

Christ is Kuan Yin (the ineffable voice) in the east, who is the same Avalokiteshvara, as well as Vishnu.

Christ is Osiris among the Egyptians, and whosoever incarnated him was an Osirified One.

Christ is the Atmic thread among the Hindustani.

The Son of Man shines with all the strength of his glory in the solemn banquet of the Pascal Lamb.

AVALOKITESHVARA

THE THIRTEENTH ARCANUM

Night has passed and a new day has arrived, then thou shall be dressed with weapons of light.

Chapter 2
The First Begotten of the Dead

Jesus Christ is the faithful witness, and the first begotten of the dead, and the prince of the kings of the earth, because He overcame death. "He loved us, and washed us from our sins in his own blood," the very sacred blood of the adorable martyr. (Revelation 1:5)

Jesus, the Blessed One, has the Elixir of Longevity. This gift of Cupid is a grace of the most high God. The Holy Masters of the Guardian Wall have this marvellous elixir. When a Master of Compassion renounces the ineffable joy of Nirvana in order to live amongst and love this poor suffering humanity, then he has the right to ask for the gift of Cupid.

This Elixir of Longevity is a gas that remains attached to the vital depth of the human organism. Then, the initiate exclaims with a great voice, "Flee, oh death, before my steps, even to the end of the world and evermore! You shall be my slave and I shall be your lord!"

The glory of the great mysteries is sublime, and the sublime images of all the Osirified ones pass through our internal and delicate garden, within a diffused light of gold and violet.

The funeral ordeals of the Thirteenth Arcanum developed as a profound opera within the great archaic mysteries.

The austere Hierophants of the great mysteries rose from within the old sepulchers of ancient times.

The old operas of the Thirteenth Arcanum resounded with their ineffable melodies in the terrifying night of the centuries within the subterranean caverns of the Earth.

To preserve the body's youth for millions of years without ever dying was always the greatest longing for the great masters of Alchemy. Nonetheless, we state the following: it is better to be an eternal Elder. A venerable Elder with the gift of Cupid is always free from the danger of falling.

Those who receive the Elixir of Longevity die, but they do not die.

The Lord of all compassion received this marvellous Elixir of Longevity and his body was embalmed for death.

The Master of supreme compassion (Jesus) arrived at the holy sepulcher on the third day, and He uttered with a great voice while invoking his body. The Angels of death and the holy women were close to him. Then **Ehecatl**, the Lord of Cosmic Movement, pronounced with a paradisiacal voice while entering into the Holy Sepulchre, "Jesus, rise with your body from within your tomb." **Ehecatl**, the Angel of Cosmic Movement, induced activity and movement into the body of Jesus.

This body penetrated within the supra-sensible worlds when He arose. The physical body of Jesus was submerged within the internal worlds. The holy women awaited him in their Astral Bodies, carrying aromatic spices.

These women administered their spices to the body of Jesus. Then the body, obeying superior commands, penetrated into the Astral Body of the Master through the superior part of the sidereal head.

Thus, this is how the Adorable One was resuscitated from the dead. Then, the body abandoned the Holy Sepulcher and was submerged within the internal worlds.

After the Resurrection, Jesus appeared before the disciples of **Emmaus** and took dinner with them. (Luke 24:30, 31)

Jesus also appeared before his eleven Apostles who were reunited, and showed them the tremendous reality of his resurrection. (John 20:19, 20)

The sacred scriptures give testimony of the various apparitions of the divine Master after his resurrection.

Thus, this is how the body of the Master remained submerged within the supra-sensible worlds. The body of the divine Rabbi of Galilee penetrated into the state of "**Jinn**." Jesus died, but He did not die.

Actually, the Master lives in Shamballa in oriental Tibet. There he lives with the same body with which he resurrected.

Other holy Masters who achieved this ineffable resurrection dwell with him in Shamballa.

The great Master Zanoni achieved the resurrection and he remained youthful for millions of years. Afterwards, he disgracefully lost his head in the guillotine during the French Revolution. He fell because of the crime of taking a woman. He fell in love with a young woman who was a choral artist in Naples. That was his mistake.

A great Tartarean Master, whose body has actually existed for millions of years, textually told us the following, "A true Master is one who has swallowed soil. Really, one is nothing but a fool before swallowing soil."

The divine Rabbi of Galilee is the first begotten of the dead because, in addition to having resurrected from the dead, He is the chief of souls.

Actually, Count Saint Germain possesses the same body with which he was known during the XVII and XVIII centuries in the royal courts of Europe.

After the resurrection, the physical body remains in the state of "**Jinn**" (meaning, submerged within the supra-sensible worlds).

Nevertheless, this body can enter into the physical world at any time the Master wishes to do so.

The Masters of compassion live in these exalted conditions solely to guide the current of life throughout the innumerable centuries.

Condemned by themselves to live for millions of years in order to guide the current of the centuries, these ineffable Saints are the silent guardians of the Guardian Wall. This protective Wall has been built with the blood of those Saints of the Blessed One. This Wall has protected humanity since the dawn of creation.

The secret path is full of infinite torments. This secret path takes us directly to the **Absolute**, where the uncreated light shines.

Actually, Jesus Christ, the first begotten of the dead, lives in Shamballa. This secret country is found in the state of "**Jinn**." There is where the blessed Adorable One has his sacred temple.

The oriental firmament shines with all of the love of the Master, and the shy little flowers of the path that the Holiest of Holies treads upon without damage deliciously shake in the perfumed breeze.

The flaming fire, the pure waters of life, the soft perfumed earth, and the tempestuous air of Tibetan Shamballa are inebriated with the glory of the Adorable One who is, who was, and who is to come.

The **Maha Avatar Babaji**, who has preserved his physical body for many millions of years, promised to publicly teach the science which permits us to immortalize the body of flesh and bones.

Lo and behold, we deliver that science here, in this book.

The promise of the immortal **Babaji** has been fulfilled.

Chapter 3
The Seven Churches

> Revelation 1:12-18:
>
> *And I turned to see the voice that spake with me* (one Word from the Army of the Voice† who was talking to the Apostle). *And being turned, I saw seven golden candlesticks.* (These are the seven chakras of the spinal medulla or the seven churches.)
>
> *And in the midst of the seven candlesticks one like unto the Son of Man* (the Word from the Army of the Voice, who was teaching the Apostle) *clothed with a garment down to the foot, and girt about the paps with a golden girdle.*
>
> *His head and his hairs were white like wool, as white as snow; and his eyes were as a flame of fire;*
>
> *And his feet like unto fine brass, as if they burned in a furnace; and his voice as the sound of many waters.* (The Word, the Verb, always sounds.)
>
> *And he had in his right hand seven stars* (these are the seven Spirits before the Throne, which are in the Macrocosmos†, and also these are the seven atomic Angels who govern the seven chakras or seven churches located in the spinal medulla, which are in the Microcosmos†): *and out of his mouth went a sharp two-edged sword* (the flaming sword): *And his countenance was as the sun shineth in his strength.*
>
> *And when I saw him, I fell at his feet as dead. And he laid his right hand upon me, saying unto me, Fear not; I am the first and the last.* (Our resplendent Dragon of Wisdom is the first and the last.)

The Beloved One lives, and was dead; and behold, He is alive for evermore. He has the keys of hell and of death.

When we departed from Eden, we divorced ourselves from the **Word** that lives within the unknown profundities of

Engraving by Albrecht Dürer.

"Fear not; I am the first and the last..."

our Being. The Beloved One died for us, but behold, he lives eternally.

The Beloved One is Hiram† who was killed by three traitors. He is Jesus condemned to death by Judas, Caiaphas, and Pilate. These three traitors constitute what we call the "**I**," the "**Ego**," and the "**Myself**" (**Satan**).

Sebal, the first traitor of Hiram, is Satan in the Astral Body of the human being; Ortelut, the second traitor of Hiram, is Satan in the mind; and Stokin, the third traitor of Hiram, is Satan in the Will-Soul. Behold the "I" in its three fundamental levels of consciousness.

This "I" is the prince of this world, the three-headed Black Dragon that we must decapitate and dissolve. The three heads are the three rebels that we carry within: the Demon of Desire, the Demon of the Mind, and the Demon of Evil Will. These are the three assassins of the **Word** (Christ). *"But behold, he is alive and he will live for ever more, Amen."* Christ has the keys of our Atomic Infernos.

He has the keys of hell and of death. - Verse 18

We need to resurrect the Son of Man within ourselves.

The seven churches exist within the Microcosmos and within the Macrocosmos.

The Apocalypse is the book of the human being and of the Universe. The seven churches of our spinal medulla happily shine with the sacred fire of the Holy Spirit. The seven churches of our spinal medulla are the doors that give us entrance into the seven glorious cathedrals of the superior worlds.

We are filled with a lot of terror and mystical trembling when we see among thunder, lightning, earthquakes, tempests and great hail, the majestic cathedral of Sardis.

The chakra of the larynx is the door that allows us to enter into the great cathedral of Sardis.

The sublime and terribly divine church of Laodicea is entirely of pure gold. Its cupola and walls are carved with the purest gold of the Spirit.

The lotus of one thousand petals, the resplendent crown of the Saints, gives access into the glorious cathedral of Laodicea. This temple really exists in the superior worlds.

We study the rituals of life and death within the seven churches of the superior worlds, until the Officiant (the **Word**) arrives.

The seven churches of the spinal medulla are united to the seven chakras or plexus of the grand sympathetic nervous system by means of very fine nerves.

The seven churches are similar to lotus flowers that are suspended from the famous **Chitra Nadi**. The canal of Shushumna exists within the medullar canal. The canal of **Chitra Nadi** is within this canal of Shushumna. The seven beautiful and divine churches are suspended from this precious medullar canal.

The spinal medulla is the candelabra. The two olive trees of the temple are situated upon the right and left side. These are the two olive branches through which the two golden pipes empty the golden oil out of themselves. That golden oil is the "**Ens Seminis**." *"These are two anointed ones that stand by the Lord of the whole earth"* (Zacharias 4: 12-14). These are the two witnesses, **Ida** and **Pingala**. These are the two sympathetic nerves that are entwined like two serpents around the spinal medulla and through which the oil of pure gold rises to the chalice (the brain).

When the serpent of metal awakens, it then enters through the "centralis canalis" of the spinal medulla and rises very slowly and with difficulty through the medullar canal, which is known in India as the Brahmanadi.

The seven churches shine with the blazing fire of the Holy Spirit. While this sacred fire rises, the seven churches open and turn upwards. The chakras or sympathetic plexus awaken in accordance with the opening of the seven churches.

The candlestick has seven lamps, which are the seven churches, and seven canals for the lamps which are upon it. These seven canals correspond to the seven degrees of the power of the fire.

All of these chakras, discs, or magnetic wheels are the senses of the Astral Body.

Our soul is enveloped in the Astral Body. The anatomy, physiology, and pathology of the Astral Body is ultra-sensible.

The senses of the Astral Body and the endocrine glands are found to be intimately related. Wherever a nervous plexus exists, a chakra of the Astral Body exists.

The mind, the willpower, the consciousness, and the spirit, etc., are within the Astral Body.

The Astral Body becomes filled with glory and beauty with the awakening of the seven churches.

Thus, this is how we transfigure and glorify ourselves completely.

"And Moses made a serpent of brass, and put it upon a pole, and it came to pass, that if a serpent had bitten any man, when he beheld the serpent of brass, he lived." - Numbers 21:9

Chapter 4
The Serpent of Metal

Enmity has existed between the woman and the serpent since the departure from Eden. The serpent beguiled Eve and from that moment the conflict began.

Jehovah said unto the serpent, *"Because thou hast done this, thou art cursed above all cattle, and above every beast of the field; upon thy belly shalt thou go, and dust shall thou eat all the days of thy life. And I will put enmity between thy seed and her seed; it shall bruise thy head and thou shall bruise his heel."* - Genesis 3:14,15

The world filled with tears when the serpent was cursed. The woman bruised the serpent's head and the serpent took revenge by bruising her heel. Thus, we cry when we are born and we cry when we die.

Moses raised the serpent of metal upon the staff, in the wilderness. This serpent became the same staff.

The struggle is terrible, "brain against sex, sex against brain, and heart against heart." We must tame and raise the serpent of metal upon the staff as Moses did in the wilderness.

We must descend into the Ninth Sphere (sex) in order to work with the fire and the water, which are the origin of worlds, beasts, human beings, and Gods. Every authentic White Initiation begins here. The key of all power is found in the union of the phallus and the uterus.

Raise well your cup, and be careful not to spill even a single drop of the sacred wine.

Kill desire. Kill even the very shadow of desire.

There is the need to celebrate the marriage of **Cana** and to transmute the water into wine.

When chaste, the human being can raise the igneous serpent of magical powers through the central canal of the spinal medulla. This Pentecostal fire has the power to open the seven churches. The advent of the sacred fire of Pentecost takes place when the solar atoms make contact with the lunar atoms in the coccygeal bone, near the Triveni. Then, the igneous serpent rises from the bottom of the sacred Ark. This Ark of the Covenant is the sexual organs.

The Ark shone like terribly divine lightning when in the sanctum sanctorum of the Temple of Solomon. Two Cherubim, whose wings were touching each other, were placed at the sides of the Ark, one to the right and the other to the left. These very sacred Cherubim were in the attitude of the man and the woman during the act of copulation.

Within the Ark were found the Staff of Aaron (symbol of the phallus), the cup or Omer which contained the manna of the desert (symbol of the uterus), and the Tablets of the Law, without which the development of the terrific serpent of metal is impossible.

The name of this divine serpent is Kundalini. Devi Kundalini only awakens with the ineffable enchantments of love. What is important is not to waste the sacred wine. Only willpower can save us while in the chamber of wine.

The Kundalini rises very slowly through the medullar canal. The seven churches are in the medullar canal. The Kundalini opens the seven churches.

The precious, immaculate, and divine light that is irradiated by Angels has its origin in the candlestick of their spinal medulla.

The spinal medulla is the sacred candlestick of the temple.

The candlestick of pure massive gold of the Temple of Solomon had seven branches. This candlestick is the spinal medulla with its seven churches.

The two olive trees of the temple, "the two anointed ones," are situated on either side of the candlestick.

The water and the fire of the Ninth Sphere rise through these two sympathetic canals (**Ida** and **Pingala**) towards the chalice (the brain) when we work with the Arcanum A.Z.F.

The saintly martyr Miguel de Molinos said,

> "The subtlest arrow that nature throws us induces us to perform illicit acts (fornication) with the pretext that they are beneficial and necessary. Oh, how many souls have been coerced and have lost the Spirit because of this golden snare. They will never taste of the silent Manna. Quod Nemo Nocet Nist Qui Accipit.
>
> "If you do not defeat (the animal ego) with perfection by dying within yourself, then you are the one who does not attempt to die in his passions and is not well disposed for receiving the power of understanding. Without this infusion it is impossible for the introversion to occur and for the Spirit to be altered. Thus, this is how those who are outside live without **Him**.
>
> "Resign, and deny yourself everything. However, the real denying is difficult in the beginning, easier in the middle, and very placid in the end. You will know that you are very far from perfection if you do not find God within everything. You will know that pure, perfect, and essential love consists of the Cross, in voluntary denying and resignation, in perfect humbleness, poverty of the Spirit, and abhorrence of yourself.
>
> "It is important to enter and remain in the innermost part of your center while in times of strong temptation, despair, and desolation, in order to see and contemplate only God, who has his throne and quietude in the depth of your soul... You will discover that impatience and bitterness of the heart are born from the bottom of the sensitive, empty, and less mortified love. When the soul is profoundly humble and is truly mortifying and despising herself, then she knows true love and its effects."

If you wish to ignite your candlestick of seven branches, remember this is achieved through the path of the razor's edge.

This path is filled with dangers inside and outside.

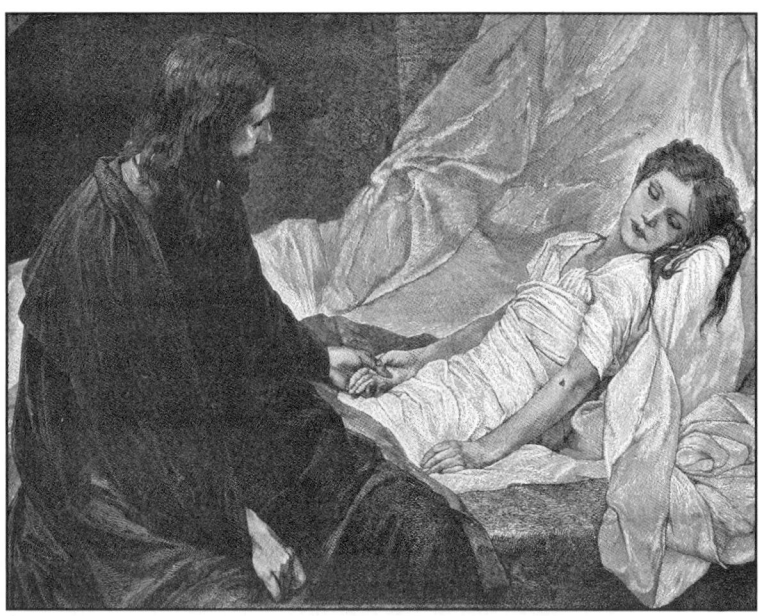

"When our mind becomes submerged within the Nothingness, then the Lamb enters the Soul in order to sup with Her."

Chapter 5
Internal Meditation

The seven degrees of ecstasy through which the mystic reaches the perfect state of the Soul are described in the school of Sufism.

The school of Sufism teaches about ecstasy. The state and secret of our level is revealed in Sufism, because this is the interior state of life in God.

We must perform the will of God on Earth as it is in heaven while on the path of interior peace. This conformity with the mild yoke takes us through the narrow stretch and difficult path that leads us towards the Light.

Everyone who works in the Magisterium of Fire must learn how to meditate on the seven churches.

The mystic must profoundly focus his concentration on the Immolated Lamb. The mystic must pray, beseeching the Adorable One to awaken the longed for chakra, disc, wheel, or faculty.

Afterwards, when the supplication is done, the mystic must then search for refuge in the Nothingness. His mind must remain silent and serene.

Illumination and ecstasy come when the mind is silent, when the mind is quiet.

Drowsiness in combination with meditation produces ecstasy.

God searches the Nothingness in order to fill it.

Ecstasy has seven degrees of power:

The first is the fire that instructs and teaches us.

The second is the Gnostic Unction, which is a soft, solar liquor, that when diffused throughout the Soul, teaches, corroborates, and prepares us in order to incarnate the Truth.

The third is the mystical exaltation of the humble and sincere disciple.

The fourth is the illumination.

The fifth is the internal joy of divine sweetness that emanates from the precious fountain of the Holy Spirit. This joy is for those who have "continuous consciousness."

The sixth is the decapitation of the "I."

The seventh is the Venustic Initiation, the incarnation of the Son of Man within ourselves.

Other degrees of contemplation and ecstasy exist, such as: rapture, liquefaction, bliss, jubilation, osculation, embracement, transformation, etc.

When our mind becomes submerged within the Nothingness, then the Lamb enters the Soul in order to sup with Her. Therefore, the Nothingness is the medium utilized by the Beloved One in order to work within our Soul, awakening centers and performing marvels. The Divine Spouse comes in order to betroth his soul through this Nothingness, within the nuptial bridal bed of Paradise.

Thus, this is the path for returning into the innocence of Paradise. The Soul will successfully experience the spiritual martyrdoms and the interior torments while submerged within the Nothingness. God searches the Nothingness in order to fill it.

Internal meditation produces changes in our internal bodies. Through it, the awakening of the consciousness arrives.

All human beings live within the supra-sensible worlds with the consciousness asleep. Meditation provokes the solemn awakening of the consciousness.

This awakening is like lightning in the night. This awakening of the consciousness occurs during the normal sleep of our physical body. We move ourselves in our internal vehicles when this body sleeps.

The Soul travels throughout the superior worlds when the body sleeps. We stop dreaming when the consciousness awakens. Then we live in the internal worlds in a state of intensified awareness. This is what is called "continuous consciousness."

Whosoever has awakened the consciousness lives awake in the Superior Worlds.

We feel the mystical beatitude of the ineffable Light while in the supra-sensible worlds. Then, the past, the present, and the future harmonize within an eternal Now.

There is no better pleasure than feeling one's soul detached. Then we taste the divine nectar of eternity, and we enter through the doors of the temples filled with joy and amidst the ineffable melodies of the great mysteries.

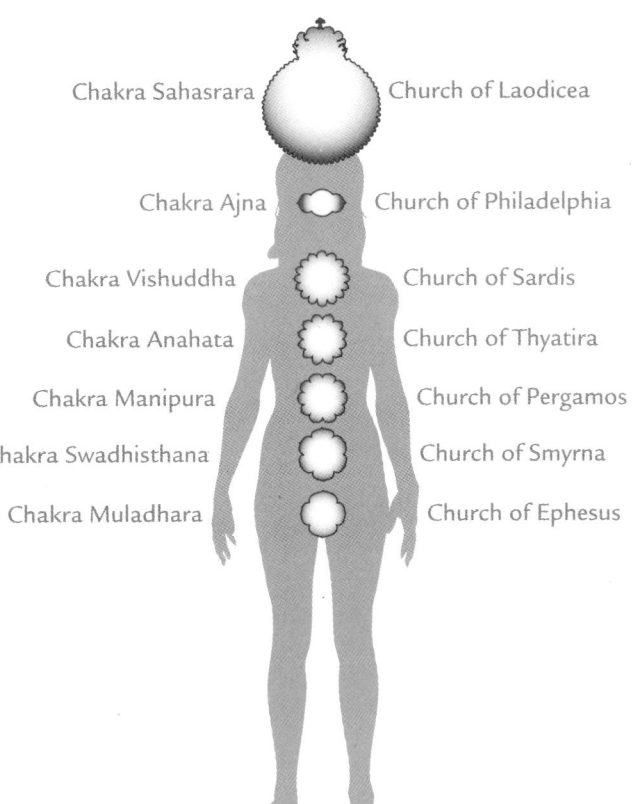

THE SEVEN CHURCHES

Chapter 6
The Church of Ephesus

The church of Ephesus is found situated exactly between the sexual organs and the anus. This is the church of the coccyx. The sacred serpent sleeps quietly within this church, awaiting the supreme moment of awakening.

The marvellous serpent awakens within the miraculous enchantments of love. Mozart's *Magic Flute* awakens memories of the profound mysteries of the sacred serpent.

The church of Ephesus is a mystical lotus flower. This flower has four petals, and anyone who profoundly meditates on the church of Ephesus penetrates into the subterranean regions of the earth. Then, the gnomes or pygmies teach us their mysteries. The Tattva Prithvi shines with glory within the church of Ephesus.

The mysteries of **Lingam Yoni** are found hidden within the church of Ephesus.

Revelation 2:1-6:

> *Unto the Angel of the church of Ephesus write* (the Word, Christ, communicates unto the atomic Angel of the Church of Ephesus); *These things* (the virtues which are needed in order to open the church of Ephesus) *saith he that holdeth the seven stars in his right hand* (the Son of Man), *who walketh in the midst of the seven golden candlesticks* (the candelabra of seven branches);
>
> *I know thy works, and thy labour, and thy patience* (patience is the virtue needed in order to open this church), *and how thou canst not bear them which are evil: and thou hast tried them which say they are apostles, and are not, and hast found them liars:* (because they are **fornicators**).
>
> *And hast borne, and hast patience* (this church is opened with suffering and patience), *and for my name's sake hast laboured, and hast not fainted.*

Nevertheless I have somewhat against thee, because thou hast left thy first love. The first love is the eternal Beloved One, the Internal God, the Ineffable One. The soul suffers terribly when she abandons the Beloved One.

Remember therefore from whence thou art fallen, and repent, and do the first works; (you have to create without fornication) *or else I will come unto thee quickly, and will remove thy candlestick out of its place, except thou repent.* The human being acts with sacrilege when the sacred wine of the temple is spilled. Then the serpent of fire descends one or more vertebrae in accordance with the magnitude of the fault. Thus, this is how the candlestick is taken out of its place and pain and remorse will hurt the heart.

But this thou hast, that thou hatest the deeds of the Nicolaitans, which I also hate.

When the priest spills the sacred wine of the altar, the blessed Mother Goddess of the world conceals her face with her veil and cries bitterly. The Beloved One then crucifies himself upon his cross and the whole of nature trembles with terror.

The sacred wine is the semen of Benjamin. This semen is a mixture of wine and water, which is contained within the chalice of Benjamin, the beloved son of Jacob.

When the priest spills the wine of the temple, the enchanted serpent descends towards the atomic infernos of the human being and converts itself into the tail of Satan.

In ancient times there were giants upon the earth who committed this sacrilege.

The cities of Carthage, Tyre, and Sidon were also affected by this crime.

Furthermore, the Canaanites performed this sacrilege.

The mysteries of **Vulcan** were betrayed, and the human being submerged himself into the abyss.

These are, "*....the deeds of the Nicolaitans, which I also hate.*"

Chapter 7
The Church of Smyrna

The church of Smyrna is the chakra of the prostate (the uterus in women). Apas is the Tattva of this chakra. *"All of you will be Gods if you depart from Egypt and travel through the Red Sea."*

The divine male sings, the ineffable female sings... Both sing together, male and female. Both of them sing the sublime opera of the centuries. This opera of light begins in Eden and ends in Eden.

The voice of this sublime male is heroic, it is terrific like the lightning which strikes, it is like the omnipotent thunder.

The voice of the woman is so sweet and melodious like *The Magic Flute* of Mozart or like the miraculous voice of a mermaid of the great ocean.

This touching duet and this lovely connubial of the Word fecundates the waters of life.

When the serpent of fire breathes upon the waters of Eden, then the church of Smyrna opens within the august thunder of thought.

Let us kneel in order to contemplate the miraculous lotus of six petals, this lotus of the Nile, which is the prostatic (uterine) chakra upon which the mermaids of the ocean stand.

Let us pray and meditate on this chakra of the prostate (uterus). We convert ourselves into Kings and Queens of the waters when the Beloved One awakens this chakra.

This chakra grants us consciousness of the nature of all beings who dwell in the internal worlds.

Whosoever drinks from the waters of pure life shall never thirst again.

The very pure waters of Eden are the divine mirror of love.

The swan of inviolable whiteness stands upon the lotus flower. This swan of love awakes among the moving murmurs of nature.

The "second Buddha" Padmasambhava (whose name means "lotus-born") emerges from the lotus which rises out of the waters.

Revelation 2:8-11:

And unto the (atomic) *Angel of the church in Smyrna write; These things saith the first and the last, which was dead and is alive;* (is alive within anyone who receives the Venustic Initiation).

I know thy works, and tribulation, and poverty, (tribulation and poverty are the fundamental conditions in order to open the church of Smyrna) *but thou art rich* (spiritually), *and I know the blasphemy of them which say they are Jews, and are not, but are the synagogue of Satan.*

Fear not of those things which thou shalt suffer: behold the devil shall cast some of you into prison (of pain), *that ye may be tried; and ye shall have tribulation ten days:* (meaning, you shall have tribulation as long as you are submitted to the wheel of reincarnation and karma) *be thou faithful unto death, and I will give thee a crown of life.*

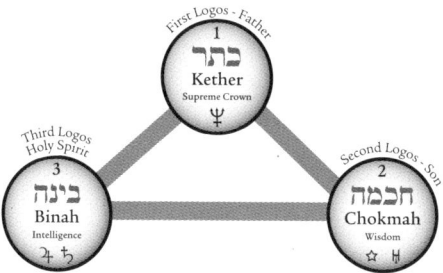

THE CROWN OF LIFE, THE SUPERNAL TRIANGLE OF THE TREE OF LIFE.

Whosoever receives the Crown of Life is free of the wheel of reincarnation and karma.

The Crown of Life is threefold. It has three aspects: the Elder of Days, the Adorable Son, and thirdly, the very wise Holy Spirit.

The crown of life is the **Man-Sun**, the **King-Sun**, who was greatly worshipped by the Emperor Julian.

The Crown of Life is our incessant Eternal Breath profoundly unknown to himself. It is the particular ray of each human being. It is the **Christ**.

The crown of life is Kether, Chokmah, and Binah.

Whosoever is faithful unto death receives the Crown of Life.

The ineffable countenances of all the Saints who have incarnated **Him** shine like **Suns** of love while at the banquet of the **Lamb**. The immaculate, white tablecloth is dyed with the royal blood of the immolated Lamb.

> He that hath an ear, let him hear what the Spirit saith unto the churches;
>
> He that overcometh shall not be hurt of the second death.

Whosoever does not overcome will be divorced from the Beloved One and will be submerged into the abyss.

Those who enter the abyss will experience the Second Death.

The demons of the abyss disintegrate very slowly over a period of many eternities; these souls are lost.

Whosoever overcomes shall not be hurt by the Second Death.

Be thou faithful unto death, and I will give thee a crown of life.
- Revelation 2:10

Whosoever knows, the Word gives power to. No one has uttered it, no one will utter it, except the one who has incarnated it (the Word, the Christ).

The Word becomes flesh within each one of us when we receive the Crown of Life.

Every Saint who reaches the Venustic Initiation receives the Crown of Life.

Our very beloved savior Jesus Christ reached the Venustic Initiation in the river Jordan.

And the Word (the Verb) *was made flesh, and dwelt among us, and beheld his glory, the glory as of the only begotten of the Father full of grace and truth.* - John 1:14

Light is come into the world, and men loved darkness rather than light, because their deeds were evil. - John 3:19

Jesus is the Savior because He brought us the Crown of Life and He gave his blood for us.

We must reach the supreme annihilation of the "I" in order to receive the Crown of Life.

We must resurrect the Lamb within ourselves. We need the Easter Resurrection.

Chapter 8
The Church of Pergamos

The blessed womb of the Mother Goddess of the world is Eden.

We departed from Eden through the door of sex, and only through this door can we enter again into Eden.

Two millennial trees exist within the orchard of Eden: the Tree of the Science of Good and Evil, and the Tree of Life.

Genesis 3:6-7:

> *And when the woman saw that the tree was good for food, and it was pleasant to the eyes, and a tree to be desired to make one wise, she took of the fruit thereof, and did eat and gave also unto her husband with her; and he did eat.*
>
> *And the eyes of them were opened, and they knew that they were naked; and they sewed fig leaves together, and made themselves aprons.*

Eighteen million years have passed and we are still naked. If we wish to return into Eden, we must dress ourselves as Kings and Priests of Nature in accordance with the order of **Melchizedek**, who is the King of Fire.

The church of Pergamos is the church of fire. This chakra is a precious lotus flower with ten beautiful petals saturated with happiness.

This chakra is situated in the region of the navel and controls the liver, the stomach, etc.

The color of this chakra is similar to that of clouds charged with rays, lightning, and living fire.

A triangular space exists within this chakra. The region of fire is situated in this ineffable space, the region of the Agni-tattva.

We can walk upon fire without being burned when we meditate on this chakra.

Whosoever develops this chakra will not fear fire but will be capable of remaining in fire for many hours without receiving any harm (see Daniel 3:23-27).

When we meditate on this chakra, we penetrate into Eden. There, we find human beings still naked. Only we, the brothers and sisters of the temple, are dressed with the vesture of fire.

We convert ourselves into Kings and Queens of fire when we develop this chakra.

The church of Pergamos is opened when the sacred serpent rises and reaches the region of the navel.

The power to govern over fire is granted unto us when we internally meditate on this precious lotus of the belly.

Revive the living flame of the Spirit with the divine nectar of love.

The fire burns the scoria of evil. You must cast the demons of desire out from the sanctuary of your soul.

Your soul must be as pure as the drop of dew which, while vibrating with love, submerges itself deliciously within the fragrant petals of the rose.

You must protect your soul from the attacks of the "I"; kill not only desire but moreover, the very shadows of the tree of desire.

Remember that the Christonic semen is the raw matter of the Great Work.

Cleanse your soul from any desire. Be chaste.

If you are certain that you have annihilated every desire, then analyze yourself deeply and search again in the profound depths of your soul. It may be that the "I" is betraying you in other levels of consciousness.

You must subdue your senses and control your mind; kill every desire of life. Do not desire anything.

Revelation 2:12-17:

> *And to the* (atomic) *Angel of the church in Pergamos write; These things saith he which hath the sharp sword with two edges, the Son of Man;*

I know thy works, and where thou dwellest, even where Satan's seat is (the chair of Satan is situated in the region of the navel. However, the atomic Angel of the Church of Pergamos is faithful): *and thou holdest fast my name, and hast not denied my faith, even in those days wherein Antipas was my faithful martyr, who was slain among you, where Satan dwelleth.*

Antipas was a man who really existed. This man was a holy martyr who died by assassination while preaching the word of the Lord. The place where Antipas was assassinated was really a synagogue of Satan. This was an historical event.

A tenebrous nuclear atom exists in the chakra of the navel. The "I" is found intimately related with this atom. This is the seat of Satan.

But I have a few things against thee, because thou hast there them that hold the doctrine of Balaam, who taught Balac to cast a stumbling block before the children of Israel, to eat things sacrificed unto idols, and to commit fornication.

All of these vulgar passions are satanic. The seat of Satan is situated in the region of the navel. Situated in the area of the stomach are gluttony, drunkenness, etc...

So hast thou also them that hold the doctrine of the Nicolaitans, which thing I hate.

Only absolute saintliness and chastity can convert us into Angels.

The Nicolaitans spill the sacred wine of the temple. They waste the oil of the lamp and remain within the darkness.

The Nicolaitans spill the raw matter of the Great Work in their practises of Sexual Alchemy. This is Black Tantrism.

Repent; or else I will come unto thee quickly, and will fight against them with the sword of my mouth.

This fight is occurring in this present day and age. We must know that since the year 1950, one **Word** is fighting against them with the flaming sword.

The Nicolaitans are submerging themselves into the abyss. The Nicolaitans converted themselves into terribly perverse demons.

> *He that hath an ear, let him hear what the Spirit saith unto the churches;*
>
> *To him that overcometh will I give to eat of the hidden manna* (the manna of the Christic wisdom), *and will give him a white stone* (the Philosophical Stone, sex), *and in the stone a new name written which no man knoweth saving he that receiveth it.*

This new name is the name of our internal God; this is the name of the Son of Man. The virtues that are necessary in order to open the church of Pergamos are the following: chastity, loyalty, faith, and obedience to the **Father**.

The initiate cannot be a glutton, drunkard, or fornicator. The Nicolaitans develop tenebrous magical powers through fornication.

The initiate must be temperate, faithful, chaste, humble, and obedient.

Chapter 9
The Church of Thyatira

The church of Thyatira is opened when the serpentine fire reaches the height of the heart.

Internal meditation and internal prayer develop and unfold the chakra of the tranquil heart.

Seven sacred centers exist in the heart and correspond to the seven degrees of the power of the fire.

The heart is the sanctuary of love. Take heed of sensual love. Do not mix sacred ecstasy with selfish love.

Love is as pure as the morning star. Love is universal. Love is impersonal, ineffable, and impartial.

You must be charitable. We sin against Christian charity when we criticize the religion of others. Cultivate respect and veneration.

Respect your neighbor's beliefs. Respect the religion of your neighbor. Do not force anyone to think your way. Do not criticize. Remember that each head is a world. Do not sin anymore against the charity of Christ.

Humanity is divided and subdivided into groups. Each group requires a special system of teaching. Each group needs its school, its religion, its sect. These are the commandments of the Blessed One.

We violate the law of the tranquil heart when we criticize others.

If your are willing to give the last drop of blood for the love of this suffering humanity, then you are one of us.

Whosoever wants to reach the altar of initiation must transform the self into the immolated Lamb upon the altar of supreme sacrifice.

It is necessary to love those who hate us, to kiss the adorable hand of the one who whips us, to clean the sandals of the one who humiliates us.

If a poor beggar invites you to eat at his table, eat with him, because that poor beggar is our brother.

If a leper cuts a piece of bread and offers it to you, take it and eat it because that poor leper is your brother; do not despise him.

Always be the last; do not aspire to be the first. Seat yourself on the last seats; never occupy the first place. Remember that you are nothing but a poor sinner. Do not be proud of perfection because only your Father who is in secret is perfect.

Your internal God is filled with glory, but you are only a poor slug that slithers in the mud. You are not perfect.

Do not hold resentments against your neighbor. Remember that your neighbour is not perfect either. Act not with resentment or revenge. Love, forgive, and kiss the hand of the executioner who whips you.

It is necessary for your "I" to be annihilated in order for the great Lord of the Light to enter into your soul.

Dress with light, my brother, my sister. Hear the **ten mystical sounds** of the tranquil heart.

The first sound is like the voice of the Son of Man that fecundates the waters of genesis in order for life to sprout.

The second is the sound **Chini-Chini**.

The third is the supreme sound of the great cosmic bell that emanates from the internal ray of each human being.

The fourth is the internal thunder of the heart whose solemn vibration is repeated within the body of each human being.

The fifth is like the delectable sound of the **lute**.

The sixth is the cymbals of the ineffable Gods that resound within the chalice of each blessed flower.

The seventh sound is that of the Magic Flute whose virginal melodies carry us to the supreme joy of the gardens of Nirvana.

The eighth sound is that of the **Bheri** (drum).

The ninth sound is that of the exotic variation of a double drum (Mridanga).

The tenth is the sound of seven uttering thunders.

When we reach the ninth hour and are crucified upon the Cross of Golgotha, we exclaim with a great voice, ***"Father, into Thy hands I commend my spirit."*** (Luke 23:46)

This supreme instant of the ninth hour occurs with terrible lightning, words, voices, and thunder. The seven thunders utter the voices of the Eternal One.

Only those who have experienced the supreme death of the "I," the **ego**, the **myself**, know how to pronounce the seventh word. The fight against **Satan** is terrible for them. The women seal the sepulchres of the initiates with a great stone, the blessed Philosophical Stone.

The supreme spear of pain passes through the hearts of the great initiates, and from their wound flows blood and water.

The raw matter of the Great Work is the sacred wine.

You will hear the ten mystical sounds when you meditate internally in the lotus of the heart.

We control the Tattva Vayu when we meditate on the lotus of the heart, and the power of winds and hurricanes is given to us.

The lotus of the heart has fifteen petals that shine with the fire of the Holy Spirit.

An octagonal space with an ineffable jet black color exists within the chakra of the heart. In this space, the ten mystical sounds of the church of Thyatira resound like a symphony of Beethoven.

The great rhythms of **Mahaban** and **Chotaban** firmly sustain the universe in its march.

The rhythms of fire are the foundation of the exquisite harmonies of the cosmic diapason. If you visit Nirvana during an ecstasy, then you must accomplish the sacred duty of singing in accordance with the rhythms of fire. Thus, this is how you will help us (the Nirvanis) with your Word. The universe is sustained by the Word.

If you want to travel consciously in the internal worlds, you must develop the chakra of the heart.

If you want to reach the Christ, then you must kill desire. You must obtain the characteristics of a lemon.

If you want to learn how to place your body in the state of "**Jinn**," then you must develop the chakra of the heart.

We can develop the chakra of the tranquil heart with the system of internal meditation.

Revelation 2:18-29:

> *And unto the* (atomic) *Angel of the church in Thyatira write: These things saith the Son of God, who hath his eyes like unto a flame of fire, and his feet are like fine brass;*
>
> *I know thy works, and charity, and service, and faith, and thy patience, and thy works; and the last to be more than the first* (charity, service, faith, and patience are the virtues required in order to open the church of Thyatira).
>
> *Notwithstanding I have a few things against thee, because thou sufferest that woman Jezebel which calleth herself a prophetess, to teach and to seduce my servants to commit fornication, and to eat things sacrificed unto idols.*

Jezebel is that harlot woman dressed in purple and scarlet. She is the intellectual mind that teaches us to fornicate and to eat things sacrificed unto idols. Jezebel is politics, journalism, diplomacy, materialistic science, intellectualism of any type and etc.

In ancient times, Jezebel taught human beings to eat things offered unto idols in the temples of black magic. Jezebel signifies intellectualism, feasts, drunkenness, orgies, gluttony, fornication, adultery, materialistic science, etc. Jezebel is symbolized by the turkey and the pig.

> *And I gave her space to repent of her fornication; and she repented not.*
>
> *Behold, I will cast her into a bed, and them that commit adultery with her into great tribulation, except they repent of their deeds.*

Jezebel is the satanic mind that does not want to repent of its evil deeds.

The times of the end have arrived and Jezebel, along with all who commit adultery with her, will be cast into a bed of pain.

The dwellers of the earth have committed adultery with Jezebel as well as the potentates of gold and silver, the vultures of war and the intellectuals who abhor the Eternal One.

And I will kill her children with death (the children of Jezebel are the dwellers of the earth: the intellectuals, the merchants of fine linen, gold and silver, silk and scarlet, precious wood, brass, iron, and marble); *and all the churches shall know that I am he which searcheth the kidneys and hearts: and I will give unto every one of you according to your works.*

When the renal (kidney) chakras shine with immaculate whiteness like the lotus flower, it is because we have reached supreme chastity.

When the renal chakras are dyed with a bloody passionate colour, woe to us! for we are fornicators and the **Word** casts us into the abyss with his sword. Woe to the inhabitants of the Earth!

The **Word** searcheth the kidneys (reins) and the hearts; and He gives unto each one of us in accordance with our works.

Whosoever wants to open the church of Thyatira must have the mind of a child.

Those who commit adultery with Jezebel who called herself a prophetess cannot know the wisdom of the tranquil heart.

Love and wisdom are the secret path of the heart. The wisdom of the seal of the heart is for children, in other words, for those who do not commit adultery with Jezebel who called herself a prophetess.

If you want to open the church of Thyatira, you must attain the lost infancy.

Jezebel is Satan. Jezebel is the "I," the **myself**, the **ego** that we carry within.

But unto you I say, and unto the rest in Thyatira, as many as have not this doctrine, and which have not known the depths of Satan, as they speak; I will put upon you none other burden.

But that which ye have already hold fast till I come.

And he that overcometh, and keepeth my works unto the end, to him will I give power over the nations:

And he shall rule them with a rod of iron: as the vessels of a potter shall they be broken to shivers: even as I receiveth of my Father.

And I will give him the morning star.

He that hath an ear, let him hear what the Spirit saith unto the churches.

When we decapitate and dissolve the "I," the **myself**, then we receive the Venustic Initiation.

Whosoever receives the Venustic Initiation incarnates his Star.

It is urgent to know that the Star crucified upon the Cross is the **Christ** of the **Abraxas**.

The Star is the Son of Man, the Truth. No one can search for the Truth. The Truth cannot be known by the "I." No one can search for the Truth because no one can search for that which they do not know.

Jezebel, who called herself a prophetess, cannot know the Truth.

The Truth cannot be studied, read, or known by the mind. The Truth is completely different, distinct from all of that which is read, studied, or known by the mind.

The Truth comes to us when we have decapitated and dissolved the "I."

The distinct truths of people are nothing else but projections of the mind.

The times of the end have arrived, and all of those who commit adultery with Jezebel who called herself a prophetess will be broken into slivers as the vessels of a potter.

When the devotee enters into the chamber of the pure Spirit, he feels a delectable terror. This sacred chamber is illuminated by an immaculate and divine light that gives life, yet does not cast a shadow upon the way of anyone.

Whosoever reaches the heights of contemplation and illumination will see in this chamber of the pure Spirit the living picture of the event of Golgotha. No wise man on earth could have painted so much beauty. This picture has its own life. The stigmatas of the Adorable One bleed, and with his blood he dyes the land of Golgotha red. His beloved temples, pierced with the cruel thorns of the crown of martyrdom, bleed painfully, and from his wounded side, pierced by the **Lance of Longinus**, flows blood and water.

This picture has abundant life. The sun sets within its bed of purple. The craniums of the executed ones and the shadow of death are at the foot of Calvary. Do not be afraid, faithful devotee, behold, the shadow of death is rising. Do not be afraid; rather, defeat it. Remember that the Lord defeated death.

Flee, oh death, before my steps even to the end of the world and evermore! You shall be my slave and I shall be your lord!

Death has fled, but behold what is in the middle of the sanctuary. It is a gigantic specter dressed in the style of the princes of the Middle Ages. He is the prince of this world, proud and perverse. He is your own "I." You must decapitate him with your flaming sword and then you must dissolve him with rigorous purifications. Thus, this is how you will reach the Venustic Initiation. Then you will incarnate the Truth. The **Word** will be made flesh in you. You will incarnate the Son of Man and you will receive the Morning Star.

"The Army of the Voice is Christ."

Chapter 10
The Church of Sardis

The church of Sardis is opened when the victorious serpentine fire ascends to the height of the thyroid gland.

The chakra of the larynx has sixteen beautiful petals that magnificently shine with the glorious Pentecostal fire.

This beautiful chakra resembles a mysterious full moon shining as an ineffable poem within the moving melodies of the infinite ether.

The hidden and terrific powers of this chakra will awaken through meditating in it.

We can preserve the physical body even during the Great Cosmic Night and avoid being disintegrated by the Great Pralaya† when we develop this chakra of the larynx.

The development of this chakra of the larynx grants us conceptual synthetism.

The great Masters of Nirvana do not rationalize.

Conceptual synthetism and intuition replace reasoning.

Desire and reasoning belong to the "I." Really, Satan is the one who rationalizes.

We comprehend the esoterism of the sacred books with the development of this chakra of the larynx.

The Tattva Akash is the Tattva of the laryngeal chakra.

We become aware of the past, present, and future, of all that exists in the universe, with the development of this chakra of the larynx.

Likewise, with the development of this chakra of the larynx, we awake the sacred ear, and then we can hear the words of paradise and the ineffable symphonies of the temples.

The power of comprehension is granted to us when we develop this chakra. Comprehension and intuition will replace reasoning.

The comprehensive mind does not judge or translate. The "I" judges and translates everything that it sees into the language of its own prejudgments, memories, mistakes, and evil deeds.

Judge not, that ye be not judged. For with what judgment ye judge, ye shall be judged: And with the measure ye mete, it shall be measured to you again. - Matthew 7:1-2

You must live in the state of alert perception. See, hear, and comprehend; do not judge so that you will not be judged. Comprehend everything.

Do not allow Satan to translate all that you see and hear. You must reconquer the innocence of Eden.

Those who meditate on the church of Sardis hear the ineffable words of Nirvana.

Have you ever attended the banquet of Nirvana? Behold, such divine beings! The Holy Masters are dressed with diamond tunics. These are the tunics of the **Dharmasayas**. Three glasses that contain three pure balsams are placed upon the table of the banquet. The first is the red balsam of fire, the second is the green balsam of the pure waters that give eternal life, the third is the immaculate pure balsam of the Spirit.

Drink from these three glasses and you will never thirst again.

Ah! When your words will be pure and beautiful like the voice of paradise.

Ah! When your phrases will be lovely, beautiful and harmonious. Then, your creative larynx will be as the divine and enchanted notes of a piano of Nirvana, like the melody of a temple, like the Word of the Holy Masters who attend the banquet of the immolated Lamb.

You must never pronounce words in vain; never pronounce disgusting words.

The throat is the uterus where the word is created. The Gods create with the power of the Word.

The Kundalini creates with the Word. The Kundalini creates in the larynx. The sexual organ of the Gods is the creative larynx.

> *In the beginning was the Word, and the Word was with God, and the Word was God, the same was in the beginning with God. All things were made by him; and without him was not anything made that was made.* John 1:1-3

The Army of the Voice is **Christ**.

In the dawn of life, the Gods sang in their golden language, teaching us the divine laws.

When the heart of the solar system began to palpitate after the Great Cosmic Night, then the Army of the Voice fecundated the Chaos in order for life to emerge.

The seven sublime Lords sang with the rhythms of the fire. The Gods and their Isis officiated in each one of the seven temples. Each one of the seven Gods (Spirits) and their Isis sang the rituals of fire. There was a priest, an Isis (priestess) and a choir of Angels in each one of the seven churches. There was a man, a woman, and a choir; a male, a female, and choir.

The waters of the Chaos were fecundated with this sexual intercourse of the creative word in order for life to emerge. Thus, this is how the universe was born. The waters of Genesis were fecundated by the sexual fire of the Word.

In the beginning, the universe was subtle, pure, and ineffable.

The dense, gross, and material state of the universe was acquired after successive condensations.

Revelation 3:1 to 6:

> *And unto the* (atomic) *Angel of the church in Sardis write: These things saith he that hath the seven Spirits of God, and the seven stars; I know thy works, that thou hast a name* (the name of your internal God) *that thou livest, and art dead* (because you did not incarnate Him yet).

Be watchful, and strengthen the things which remain, that are ready to die: (strengthen the death of your "I") *for I have not found thy works perfect before God.*

Remember that all of the deeds of your "I" are evil. Resolve to die. Take from the "I" its nourishment and the "I" will be disintegrated. The nourishment of the "I" is the defects.

Do not justify your defects and do not condemn them, but rather, comprehend them.

The defects are disintegrated when we consciously comprehend them.

The "I" dies when it is not being fed. First we must decapitate Satan, then we must dissolve it. You know this.

Remember therefore how thou hast received and heard, and hold fast, and repent. If therefore thou shalt not watch, I will come on thee as a thief, and thou shalt not know what hour I will come upon thee.

Remember that the times of the end have arrived and that we are in them. The great cataclysm of fire will occur sooner or later. You know this. The Lord will come as a thief in the night, in an unexpected hour.

Thou hast a few names even in Sardis which have not defiled their garments; and they shall walk with me in white: for they are worthy.

He that overcometh, the same shall be clotheth in white raiment; and I will not blot out his name out of the book of life. But I will confess his name before my Father, and before his Angels.

Whosoever incarnates **Him** is a conqueror.

He that hath an ear, let him hear what the Spirit saith unto the churches.

Remember that the sacred wine is the **Ens Seminis**. You know this.

The whole power of the **Word** is found enclosed within the **Ens Seminis**.

The **Staurus**† of the Gnostics is formed with the intersection of the vertical phallus with the horizontal cteis†.

The cteis is the house of the phallus. Creation is the house of the **Word**.

The secret key of the awakening of the fire is found in the cteis and the phallus well united.

It is important to avoid the orgasm in order to impede the raw matter of the Great Work from being spilled from its receptacle. Our motto is **Thelema** (willpower).

All of the **Ens Virtutis**† of the sacred fire is contained within the **Ens Seminis**.

However, there are some doctors who affirm that this scientific process can cause us damage in many ways (**Loedere**†). We affirm that this is not so, because the **Ens Seminis** is completely transmuted into light and fire.

Actually, within our creative organs a slow coition (**Digerere**†) exists, which reduces the **Ens Seminis** into its primordial, energetic principles.

The solar and lunar atoms of the seminal system ascend towards the brain through the two sympathetic canals. These two canals are two fine cords that rise from the testicles or ovaries up to the brain.

In the East, these two canals are known as **Ida** and **Pingala**. These are the two witnesses.

You must light the fire in order to incarnate the **Word**. Without the fire, you cannot speak the Word of gold of the first instant.

The igneous serpent of our magical powers awakens when the solar and lunar atoms make contact in the coccyx. Thus, this is how we convert ourselves into ardent flames.

The key of fire is in the intersection of the vertical phallus with the horizontal cteis. However, you must be careful not to spill the wine of the altar.

All of the atoms of all the languages that we spoke in our past lives exist within the **Ens Seminis**. When the atomic substances of the Word rises to the creative larynx, then we are able to speak all of those languages again. Therefore, only the Holy Spirit can give us this Power of Tongues.

Within the **Ens Seminis**, there also exist transformative atoms of a high voltage. These atoms transform us completely.

Within the **Ens Seminis** live the atoms of the cosmic grammar. The very pure rising of the divine language runs like a river of gold through a thick, sunny jungle.

We reach perfect beatitude when the **Word** is made flesh in us.

Whosoever overcometh will be dressed with white vestures because this one is a Master of the Day, a Master of the **Mahamanvantara**. *"His name will be written in the book of life and I will confess his name before my Father, and before his Angels."* (Verse 5)

It is necessary to be born again in order to enter into the kingdom of heaven.

The **Word** is always born from Immaculate Conceptions. The **Word** is always the child of very pure Virgins. The mother of the **Word** is always a woman.

When **Jesus** was crucified upon his cross and was bleeding, filled with pain, He uttered to his mother the following, *"Woman, behold thy son."* (John 19:26) He was indicating John who stood beside Mary. Then, after he said to his disciple, *"Behold thy mother! and from that hour that disciple* (John) *took her unto his own home."* (John 19:27)

John is a word which must be sounded into five divided vowels in the following way: **I.E.O.U.AN.** We form the **mantras** with these five vowels. **John** is the **Verb**, the **great Word**.

> *Verily, verily I say unto thee, except a man be born of Water* (semen) *and of the Spirit* (fire), *he cannot enter into the kingdom of God.* - John 3:5

All of these verses of the third chapter of the Gospel of Saint John enclose the Great Arcanum. The Arcanum A. Z. F. is the Great Arcanum.

> *And as Moses lifted up the* **serpent** *in the wilderness, even so must the* **Son of Man** *be lifted up.* (John 3:14) Whosoever

incarnates Him is lifting Him up, resurrecting Him within himself.

Verily, verily, I say unto thee, we speak that we do know, and testify that we have seen; and ye receive not our witness. (John 3:11) Our divine Savior gave testimony of what he saw and experienced.

Jesus is a son of the water and the fire. The mother of the **Word** is always a woman.

And no man hath ascended up to heaven, but he that came down from heaven, even the Son of Man which is in heaven. (John 3:13)

We must dissolve the "I." The "I" did not come from heaven. Therefore, the "I" cannot ascend to heaven. Only the Son of Man can ascend to heaven, because He descended from heaven.

Everything lives because of the **Word**. Everything is sustained by the **Word**.

The five vowels **I.E.O.U.A.** resound like a miraculous harp of the infinite cosmos within the flaming fire, within the impetuous air, within the boisterous waves, and within the perfumed earth.

The vowel "**I**" (sounded *eee*) causes the frontal chakra to vibrate.

The vowel "**E**" (sounded *ehhh*) causes the chakra of the larynx to vibrate.

The vowel "**O**" (sounded *ooo*) causes the chakra of the heart to vibrate.

The vowel "**U**" (sounded *uuu*) causes the chakra of the solar plex to vibrate.

The vowel "**A**" (sounded *aaahhh*) causes the chakra of the lungs to vibrate.

These chakras, discs, or magnetic wheels of the Astral Body develop and improve when the seven vowels are vocalized daily for one hour.

The Prana, life energy, must be inhaled through the nasal cavities and then exhaled through the mouth while vocalizing.

Each vowel is powerful. Each vowel must be prolonged and sustained in order to awaken the chakras.

The sound of these vowels vibrated within our organism when we dwelled in Eden. Now, we must awaken these miraculous sounds of nature again in all of the chakras of the Astral Body.

We were paradisiacal human beings, there, in **Arcadia**, in those ancient times of Nature. Disgracefully, the lyre of Orpheus fell upon the floor of the temple and broke into pieces.

Now, we must pray, meditate, transmute, and vocalize in order for the Phoenix Bird to resurrect from its own ashes.

Chapter 11
The Church of Philadelphia

The church of Philadelphia shines with mystical happiness within each exquisite note of a piano, and within each melody of Nirvana.

The frontal chakra awakens when the sacred fire opens the church of Philadelphia.

This chakra is found situated between the eyebrows. The mystic is filled with ecstasy when contemplating this lotus flower within the cavernous plex.

This immaculate lotus resembles a poem of love within the sublime enchantments of the starry night.

This precious lotus flower is rooted in the pituitary gland.

The frontal chakra shines with the immaculate colors of a romantic moonlight.

The frontal chakra has many divine splendors, yet it has only two fundamental petals.

The total and complete development of the frontal chakra signifies supreme beatitude and absolute liberation. The frontal chakra has eight major powers and thirty-six minor powers.

The frontal chakra causes us to be clairvoyant. The clairvoyant must have a child-like mind. But, when he permits the "I" to translate his visions, he can also convert himself into a calumniator.

The clairvoyant must be simple and humble like the little timid and perfumed flower existing during the starry night.

The clairvoyant must be as a garden sealed with seven seals.

The true seer never says that he is a seer. The true seer must be humble and modest.

The seer must learn how to see without the presence of the "I," to see without translation, and without judgement.

The frontal chakra develops with internal meditation.

Revelation 3:7-13:

And to the Angel of the church in Philadelphia write: These things saith he that is holy, he that is true, he that hath the key of David, he that openeth, and no man shutteth; and shutteth, and no man openeth.

The key of David is the key of the internal temple of each human being. We must build the temple upon the living rock (sex). The key of the temple is the key of the Ark of Science.

This key is the Arcanum A.Z.F. The Son of Man openeth and no man shutteth, and shutteth, and no man openeth.

Do not throw stones from the interior of the temple. Do not use clairvoyance in order to hurt neighbors; have pity for those who suffer, have pity for those who cry. Do not hurt them, but rather love them. Do not transform the temple into a den of thieves.

I know thy works: behold I have set before thee an open door (the door of the frontal chakra), *and no man can shut it: for thou hast a little strength, and hast kept my word, and hast not denied my name.*

Behold, I will make them of the synagogue of Satan, which say they are Jews, and are not, but do lie; behold I will make them to come and worship before thy feet, and to know that I have loved thee.

Authentic Jews are only the children of the lion from the tribe of Judah, meaning, the **Christified Ones**.

Those who say that they are Jews (illuminated ones) and are not, do lie. Really, these people belong to the synagogue of Satan. These people cannot enter the temple of Philadelphia.

When the clairvoyant is a black magician, the frontal chakra is controlled by Jezebel, the woman who called herself a prophetess.

The black magician develops tenebrous clairvoyance. The frontal chakra of the black magician works only in the abyss. The tenebrous ones take the shape of Masters and also friends of Masters in order to perform horrible acts within the atomic infernos of nature.

Actually, the clairvoyants of Jezebel calumniate their neighbors when they are in contact with these disguised tenebrous beings.

The truly illuminated clairvoyant is not capable of calumniating his neighbor. The truly illuminated clairvoyant sees without the presence of the "I." The illuminated clairvoyant uses his faculty with supreme wisdom in order to advise and help his neighbor.

We need to decapitate Jezebel. We need to place clairvoyance under the service of the immolated Lamb. We need to prophesy with wisdom.

> *Because thou hast kept the word of my patience, I also will keep thee from the hour of temptation, which shall come upon all the world, to try them that dwell upon the earth.*

We are now in the hour of the great temptation.

> *Behold, I come quickly: hold that fast which thou hast, (the fire) that no man take thy crown.* Do not let Satan take it from you. Do not waste the sacred wine; be chaste.

> *Him that overcometh will I make a pillar in the temple of my God, and he shall go no more out; and I will write upon him the name of my God, and the name of the city of my God, which is new Jerusalem, which cometh down out of heaven from my God: and I will write upon him my new name.*

> *He that hath an ear, let him hear what the Spirit saith unto the churches.*

The sixth sense, the divine clairvoyance, awakens during the ascension towards the superior worlds.

And He will write upon him, on his forehead, the name of the Lamb and the name of the new Jerusalem from above, from the superior worlds where we are received with palms and praises and feasts when we liberate ourselves from the four bodies of sin. And the new Jerusalem comes down from God out of heaven, prepared as a bride adorned for her husband.

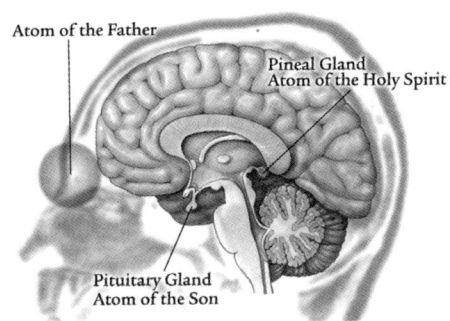

THE GLANDS AND THE THREE ATOMS

Chapter 12
The Church of Laodicea

The church of Laodicea is opened when the igneous serpent of our magical powers reaches the pineal gland, which is situated in the brain.

The pineal gland is situated in the superior part of the brain and is the queen of all glands.

A very subtle and small canal exists between the pituitary gland and the pineal gland; this canal vanishes in cadavers. The fire must pass through this small canal towards the point between the eyebrows. Then, the fire travels towards the root of the nose. A special magnetic field exists in the root of the nose; here is where the atom of the Father resides.

When we aspire to the great Light, then we inhale billions of aspirant atoms that travel through the nasal cavities towards the magnetic field of the root of the nose where the atom of the Father is situated.

The sexual glands and the pineal gland are found to be intimately correlated. The potency of the pineal gland depends upon the potency of the sexual glands.

The atom of the Holy Spirit is in the pineal gland. The atom of the Son (**Christ**) is in the pituitary gland. The atom of the Father resides in the magnetic field of the root of the nose.

The pineal gland is only five millimetres in diameter and is surrounded by fine, sandlike particles.

The lotus flower of the pineal gland has one thousand petals that shine when forming the Crown of the Saints. An entire cosmic zodiac shines and gleams within the microcosmical human being. This is the glowing halo above the heads of the Saints.

As above, so below. The zodiac of the starry sky is governed by twenty-four Elders.

The zodiacal human being is also governed by twenty-four Atomic Gods who have their throne in the brain. The halo of the twenty-four Atomic Gods gleam and shine in the Crown of the Saints.

Above, in the starry sky, the seven Spirits are before the throne of the Lamb. Here below, the seven Atomic Angels who govern the seven churches of the spinal medulla are within the microcosmical human being. "**As above, so below.**"

The pineal gland is the window of **Brahma**, the diamond eye, the eye of polyvoyance.

The intuitive sight resides in this chakra, the eye of the Spirit. This splendorous and divine chakra is associated with the crown of thorns that pierces the temples of all the Christified Ones and causes them to bleed.

We can study the divine wisdom of Nirvana with this chakra.

This chakra permits us to see and to instantaneously know. Seeing with the diamond eye allows us to transport ourselves to the place that we are seeing.

Whosoever has developed this coronary chakra can instantly abandon his vehicles whenever he so wishes. We reach perfect ecstasy when the **Innermost** functions without any type of vehicles in the world of the mist of the fire.

We arrive at the First Initiation of Fire when the fire touches the atom of the Father.

Both glands, epiphyses and hypophyses (pineal and pituitary), respectively radiate and have their own aura. A current of light departs through the door of the frontal chakra when these glandular auras are mixed. The initiate receives the initiation when reaching these esoteric heights. The initiate must raise the seven degrees of the power of the fire.

The Pentagonal Star gleams and shines with immaculate whiteness in the frontal chakra of the great initiates.

Some initiates resurrect in the fire, others in the fire and in the light. We must first resurrect in the fire, then after in the light.

When we aspire to the light, millions of aspirant atoms reach the magnetic field of the nose and then they move towards the heart. In the heart resides the atom "**Nous**"; this atom governs all of the atoms of the organism.

A master atom† exists within the seminal system. This atom rises towards the brain with Sexual Alchemy in order to teach the wisdom of nature.

Whosoever reaches the Fifth Initiation of Major Mysteries becomes a major brother of humanity.

Before you can reach the valley of refuge, which is referred to us as the path of pure knowledge, you have to sacrifice yourself for the love of humanity.

The Fifth Path is supreme love, supreme charity, and supreme obedience to the Father.

Part of the fire escapes and enters the exterior world when the sacred serpent passes through the cerebral center, which is situated where the frontal fontanel of a newborn would be found. The entire aura shines with fire in those instances, and the immaculate white dove of the Holy Spirit enters within us.

All of the vehicles of the initiate must be crucified and stigmatized in the Golgotha of supreme sacrifice. The Golgotha of the Father is the brain. We must rise to the Golgotha with the cross on our back.

The twenty-four Elders cast their crowns at the feet of the Lamb. Whosoever opens the church of Laodicea must humbly toss his crown to the feet of the Lamb.

The resplendent lotus of one thousand petals develops and unfolds with internal meditation.

Those who throw their crowns to the feet of the Lamb must remember that whosoever wishes to reach the mystical science must deny and release the self from these five things:

1. The human passions, distractions, and vices of the multitudes
2. The vain and futile things of the world

3. Attachment to hidden powers. If you have such powers in abundance, act as if you do not.
4. Release yourself from your own self. Convince yourself that even though your internal God is very exalted and grandiose, you are nothing else but a shadow of your God, a sinning shadow that must be annihilated; and
5. Resolve yourself to die. Do not aspire to immortalize your "I." Resolve to die completely, for you are nothing more than a poor shadow. Thus, this is how you will be lost within your internal God and only the Son of Man will remain dwelling within your Christified Soul.

To you who have opened the seven churches, remember that the hidden powers are very divine, yet also very dangerous. If we do not dissolve the "I," then when it is armed with all of these powers it will desire to do something with them; this "I" will desire to be great and almighty.

Those initiates who are attached to magical powers are departing from humbleness and from nothingness, therefore they fall into the abyss of perdition.

If you want to incarnate the Lamb, remember your own misery in every instant. Nothingness is the acknowledgment of your own sin and misery; it is the way for your God who is waiting to perform marvels and prodigies within you.

You must fast, pray, cover yourself with sackcloth, and make penance.

Tell your sacred visions to no one. Remember that Jezebel who called herself a prophetess enjoys when she tells people of her visions.

You who throw your crown at the feet of the Lamb must learn to be quiet. Never speak of the initiations of the Beloved One. The initiations are very sacred.

The Beloved One can be filled with initiations and powers, but you are nothing but a sinning shadow. It is urgent that you arrive to the annihilation of your "I." Never say how many initiations you have or someone else has because your "I" never receives initiations. The initiations are very sacred. Only the **Innermost** is the unique One who receives initiations, degrees, and feasts. The initiations are for the **Innermost**. You are nothing but a shadow that must be annihilated.

Revelation 3:14-22:

> *And unto the* (atomic) *Angel of the church of the Laodiceans write: these things saith the Amen, the faithful and the true witness, the beginning of the creation of God:*
>
> *I know thy works, that thou art neither cold nor hot: I would thou wert cold or hot.*
>
> *So then because thou art lukewarm, and neither cold nor hot, I will spue thee out of my mouth.*

Woe for those who are lukewarm! Truly they will not enter unto the Secret Path. The lukewarm are parasites of nature.

A great sinner is often closer to redemption than a lukewarm devotee. *"I will spue thee* (the lukewarm) *out of my mouth."*

Really, the one who is lukewarm says, *"I am rich* (I am filled with science etc.), *and increased with goods, and have need of nothing: and knowest not that thou art wretcheth, and miserable, and poor, and blind, and naked:*

> *I counsel thee to buy of me gold tried in the fire* (by means of the sexual fire, we must transmute the lead of the personality into the very pure gold of the divine Spirit), *that thou mayest be* (spiritually) *rich; and white raiment, that thou mayest be clothed, and that shame of thy nakedness do not appear; and anoint thine eyes with eyesalve, that thou mayest see.*

The eyesalve of chastity is the raw matter of the Great Work. It is the Holy Collyrium† which opens our eye with polyvoyance. The potency of the pineal gland depends upon the potency of the sexual glands.

> *As many as I love, I rebuke and chasten: be zealous* (vigilant) *therefore, and repent.*

Behold, I stand at the door, and knock; if any man hear my voice, and open the door (the pineal gland is the door of the soul), *I will come in to him, and will sup with him, and he with me.*

The Lamb enters within us through the door of the pineal gland. The Lamb transforms himself into the Soul and the Soul into **Him**, when **He** enters within the Soul. Then, the Son of Man resurrects within our own selves.

To him that overcometh will I grant to sit with me in my throne, even as I also overcame, and am set down with my Father in his throne.

The Soul mixed with the Lamb is that Son of Man who sits in his throne. The Son of Man is a conqueror. He defeated Satan. He has the right to sit in the throne of the Father because the Son is one with the Father and the Father is one with the Son.

He that hath an ear, let him hear what the spirit saith unto the churches.

The Lamb must enter the Spirit (the **Innermost**), the Soul, and the body of the human being.

Those who throw their crowns to the feet of the Lamb, remember that you must build the temple upon the living stone in order for the Lamb to enter and sup with you.

The temple of wisdom has seven columns of living fire.

If you want the initiation, write it upon a staff.

Only with INRI will you reach the Golgotha of the Father.

Chapter 13
The Jinn States

"As above, so below." The infinitely small is analogous to the infinitely great. An atom is a complete, tiny solar system.

The heavenly Jerusalem exists in the macrocosm. The heavenly Jerusalem also exists within the microcosmic human being.

A new heaven and a new earth will exist. This will be the future new, heavenly Jerusalem of the macrocosm.

When a human being is Christified, then he becomes transformed into the new heavenly Jerusalem of the microcosm. "As above, so below." This is the Law.

The new Jerusalem, in the macrocosm as well as in the microcosm, descends from the superior worlds and is filled with terribly divine powers.

The new Jerusalem, either in the future planet Earth or in the planet human being, is illuminated by the immolated Lamb.

In the macrocosm, the purified planet of the future, as well as its internal bodies, will be the heavenly Jerusalem of the future.

The Christified body of the human being with his Christified internal bodies constitute the heavenly Jerusalem of the microcosmic human being.

Everything that happens in the heavenly Jerusalem of the macrocosm is repeated within the heavenly Jerusalem of the microcosmic human being. "As above, so below."

The Christified souls will abide in the future heavenly Jerusalem of the planet Earth. Only the Christified soul of the initiate abides in the heavenly Jerusalem of the human body.

The physical body of an initiate is the heavenly Jerusalem of the microcosm. This Christified body is filled with terrific powers.

The eight major powers of the mystic are the following:

Anima: the power to reduce the size of the physical body to the size of an atom.

Mahima: the power to enlarge the physical body to the point of touching the sun and the moon with the hand.

Laghima: the power to decrease the weight of the physical body to that of a feather. We can float in the air with the physical body, thanks to this power.

Garima: the power to willingly increase the weight of the physical body to that of a mountain.

Prapti: the power of prophecy, the power of clairvoyance, the sacred ear, psychometry, telepathy and intuition, the power of understanding the language of the animals. Apollonius of Tyana and Saint Francis of Assisi were able to communicate with animals of the forest.

Prakamya: the power that permits the mystic to submerge within the waters and to live submerged in the waters without receiving any harm. The great Guru-deva Sivananda told us of the case of the Swami Trillinga of Benares (India), who was accustomed to live six months of the year submerged within the waters of the river Ganges.

Vashitvam: the power with which the mystic can dominate the wildest animals; also the power to pronounce words which enchant and quiet poisonous serpents.

Ishitvam: the power that permits the Saint to resurrect the dead. Whosoever reaches this height is a liberated one, a Lord of the living and of the dead.

Everyone who walks on the path of Christification must develop these eight powers.

These powers of the heavenly Jerusalem are conquered with internal meditation, with the condition of absolute chastity.

When the human body is converted into the heavenly Jerusalem, then it becomes a marvellous Christic body.

Practice

1. The mystic must lie down on his bed with tranquility.
2. Ask the Lamb for the assistance of an Angel which specializes in the "**Jinn**" science.
3. The mystic must beseech the Angel and the immolated Lamb to take him (or her) with his physical body into the superior worlds.
4. We, the brothers and sisters of the temple, advise you to invoke the Angel **Harpocrates** who is a specialist in the "**Jinn**" science. Beg the Lamb, beseech Him to send the Angel **Harpocrates** to you.
5. Release all your thoughts from your mind, clear your mind. It is necessary for you to place your mind in quietude and tranquility.
6. You must provoke sleep. Let yourself fall asleep without thoughts.
7. While conserving your sleep like a precious treasure, rise from your bed and leave your bedroom.

If the practice has been performed well, then your body will enter the "**Jinn**" state, meaning that it will submerge within the supra-sensible worlds.

A body while in the "**Jinn**" state can float in the air (**Laghima**) or be submerged within the waters (**Prakamya**), or pass through fire without being burned, or be reduced to the size of an atom (**Anima**), or be enlarged to the point of touching the sun or the moon with the hand (**Mahima**).

A body submerged within the supra-sensible worlds is submitted to the laws of those worlds. Then, this body is plastic and elastic, so it can change form, decrease its weight (**Laghima**), or increase its weight (**Garima**) willingly.

The Yogi of Benares was able to submerge himself within the waters for six months because, firstly, he was placing his body in the "**Jinn**" state.

Some devotees who were practicing meditation in order to place the physical body in "**Jinn**" state were feeling the sensation

ST. PETER DELIVERED FROM PRISON

And, behold, the angel of the Lord came upon him, and a light shined in the prison, and he smote Peter on the side, and raised him up saying, Arise up quickly. And his chains fell off from his hands... - Acts 12:7

of being enlarged or inflated like a balloon. If those devotees would have risen from their beds in those moments when they were feeling that sensation, then they would have had the joy of entering into the "**Jinn**" state.

When Jesus was walking upon the waters of the Sea of Galilee, he had his body in the state of "**Jinn**."

Peter was able to liberate himself from the chains and to leave the prison, thanks to the assistance of an Angel who helped him place his body in the state of "**Jinn**."

The heavenly Jerusalem of the microcosmic human being is filled with formidable divine powers.

You will develop the eight great mystical powers with internal meditation, and then you will become a living model of the future heavenly Jerusalem.

A great deal of patience and many years of practice are needed in order to educate, develop, and completely strengthen the eight great mystical powers.

The devotees must be patient with these practices of "**Jinn**." To persevere days, months, and years is necessary, until educing, developing, and totally strengthening the eight great mystical powers.

We are able to work with nature while in the "**Jinn**" state, with the powers of the seven churches.

To have faith, tenacity, patience, chastity, charity, and supreme love for humanity is necessary. All of these virtues are indispensable. Thus, this is how you will obtain the development of the eight great mystical powers of your own heavenly Jerusalem.

These eight great mystical powers belong to the seven churches.

Those who become weary and who are inconsistent, and those who commit adultery with Jezebel who called herself a prophetess, will never obtain the development of the eight mystical powers of the Saints.

We perform the perfect priesthood of the seven churches while we are in the "**Jinn**" state.

Every human being who is Christified becomes a living exponent, a living example, of the future Jerusalem.

All of the internal vehicles of the human being shine with the glory of the Lamb when they have been Christified and stigmatized. Really, this is the holy tabernacle of God and human beings.

The Lord dwells within his holy tabernacle. This is the heavenly Jerusalem endowed with terribly divine powers.

The sun and the moon do not need to shine upon the heavenly Jerusalem because the immaculate clarity of the **Eternal One** illuminates it and the Lamb is its light.

The Holy Eight is the sign of infinity. The two witnesses of the Apocalypse are entwined around the spinal medulla, thus they form the Holy Eight.

All of the mystical powers of the heavenly Jerusalem emanate from this Holy Eight. Now the devotees can better comprehend why we speak of eight mystical, ineffable powers.

> *And he measured the wall thereof, an hundred and forty and four (144) cubits, according to the measure of a man, that is of the Angel.*

$1 + 4 + 4 = 9$. It is necessary to descend into the Ninth Sphere (sex) in order to work with water and the fire. This is the source of worlds, beasts, human beings, and Gods. Every authentic White Initiation begins here.

The Son of Man is born from the water and the fire. *"And he that spoke with me had a golden reed to measure the city, and the gates thereof, and the wall thereof."* This golden reed is the spinal medulla.

The seven degrees of the power of the fire rise through the spinal medulla. Grasp your reed strongly so that you can perform the priesthood of the Saints.

You can become citizens of the future Jerusalem with anticipation. Just as the birds enjoy the breaking of the dawn in the East and fill the forest with the sweet sounds of their touching songs, as well, the dawn of the Eternal One shines with living examples of the new Jerusalem, before the future ineffable Jerusalem.

Let your internal powers be developed. Do not covet powers. Do not wish for powers. Cultivate your lotus flowers with disinterested love. Cultivate your precious and delicate internal garden just as the poor gardener cultivates his garden.

When your lotus flowers begin to shine, remember that all of your powers are nothing but miserable candlelights that shine like glow worms before the resplendent Sun who is your immolated Lamb.

You are not the Master; you are only the sinning shadow of He who has never sinned. Remember that only your internal Lamb is the Master.

Remember that even though your internal God is a Hierarch of Fire, you, poor slug, are only a human being, and as a human being you will always be judged.

Your internal Lamb could be a planetary God, but you, poor slug of the mud, do not forget, always remember, that you are only the shadow of your God. Poor sinning shadow..!

Do not say "I am this God" or "I am that Master," because you are only a shadow that must resolve to die and be slaughtered in order not to serve as an obstacle for your internal God.

It is necessary for you to reach supreme humbleness.

THE DRAGON AND THE BEAST BY ALBRECHT DÜRER

And I stood upon the sand of the sea, and saw a beast rise up out of the sea, having seven heads and ten horns, and upon his horns ten crowns, and upon his heads the name of blasphemy. And the beast which I saw was like unto a leopard, and his feet were as the feet of a bear, and his mouth as the mouth of a lion: and the dragon gave him his power, and his seat, and great authority. - Revelation 13:1-2

PART TWO

The Sealed Book

IN OMNIBUS DEBEMOS SUBJICERE
VOLUNTATEM NOSTRAM VOLUNTATI DIVINAE

THE THRONE IN HEAVEN BY ALBRECHT DÜRER

Chapter 14
The Throne in Heaven

Revelation 4:1-10:

After this I looked, and, behold, a door was opened in heaven (the door of the pineal gland): *and the first voice which I heard was as it were of a trumpet talking with me; which said, Come up hither, and I will shew thee things which must be hereafter.*

And immediately I was in the Spirit: and, behold, a throne was set in heaven, and one sat on the throne (the Lamb).

And he that sat was to look upon like a jasper and a sardine stone: (the Son of Man is the son of the living stone, and all the Masters are children of the precious stones of the temple. The cubic stone of Yesod is **sex**) *and there was a rainbow round about the throne, in sight like unto an emerald.* This is the aureole of wisdom. The Son of Man is the Spirit of wisdom.

And round about the throne were four and twenty seats: and upon the seats I saw four and twenty elders sitting (the four and twenty Elders which govern the zodiac), *clothed in white raiment; and they had on their heads crowns of gold.*

And out of the throne proceeded lightnings and thunderings and voices: and there were seven lamps of fire burning before the throne, which are the seven Spirits of God.

The four and twenty Elders exist in the Macrocosm and in the Microcosm. They exist above and below, in the firmament of heaven and within the atomic firmament of the human being.

The seven Spirits before the throne exist above and below. They exist in the firmament of heaven and within the atomic firmament of the human being. As above, so below.

A zodiac exists in heaven and also on earth. The zodiac on earth is the human being.

And before the throne (the throne of the Lamb which is as much in heaven as in the human being) *there was a sea of glass like unto crystal* (the **Ens Seminis**): *and in the midst of*

> *the throne, and round about the throne* (which is above and below, in the universe and within the human being) *were four beasts full of eyes before and behind.* These four animals symbolize the entire science of the Great Arcanum.
>
> *And the first beast was like a lion* (the sacred fire), *and the second beast like a calf* (the salt, or, in other words, the matter), *and the third beast had a face as a man* (the mercury of the secret philosophy, the **Ens Seminis**), *and the fourth beast was like a flying eagle.* The flying eagle represents the air.

The philosophical fire must be searched for within the **Ens Seminis**. In the beginning, this fire is nothing more than a dry and terrestrial exhalation incorporated into the seminal steam.

This dry and terrestrial exhalation is transmuted into the marvellous lightning of Kundalini when the priest learns how to withdraw from the altar without wasting even a single drop of the sacred wine.

We receive the flaming sword when reaching these heights. When the **Ens Seminis** is fecundated by the fire, it becomes the Master and the regenerator of the human being.

The fire nourishes itself with the vital air, with the Prana or universal life.

Really, the sexual fire, which is constantly inhaled and exhaled during the supreme ecstasy of love, becomes transformed into that terrific lightning that opens the seven churches upon rising through the medullar canal.

We must decapitate the "I" with the flaming sword of cosmic justice.

> *And the four beasts* (of Sexual Alchemy) *had each of them six wings about him; and they were full of eyes within, and they rest not day and night, saying, Holy, holy, holy, Lord God Almighty, which was, and is, and is to come.* This is the tremendous Sixth Arcanum of the Tarot.

Remember that a spring of the pure waters of life poured forth when Moses smote the Philosophical Stone.

The man is the priest and the woman is the altar. The **Ens Seminis** is the sacred wine, the pure waters of life.

Remember the brazen serpent of Moses that was entwined around the **Tau**, or in other words, around the generating **Lingam**.

Remember, beloved devotee, the double tail of the serpent that forms the legs of the solar rooster of **Abraxas**.

The entire process of the Great Work consists of releasing oneself from the enchanted rings of the tempting serpent, by taming it, defeating it, and by putting one's foot upon its head. Then, it must be raised through the medullar canal, in order to open the seven churches.

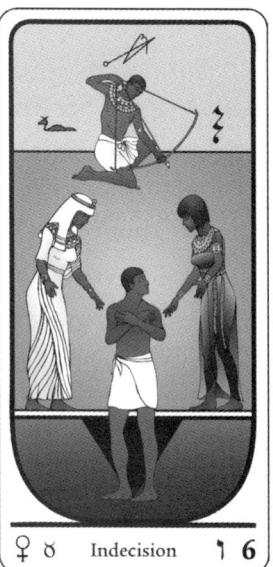

Abraxas

The Sixth Arcanum is the struggle between God and the devil; it is the antagonism between love and animal passion.

The six wings of the four beasts are full of eyes that watch us above and below. They watch us in heaven and in the abyss.

> *Woe of thee! oh warrior, oh fighter, if your servant collapses.*

Do not spill the sacred wine of your temple.

> *And when those beasts give glory and honour and thanks to him* (the Lamb) *that sat on the throne* (which is within the human being and within the universe), *who liveth for ever and ever.*

Then...

> *The four and twenty elders* (within the Macrocosm and within the Microcosm) *fall down before him that sat on the*

throne, and worship him that liveth for ever and ever, and cast their crowns before the throne, saying,

Thou art worthy, O Lord, to receive glory and honour and power: for thou hast created all things, and for thy pleasure they are and were created.

The four and twenty Elders of the zodiacal heaven cast their crowns before the feet of the Lamb. This event is repeated in the zodiacal human being. The four and twenty atomic Elders of the brain cast their crowns before the feet of the Lamb. "As above, so below."

Everything which takes place within the infinitely large, is repeated within the infinitely small.

The Lamb is the multiple, perfect unity. There are as many Lambs in heaven as there are human beings on the earth. Really, all human beings have their own Lamb.

The Lamb is not the Theosophical Septenary[†].

The Lamb is the **Logoic Ray** from which the entire Theosophical Septenary emanates.

Upon opening the seven churches, the **Innermost** must cast his crown before the feet of the Lamb.

The **Innermost** is the **Spirit**, the **Monad**, the **Being**.

The **Innermost** is not the **Lamb**.

The **Innermost** emanated from the **Lamb**.

The Initiate delivers his Spirit unto the Lamb when he pronounces the seven tremendous words of Golgotha. He exclaims, *"Father, into thy hands I commend my Spirit."* Luke 23:46

Chapter 15
The Sealed Book

We, the brothers and sisters of the temple, have suffered greatly in this night for the sake of this poor humanity who we greatly adore. The sky of this night is dressed with black, stormy clouds.

These are lion-colored clouds, illuminated by a lightning flash. The sky is full of lightning, thunder, tempests, rain, and very great hailstones.

During this night, we, the brothers and sisters, have entered through the doors of the temple, filled with a very great tribulation. We have suffered immensely for the great orphan who we love dearly. Poor humanity! Poor mothers! Poor elders!

We, the brothers and sisters, have lain upon beds of profound pain.

An apocalyptic drama is being represented in the temple.

We, the brothers and sisters, are simultaneously spectators and actors of this sacred drama.

The priests joined two things: a child and a book. The sealed book shines upon the chest of the apocalyptic child. The fine and cruel hemp cords envelop the delicate and tender body of the beautiful, anguished, and suffering child. The cruel ropes pass over the sealed book. The book is upon the immaculate chest of the child.

This child is our beloved Son.

We beseech, we cry, we ask for mercy, then the anguished child and the sealed book is liberated.

Now we open the book, and with it we prophesy to a woman dressed in purple and scarlet. This is the great harlot whose number is 666, and with whom all the kings of the earth have committed adultery.

This woman listens to us and says, "I did not know that you could prophesy me with that book."

To which we respond, "We came to prophesy and to teach with this book."

Thus, this is how we spoke to the woman dressed in purple and scarlet, and as we spoke with her, the images of five mounts passed by in our imagination. These are the five Root Races which have existed. Each Root Race ends with a great cataclysm.

Our fifth Root Race will soon come to its end.

Revelation 5:1-14:

And I saw in the right hand of him that sat on the throne a book written within and on the backside, sealed with seven seals.

And I saw a strong Angel proclaiming with a loud voice, Who is worthy to open the book, and to loose the seals thereof?

And no man in heaven, nor in earth, neither under the earth, was able to open the book, neither to look thereon. Truly, this book can only be opened by the incarnated Lamb.

And I wept much, because no man was found worthy to open and to read the book, neither to look thereon.

And one of the elders saith unto me, weep not: behold, the Lion of the tribe of Juda (the **Word**, who is the initiator of the age of Aquarius), *the Root of David, hath prevailed to open the book, and to loose the seven seals thereof.* This is ignored by this humanity, the great harlot.

And I beheld, and lo, in the midst of the throne and of the four beasts, and in the midst of the elders, stood a Lamb as it had been slain, having seven horns and seven eyes, which are the seven Spirits of God sent forth into all the earth. They were sent in order to work in accordance with the law.

And he came and took the book out of the right hand of him that sat upon the throne.

And when he had taken the book, the four beasts and four and twenty elders fell down before the Lamb, having every one of them harps, and golden vials full of odours, which are the prayers of the saints.

And they sung a new song, saying, Thou art worthy to take the book, and to open the seals thereof: for thou wast slain and hast redeemed us to God by thy blood out of every kindred, and tongue, and people, and nation. Really, the sealed book can only be opened by the Lamb.

And hast made us unto our (internal) *God kings and priests: and we shall reign on the earth.* Really, our internal God is the king and the priest.

And I beheld, and I heard the voice of many Angels round about the throne (which is in heaven and within the heart of the human being) *and the beasts and the elders: and the number of them was ten thousand times ten thousand, and thousands of thousands;*

Saying with a loud voice, Worthy is the Lamb that was slain, to receive power, and riches, and wisdom, and strength, and honour, and glory, and blessing.

And every creature which is in heaven, and on earth, and under the earth, and such as are in the sea, and all that are in them, heard I saying, Blessing, and honour, and glory, and power, be unto him that sitteth upon the throne, and unto the Lamb for ever and ever.

And the four beasts (of Sexual Alchemy) *said, Amen. And the four and twenty elders fell down and worshipped him that liveth for ever and ever.*

Really, the internal Lamb of every human being is absolutely perfect and worthy of all honor. We, the human beings, are nothing but poor, sinning shadows.

Some people say, "I believe in the 'I want,' in the 'I can', as well as in the 'I do.'" This is what they consider to be positive. But, in reality, these people fortify Satan with these affirmations.

The Lamb is not the "I." The Lamb is neither a superior "I," nor by a long shot an inferior "I."

When the Lamb says, "**I AM**," we must interpret this as, "**HE IS**," because the Lamb is the one who is uttering it, and not the human being.

The Lamb is deprived of the "I" and deprived of any seal of individuality, as well as of any vestige of personality.

If your internal God is the God of a Sun or the God of any constellation, then you must be even more humble, since you are nothing but a poor **Bodhisattva**, or in other words, a poor human being, more or less imperfect.

You must not commit the sacrilege of saying, "I am such God, or the great Master so-and-so," because you are not the Master, you are not the Lamb. You are only the sinning shadow of the One who has never sinned.

The "I" is formed with the atoms of the secret enemy. This "I" wants to stand out, to rise to the top, to be noticed, to climb to the top of the ladder, etc. But, you must recognize your own misery, and praise and worship the Lamb.

You must vanish and look for shelter within the nothingness, since you are nothing. Thus, through this way of supreme humbleness, you will return to the innocence of Eden. Then, your soul will be absorbed within the Lamb. The spark will return to the flame from where it came forth.

You are the spark; the Lamb is the flame.

So, in the days when your soul returns to the Lamb, you must multiply your vigilance. Remember that the "I" sprouts as an evil weed. Only the Lamb is worthy of any praise, honor, and glory.

You must not divide yourself into two "I's," one superior and another inferior, since only one "I" exists, and the so-called "superior 'I'" is nothing but a refined concept of Satan. This is a sophism of the "I."

You must not desire anything; kill every desire of life. Remember that the "I" is nourished with every desire. You must kiss the feet of the leper. You must dry the tears of your worst enemies. Do not hurt anyone with your words, and do not search for shelter, because you must resolve to die in all of the planes of cosmic consciousness.

Give away your goods to the poor, give away the last drop of your blood for the sake of this poor suffering humanity, renounce all happiness. Then, the immolated Lamb will enter into your soul. He will make his abode within your soul.

Some philosophers affirm that Christ brought the doctrine of the "I," because he said: "**I AM** the way, the truth, and the life." John 14:6

Certainly, the Lamb said, "**I AM,**" and only the Lamb can say "**I AM**." This phrase was spoken by the Lamb, but this phrase cannot be uttered by us (poor sinning shadows) because we are not the Lamb.

Really, the exact and axiomatic translation of "**I AM**" which was uttered by the Lamb, must be as follows: "**HE IS**" the way, the truth, and the life."

"**HE IS**" because **HE** was the One who uttered it. We did not utter it; the One who uttered it was **HIM, HIM, HIM**.

HE lives within the unknown profundities of our Being. "**HE IS**" the way, the truth, and the life. He transcends any concept of "I," any individuality, and any vestige of personality.

Really, *"Worthy is the Lamb that was slain, to receive power, and riches, and wisdom, and strength, and honour, and glory, and blessing."* He is the only one worthy to take the book, and to open the seals thereof.

The Lamb is the divine **Augoeides**†. Truly, the only great and divine One is the **immolated Lamb**.

THE FOUR HORSES BY ALBRECHT DÜRER.

Chapter 16
The Seven Seals

Revelation 6:1-17

And I saw when the Lamb opened one of the seals, and I heard, as it were the noise of thunder, one of the four beasts saying, Come and see.

And I saw, and behold a white horse (the white race): *and him that sat on him had a bow; and a crown was given unto him: and he went forth conquering, and to conquer.* The white race defeated Japan, and the illustrations of the conquerings of this race against Japan are being shown in many ways.

And when he had opened the second seal, I heard the second beast (of the Great Arcanum) *say, Come and see.*

And there went out another horse that was red: (the Atlantean red Root Race from which descended the red skinned natives of the United States of North America) *and power was given to him that sat thereon* (Uncle Sam) *to take peace from the earth, and that they should kill one another: and there was given unto him a great sword.*

Presently, this red horse with its wild, bristly mane and silver hooves eats peacefully within the stables of Augeias.

This brave, agile, and speedy red-skinned stallion reminds us of the warrior-like Atlantean Root Race, whose last noble and strong offspring were destroyed by the Yankees.

The blond citizens of the United States of North America carry in their veins the red blood of those ancient warriors, whose royal trunk was born in the Atlantean continent.

Presently, in this year of the twentieth century (1958), this red horse eats peacefully, and the citizens of the United States are preparing themselves for the atomic war. Very soon, the tempest will explode in the United States. Horribly, the hurricane will howl in the United States. The sky will be filled with pitch black clouds, and there will be much mourning, tears, and very great tribulation.

And when he had opened the third seal, I heard the third beast (of the Great Arcanum) *say, Come and see. And I beheld, and lo a black horse* (the black race and any dark skinned race, such as the Hindustani, African, etc. This horse also represents honest labor): *and he that sat on him* (the black race and any dark skinned race, Arab, Hindustani, etc.) *had a pair of balances in his hand* (slavery).

And I heard the voice in the midst of the four beasts say, A measure of wheat for a penny, and three measures of barley for a penny; and see thou hurt not the oil and the wine.

Lo and behold, the necessary hard labor and work in order to obtain our daily bread. But the initiates want peace, and they say, *"See thou hurt not the oil and the wine."* Do not hurt the sacred wine neither the oil of pure gold that nourishes the fire of the candlestick.

You must work in peace and strive for peace, *"That ye love one another, as I have loved you"* (John 15:12) and take care of the wine and the oil in order for your soul to become betrothed with the Lamb.

Nonetheless, the dwellers of the earth only want wars!

And when he had opened the fourth seal, I heard the voice of the fourth beast (of the Great Arcanum) *say, Come and see.*

And I looked, and behold a pale horse (the yellow race): *and he that sat on him* (China) *was Death, and Hell followed with him. And power was given unto them over the fourth part of the earth, to kill with sword, and with hunger, and with death, and with the* (human) *beast of the earth.*

The war between east and west will be horrible. China will kill millions of human beings. The Chinese threat is terrifying. The Chinese horse drags death and hell before him. There has never been such a terrible threat.

The Chinese army is terribly powerful, and is armed with all types of deadly weapons.

The times of the end have arrived, and the war between the east and the west is inevitable.

The agile pale horse filled with great anger furiously neighs, with death and hell following him.

And when he had opened the fifth seal, I saw under the altar the souls of them that were slain for the word of God, and for the testimony which they held:

And they cried with a loud voice, saying, How long, O Lord, holy and true, dost thou not judge and avenge our blood on them that dwell on the earth? The prophets have been killed by the dwellers of the Earth who abhor the eternal One.

And white robes were given unto every one of them; and it was said unto them, that they should rest yet for a little season, until their fellow-servants also and their brethren (the initiates), *that should be killed as they were, should be fulfilled.*

And I beheld when he had opened the sixth seal, and, lo, there was a great earthquake; and the sun became black as a sackcloth of hair, and the moon became as blood.

The radioactive particles of the nuclear explosions will profoundly alter the superior zones of the terrestrial atmosphere. These superior zones are the supreme filter for the solar rays. When this filter becomes totally altered by the atomic explosions, it will no longer classify and decompose the solar rays into light and fire. Therefore, the result will be that we will see the sun black as a sackcloth of hair.

The human beings will disembark to the moon. The conquering of the moon is inevitable. The vultures of war will conquer the moon and it will become as blood.

There will be earthquakes everywhere, darkness, famine, unknown sicknesses, blasphemies, and a very great tribulation. The atomic explosions will provoke all of these calamities.

The times of the end have arrived. Woe! Woe! Woe! of those who as in the days of Noah were eating and drinking, marrying and giving in marriage saying, "Still we have time for joy."

Woe to the inhabitants of the Earth, since the times of the end are at hand.

The atomic explosions will bring plagues, earthquakes, famine, seaquakes, and terrible cataclysms.

The sound of the sea will be filled with frightful turbulence, and there will exist monstrous tidal waves as never seen before.

There will be deadly wars, and behold, the pale horse is followed by death and hell.

The beginning of the end has already begun!

Nonetheless, all of these calamities are nothing but the warning, the preface, the prelude of the final event.

The human beings are building the Tower of Babel again. The summit of this tower is the Moon. Any illuminated clairvoyant can see within the superior worlds a hollow tower of fragile crystal (the Tower of Babel). This is treason against the Eternal One; soon this tower will be destroyed.

The ships (rockets) of "**Babylon the great, the mother of harlots and abominations of the earth**" ascend and descend through this fragile and hollow tower that is deprived of divine wisdom.

In this day and age, this Tower of Babel is represented by the hollow, superficial, and vain science of materialistic scientists.

God will confuse their tongues, and the Tower of Babel will be fulminated by the terrible ray of cosmic justice.

This fragile and hollow tower that is deprived of any type of spirituality is in these present times, as well as in ancient times, threatening the starry heaven.

The atheists, enemies of the Eternal One, want to take heaven by assault, and to conquer other worlds of space. But, soon they will be wounded to death.

The terror of love and law reigns within the sacred space where the innumerable worlds move and palpitate. The interplanetary voyages are only for divine humanities of the starry space. The human being of the Earth is not yet worthy to penetrate the starry space. Let us put a chimpanzee or any other ape inside a laboratory and observe what will happen...

When these human beings conquer the moon, when the atheists (enemies of the Eternal One) profane the sacred space, when the wise men of this great Babylon, filled with pride and arrogance, prepare themselves to conquer other worlds, then the end will come.

The Tower of Babel will fall fulminated, and from all of this, the great Babylon (humanity) will not remain, not with even one stone upon the other.

A world is approaching; it is approaching the planet Earth. Woe to the dwellers of the Earth! The day of the Lord (the new Aquarian Age) is at hand. This world that is approaching will pass through the atmosphere and will burn with living fire. Therefore, when falling upon the Earth, the elements and all things with life therein shall melt with fervent heat.

Also, there will be a great earthquake, so mighty an earthquake and so great as there has never been since human beings have existed upon the Earth.

> *And the stars of heaven* (these great geniuses of the Tower of Babel, these great luminaries of the intellectual firmament, the great lords of this great Babylon) *fell unto the earth, even as fig tree casteth her untimely figs, when she is shaken of a mighty wind.*

The spikes of this materialistic science have already become ripe, and the human beings will harvest the fruits of desire. Now human beings will harvest the result of this civilization with no God and no law.

> *And the heaven departed as a scroll when it is rolled together; and* (with the planetary collision) *every mountain and island were moved out of their places.*

The new planetary mass, mixed with the terrestrial mass, will form a new world. There will be new heavens and a new Earth for the future sixth great Root Race.

> *And the kings of the earth, and the great men, and the rich men, and the chief captains, and the mighty men, and every bondman, and every free man* (already physically dead and in their Astral Bodies), *hid themselves in the dens and in the rocks of the mountains* (since they will be terrified and surprised by a cataclysm which they do not expect or even remotely suspect.)

And said to the mountains and rocks, Fall unto us, and hide us from the face of him that sitteth on the throne, and from the wrath (justice) of the Lamb:

For the great day of his wrath is come; and who shall be able to stand?

Really, only those who have built the church for the Lamb upon the living rock (sex), will be able to firmly stand.

Those who build their church upon the sands of theories, will tumble to the abyss, into the submerged worlds, into the atomic infernos of this great nature. These are the lost ones.

In these future days, only the just ones will be secretly saved. These select people will be those who were capable of lifting up the serpent upon the staff, as Moses did in the wilderness.

The seed plot for the future sixth great Root Race will come from these select people.

The times of the end have arrived and we are in them. *"Many are called and few are chosen."* Matthew 20:16

The great Master Jesus said, *"From a thousand men who seek me, one finds me. From a thousand who find me, one follows me. From a thousand who follow me, one is mine."*

Chapter 17
The Four Angels

We, the brothers and sisters, while in the supreme instant of ecstasy, have entered through the doors of the Temple of Jerusalem. The Wailing Wall is all that remains in this valley of bitterness. Nonetheless, this temple still exists within the superior worlds. Filled with pain, we walk through its courtyards and its passageways.

We contemplate its magnificent Olympian columns with its beautiful steeples and its chambers, its golden and silver cups, as well its purple kneeling desks.

The glory of the Lord Jehovah no longer shines within the *sanctum sanctorum* of the temple because this sanctuary has been desolated. This sanctuary has been profaned.

The Ark of Science with its sacred and terribly divine coupled Cherubim is no longer there.

Now, only the Lord of Anguish is who we see within the sanctum sanctorum of the temple. Only His sacred image is there, and it is a living image.

So, the image of the Adorable One is there, but the Jews laugh at Him, and they say, "This is the One who dreamed to be the promised Messiah, but we do not believe in Him."

All of them laugh. Therefore, the sanctuary has been profaned. The veil of the temple was rent in twain because the sanctuary had already been profaned.

With the killing of Christ, the sanctuary was profaned.

We, the brothers and sisters of the temple, walked throughout the interior of this temple. The courtyard of the priests was filled with sportsmen and merchants. Thus, this is what the Temple of Jerusalem became in the end.

This humanity crucified the Christ, so they signed their own death sentence with innocent blood.

Nonetheless, infinite mercy granted us a short space of time in order for us to define ourselves for Christ or for Javhe (Javhe is not Jehovah), to define ourselves for the White Lodge or for the Black Lodge.

We all deserved to have been destroyed because of the dreadful and horrible sacrilege. Christ was assassinated and the sanctuary profaned. However, infinite mercy granted to us a short space of more time in order for us to study the doctrine of Christ and to choose the path.

Revelation 7:1-17:

> *And after these things* (which happened in Jerusalem) *I saw four Angels standing on the four corners of the earth,* (the four archivists of Karma, the four Devarajas) *holding the four winds of the earth, that the wind should not blow on the earth, nor on the sea, nor on any tree.* They govern the four winds and they control the four corners of the Earth with the law.

The prophet saw these four saints holding the law, holding the four winds of the earth, that the wind should not blow on the earth, nor on the sea, nor on any tree.

These four saints hold the law, that is to say, they hold the punishment that weighs upon the head of this humanity who assassinated Christ.

Infinite mercy granted us time in order to study the doctrine of the Lord and to turn back towards the path of righteousness.

> *And I saw another Angel ascending from the east, having the seal of the living God* (the Seal of Solomon): *and he cried with a loud voice to the four Angels, to whom it was given to hurt the earth and the sea.*
>
> *Saying, Hurt not the earth, neither the sea, nor the trees, till we have sealed the servants of our God in their foreheads.*

The Bodhisattva of the Angel who has the seal of the living God in his hands is presently reincarnated in this twentieth century in a feminine body and is a marvellous specialist in "**Jinn**" states. We must not divulge this Angel's sacred name.

This Angel told to all of us the following truth, "We are going to save the people of this street in ten days." We understood that this street is the street of the just ones, one of the streets of this great Babylon. The ten days symbolize the wheel of the centuries, which is the wheel of reincarnation and karma.

A short time was necessary in order for the people to study the doctrine of Christ and to become defined for Christ or for Javhe, for the White Lodge or for the Black Lodge.

The servants of God were already sealed in their foreheads. As well, the servants of Satan were already sealed in their foreheads.

The times of the end have arrived and we are in them. The ten days are already past due, and the times of the end are at hand.

The Seal of Solomon is the supreme affirmation of the Lamb and the supreme negation of Satan. **Hilarion IX** said, *"Its two triangles that join or separate love are the two shuttles with which the ineffable mystery of eternal life in the loom of God is woven or unwoven."* The six points of the Seal of the living God are masculine, and the six deep angles that are form between the points are feminine (in synthesis, this Seal of the living God has twelve rays: six masculine and six feminine).

These twelve rays crystallize in the twelve zodiacal constellations by means of Sexual Alchemy. These twelve zodiacal constellations are the twelve sons of Jacob.

All of humanity is divided into twelve tribes; these are the twelve tribes of Israel.

Humanity remains classified with the Seal of the living God. The majority have already received the mark of the beast on their foreheads and on their hands. A few have received the sign of the Lamb on their foreheads.

And I heard the number of them which were sealed: and there were sealed an hundred and forty and four thousand of all the tribes of the children of Israel.

By Kabbalisticaly adding the numbers to themselves we have the number nine: 1+4+4=9. **Nine** is the Ninth Sphere (sex). Only those who have attained absolute chastity will be saved.

Presently, in this year of 1958, on the fifth of September, a great tempest is approaching. The sky is filled with black and threatening clouds that are illuminated by lightning. A cold, deadly breeze blows everywhere. All of us have been crying greatly. We have beseeched a holy and almighty vigilant, we have begged him, we have made him business proposals in order to conjure the terrible tempest that is approaching this poor suffering humanity in a most dreadful way. We have asked for a clue in order to conjure this tempest. Nevertheless, all has been in vain.

The times are finished, and those who did not accept the doctrine of the Lord will sink into the abyss. Only the just ones will be saved. They will be the ones who have already received the sign of God on their foreheads. They are the ones who have already reached supreme chastity.

One hundred and forty and four thousand are the just ones who will be saved. Really, only with supreme chastity and supreme love towards this suffering humanity will we attain the divine miracle of our Christification.

With supreme adoration, we must kiss the whip of the executioner who hates us. We must purge our mind of any desire.

We must watch over the "I" within all of the levels of consciousness, because many loyal and sincere devotees who achieved chastity in this valley of tears became terrible fornicators within the world of the cosmic mind.

Have you ever meditated even once on the danger of erotic images? Remember that within your mind you have a skillful translator. This translator is the "I," who always betrays the devotees of the path. This "I" creates mental effigies, living demons of the Mental Plane. The devotees fornicate with these demons in the Mental Plane.

Movie theaters are true temples of black magic of the Mental Plane, because the mind creates living effigies, tempting demons that are absolute duplicates of the erotic images that we have seen in the movies or in the newspapers or in pornographic magazines.

The "I" betrays us in other levels of consciousness. A simple erotic word becomes fornication within the Mental World.

An ironic word signifies violence within the Mental Plane, therefore, we need to love, to adore our worst enemies.

We need to attain supreme chastity in all of the levels of consciousness, and we need to give even the last drop of blood for this adorable humanity.

Our lips must kiss the feet of those who hate and damn us the most. Our hands must only be lifted up in order to bless the enemy who spits on us and whips us.

One hundred and forty and four thousand are the Christified Saints, that is to say, we must wash our feet in the waters of renunciation. This signifies supreme chastity, supreme sanctity, and supreme love for all the millions of beings who populate the world.

It is necessary to descend into the Ninth Sphere in order to work with the fire and the water, which are the origin of worlds, beasts, human beings, and Gods. Every authentic White Initiation starts here.

To work with the Arcanum A.Z.F. is necessary, for this is the only way possible in order to receive the sign of the living God on the forehead.

> *And I heard the number of them which were sealed: and there were sealed an hundred and forty and four thousand of all the tribes of the children of Israel.*

Of the tribe of Judah were sealed twelve thousand. Of the tribe of Reuben were sealed twelve thousand. Of the tribe of Gad were sealed twelve thousand.

Of the tribe of Aser were sealed twelve thousand. Of the tribe of Nepthalim were sealed twelve thousand. Of the tribe of Manasses were sealed twelve thousand.

Of the tribe of Simeon were sealed twelve thousand. Of the tribe of Levi were sealed twelve thousand. Of the tribe of Issachar were sealed twelve thousand.

Of the tribe of Zabulon were sealed twelve thousand. Of the tribe of Joseph were sealed twelve thousand. Of the tribe of Benjamin were sealed twelve thousand. Revelation 7: 4-8

All of this poor humanity is divided into twelve tribes. All of humanity is unfolded and developed within the zodiacal womb. The zodiac is a uterus in which humanity is gestated. The twelve tribes can only receive the seal of God on their foreheads by practicing with the Arcanum A.Z.F.

Only twelve thousand were sealed in each of the twelve zodiacal tribes. Behold here the Twelfth Arcanum of the Tarot.

This Arcanum is represented by a human being who is hung by his foot. His tied hands on his head force him to form a triangle with his arms, with the vertex pointing downwards, and with his legs he forms a cross which is above the triangle. Behold here the union of the cross with the triangle.

Behold, here in the Twelfth Arcanum, sexual magic. Behold here the Arcanum A.Z.F. Behold here the realized work, the living human being who does not touch the earth, but only with thought.

The whole science of Sexual Alchemy was carved by Hermes in

the *Emerald Tablet*. Behold here the precepts that are related to the Great Work:

> *Separate that spirituous earth from the dense or crude by means of a gentle heat, with much attention.*
>
> *In great measure it ascends from the earth up to heaven, and descends again, newborn, on the earth, and the superior and the inferior are increased in power.*
>
> *By this thou wilt partake of the honours of the whole world, and darkness will fly from thee.*
>
> *This is the strength of all powers, with this thou wilt be able to overcome all things, and to transmute all what is fine and what is coarse.*
>
> *In this manner the world was created.*
>
> The Emerald Tablet of Hermes

The fundamental key of the Great Work is found in sexual union.

The Latin formula of the Great Arcanum is the following: "**Inmisio membri virili in vagina feminae sine ejeculatium seminis.**"

Do not ever ejaculate the Mercury of the secret philosophy. Avoid the physiological orgasm. This is the fundamental clue of the Great Work.

Certainly, in its depth, the entity of semen becomes the same Mercury of the secret philosophy, which when fecundated by the sulphur (**living fire**) becomes converted into the Master and regenerator of the salt (the terrestrial man).

Only the sealed twelve thousand of each of the twelve tribes of Israel will be saved from the great cataclysm (this quantity is symbolic). Only those who have achieved the union of the cross/man with the triangle/Spirit will be saved.

> *After this I beheld, and, lo, a great multitude, which no man could number, of all nations, and kindreds, and people, and tongues, stood before the throne, and before the Lamb, clothed with white robes* (tunics of Masters), *and palms* (of victory) *in their hands;*

And cried with a loud voice, saying, Salvation to our God which sitteth upon the throne, and unto the (internal) *Lamb* (of every human being).

And all the Angels stood round about the throne, and about the elders and the four beasts (of the Great Arcanum)*, and fell before the throne on their faces, and worshipped God.*

Saying, Amen: Blessing, and glory, and wisdom, and thanksgiving, and honour, and power, and might, be unto our God for ever and ever, Amen.

And one of the elders answered, saying unto me, What are these which are arrayed in white robes? and whence came they?

And I said unto him, Sir, thou knowest. And he said to me. These are they which came out of great tribulation, and have washed their robes, and made them white in the blood of the Lamb.

This Lamb is inside of everyone. Really, we can incarnate the Lamb only by working with the Arcanum A.Z.F.

There is the need to descend into the flaming forge of Vulcan (sex) in order to re-temper the sword and to attain the Venustic Initiation. Hermes descended into this forge in order to clean the internal stables of the Soul with the sacred fire, and Perseus also descended in order to cut the head of the prince of this world with the flaming sword.

Thus, this is how we can whiten our internal bodies with the blood of our internal Lamb.

Therefore are they before the throne of God, and serve him day and night in his temple: and he that sitteth on the throne shall dwell among them. The Father is glorified in the Son and the Son is glorified in the Father. The Father is one with the Son and the Son is one with the Father.

They shall hunger no more, neither thirst any more; neither shall the sun light on them, nor any heat.

For the Lamb (their own interior Lamb) *which is in the midst of the throne shall feed them, and shall lead them unto living mountains of waters: and God shall wipe away all tears from their eyes.*

We, as **egos**, have to resolve to die in all of the planes of cosmic consciousness. We have to recognize our own misery and sin in order for our diamond soul to be lost within the Lamb.

The internal Lord will shepherd and guide us towards fountains of living waters. Whosoever drinks from these fountains of pure waters of life will never thirst, and a well of water springing up into everlasting life will spring from his belly.

We need to pass through a true revolution of the consciousness.

The experiences of life complicate and strengthen the "I." We have been evolving for many millions of years... so what? What did we gain with these many experiences?

The simple human being of eighteen million years ago is now the complicated, perverse, sly, and selfish person of these great cities. Is this progress?

Let us see the child! How beautiful he is! How innocent! But while this child grows, while he evolves and acquires experiences throughout the distinct phases of life, he complicates himself more and more, he turns more and more sly. So when this person reaches the elderly age, he is filled with maliciousness, selfishness, distrust, resentments, evilness, etc. Is this evolution?

The experiences of life complicate and strengthen the "I." Therefore, we need to dissolve the "I."

When we have dissolved the "I," then there will exist a total revolution of the consciousness.

Truly, the only thing that the "I" is useful for is for doing evil. Therefore, we need to descend into the Ninth Sphere (sex) in order to decapitate the "I."

The "I" strengthened and fortified itself with experiences throughout the centuries of evolution. Therefore, we do not need evolution now. What we need is a revolution.

The internal Lamb will enter into the Soul when we dissolve the "I."

When the internal Lamb enters into the Soul, He transforms himself into the Soul. He (the Lamb) transforms himself into Her, and Her into Him.

That which we call the Son of Man is born from this divine and human symbiosis, and this is what is called the revolution of the consciousness.

The four Angels hold the four winds; they postpone the Karma which weighs upon this humanity in order for us to study the doctrine of the Adorable One.

We became tremendously destructive and perverse with evolution.

Now we need a total revolution of the consciousness.

We need to decapitate and dissolve the "I."

We need to incarnate the immolated Lamb.

> *And I heard the number of them which were sealed: and there were sealed an hundred and forty and four thousand of all the tribes of the children of Israel.*

Chapter 18
The Seventh Seal

> Revelation 8:1-13:
>
> *And when he had opened the seventh seal, there were silence in heaven about the space of half an hour.*

The adorable Savior of the world confesses the sins of humanity before his Father, and before his Angels. This great orphan (humanity) must enter into the Hospital of the Angels.

The Divine Spouse wants to save his children. The tenebrous ones want to take away his little children, but he gathered his children together under his loving arms, even as a hen gathered her chickens under her wings.

The fact of this matter is to extract a cancerous tumor from within the womb of this great orphan.

> *And... there was silence in heaven about the space of half an hour.*

Inevitably, this scientific operation is very painful.

There will be some survivors from the great catastrophe, and there will be silence about the space of half an hour. A very short space of time, but enough, so much as to secretly save the just ones.

The great apocalyptic events take place at the shores of the immense sea of life.

> *And I saw the seven Angels* (Gabriel, Raphael, Uriel, Michael, Samael, Zachariel, Orifiel) *which stood before God; and to them were given seven trumpets.*
>
> *And another Angel came and stood at the altar, having a golden censer and there was given unto him much incense that he should offer it with the prayers of all saints upon the golden altar which was before the throne.*
>
> *And the smoke of the incense which came with the prayers of the saints, ascended up before God out of the Angel's hand.* The Saints will be cruelly persecuted by the atheists; these Saints will have to do much praying.

The Angels with Trumpets by Albrecht Dürer.

> *And the Angel took the censer, and filled it with the fire of the altar, and cast it into the earth: and there were voices, and thunderings, and lightnings, and an earthquake.*

Then the Gnostics will be persecuted to death. *"And this Gospel of the Kingdom shall be preached in all the world for a witness unto all nations: and then shall the end come."* - Matthew 24:14

The materialistic, atheistic enemies of the Eternal One are filled with false science.

These atheists will persecute the Gnostics with great fury. Sexual magic is mortally hated by these atheists. Therefore, this will be their reason to persecute the Gnostics to death.

Sex is the door of Eden, and the enemies of the Eternal One do not want the people to enter through this door.

The Gnostics will multiply themselves to the millions, but they will be cruelly persecuted and hated.

> *And the seven Angels which had the seven trumpets prepared themselves to sound.*
>
> *The first Angel* (Gabriel) *sounded, and there followed hail and fire mingled with blood, and they were cast upon earth: and the third part of the trees was burnt up, and all green grass was burnt up.*

The stone of the philosophers is sex. The ancients worshipped the Sun under the figure of a black stone, which they named Heliogabalus.

Our adorable Savior taught us to build upon the living rock. Therefore, the adorable one said to Peter, *"Thou art Peter,* (Petros), *and upon this rock* (petra) *I will build my church."* - Matthew 16:18

The Philosophical Stone is the foundation of science, philosophy, and religion.

> "It may be said therefore that the Philosophical Stone is square in every sense, like the heavenly Jerusalem of St. John; that one of its sides is inscribed with the name of Adam and the other with that of Eve, and the two others those of Azoth and INRI." - Eliphas Levi

The Philosophical Stone is very sacred.

This sacred stone has been profaned by the science of the Antichrist. Unveiled sanctuary... profaned sanctuary!

The precious stones of the temple are very sacred. All Masters are children of these sacred stones.

None of the Galen (male physicians) should touch the stones of the temple. Sick women should be attended by female physicians.

Nonetheless, the times of the end have arrived, and when the first Angel sounded his trumpet, there was hail and fire mingled with blood. Iced waters mingled with fire and blood, or, in other words, **science**, **blood**, and **passion**.

The temple of science was profaned by the Antichrist, and the followers of Esculapius committed fornication and adultery with the poor sick women. *"And all green grass was burnt up,"* that is to say, every honor was raped.

The sacred Caduceus of Mercury fell on the floor of the temple and smashed into pieces.

The spikes of science have already ripened and human beings will now harvest with full hands the poisonous fruits of desire. The trumpet of the regent Angel of the Moon has sounded.

> *And the second Angel* (Raphael) *sounded, and as it were a great mountain burning with fire was cast into the sea:* (this mountain is the head of the whole of humanity) *and the third part of the sea became blood.* Entire billions of human beings will perish.

Before the great cataclysm, the karmic debts of each and every human being will be precisely inspected.

Exact mathematical calculations will be performed before the great cataclysm.

The number is holy, is infinite, is eternal. Everything is directed by the holy number.

Therefore, after the inspection of all debts in the books, and when the mathematical calculations are done, then the great catastrophe will come.

And the third part of the creatures which were in the sea, and had life, died, and the third part of the ships were destroyed. Entire billions of human beings will perish.

It is understood that the perfect triangle is what is meant by "the third part," because the great catastrophe which is approaching has a triple consequence: physical, psychological, and spiritual.

The physical, psychological, and spiritual worlds conjointly correspond with each other through the thirty-two paths of light, which are the sacred steps of the Holy Ladder.

Raphael, the regent Angel of Mercury, has sounded his trumpet, and the mathematical calculations are being made within the internal temples of Karma.

The **Bodhisattva** of the Angel Raphael is incarnated, but disgracefully, this Bodhisattva is now fallen.

Nevertheless, this humble Bodhisattva is presently struggling in order to rise up again.

And the third Angel (Uriel) sounded, and there fell a great star from heaven (the star of bitterness), *burning as it were a lamp, and it fell upon the third part of the rivers, and upon the fountains of waters;*

And the name of the star is called Wormwood (bitterness): *and the third part of the waters became wormwood; and many men died of the waters, because they were made bitter.*

The Angel of Venus has sounded his trumpet. Every event is of a triple consequence. The star of bitterness is of a triple consequence. The three worlds: physical, psychological, and spiritual, correspond to each other through the thirty-two paths of light, which are the sacred steps of the Holy Ladder.

Father, mother, and son are a perfect ternary. Every home became full of bitterness. This ternary is: fecundity, generation, nature.

The waters are families, crowds, countries, and tongues.

"*The waters became Wormwood*" because all homes on the Earth became filled with fornication, hatred, adultery, and very great tribulation.

And the fourth Angel (Michael) sounded, and the third part of the sun was smitten, and the third part of the moon, and the third part of the stars; so as the third part of them was darkened, and the day shone not for a third part of it, and the night likewise.

All cosmic events have a triple consequence: the Law of the Triangle governs every cosmic manifestation.

The highest zones of the terrestrial atmosphere will be totally altered by atomic explosions. Then, as a logical consequence, these zones will not filtrate and segregate the rays of the Sun, Moon, and stars.

Soon, we will see the Sun black as a sackcloth of hair and the Moon as blood. Therefore, the stars will become darkened.

There will be no light, and a ferruginous reddish color will cover the face of the Earth.

All of these great cosmic events are always of a triple consequence. The Law of the Triangle governs the whole of creation.

Terrible earthquakes and great seaquakes will occur because of the complete alteration of the superior zones of the terrestrial atmosphere.

The ocean will have a mysterious and strange sound. Monstrous and terrible tidal waves will strike the beaches.

Many cities will become a mass of ruins because of the movements of the earthquakes.

Radioactivity will increase each day, and with it many epidemics and unknown sicknesses will appear, as well as famine, misery, and terrible tribulation.

The plantations will be lost and even the fish of the sea will perish.

But, woe unto them that are with child, and to them that give suck in those days! For there shall be great distress in the land, and wrath upon this people.

And there shall be signs in the sun, and in the moon, and in the stars; and upon the earth distress of nations, with perplexity; the sea and the waves roaring.

Men's hearts failing them for fear, and for looking after those things which are coming on the earth: for the powers of heaven shall be shaken. - Luke 21:23,24,26

And I beheld, and heard an Angel flying through the midst of heaven, saying with a loud voice, Woe, woe, woe, to the inhabitants of the earth by reason of the other voices of the trumpet of the three Angels, which are yet to sound!

The prince of this world is that "I," that ego, that myself, which all of us carry within. This "I," with its fatal mind, supposes that the Aquarian Age will be a comfortable age without any type of problems and full of great securities, since the prince of this world is a distinguished lord of commodities!

Woe to the dwellers of the Earth: the Age of Aquarius is approaching, and the ray of justice will fall upon "**Babylon the great, the mother of harlots and abominations of the earth.**"

Aquarius has influence over the terrestrial atmosphere, and Peter the chief of the Apostolic College said, *"But the day of the Lord will come as a thief in the night; in which the heavens shall pass away with great noise, and the elements shall melt with fervent heat, the earth also and the works that are therein shall be burned up."* - Second Epistle of Peter 3:10

Aquarius signifies the end of this great Babylon. The times of the end have arrived. The second coming of Christ signifies total revolution upon the face of the Earth.

The ancient Earth was destroyed by water.

This Earth that is inhabited by the Aryan Root Race will be destroyed by the fire of Aquarius.

The just ones must not be afraid; they will be secretly saved before the great cataclysm.

Lot, the just one, was taken away from Sodom when Sodom and Gomorrah were going to be destroyed by the terrifying fire of the volcanoes of the Earth.

The just ones will be secretly evacuated from this great Babylon.

The just ones will not be punished because of the sinners; this only happened once before, and that time is already in the past.

Chapter 19
The Fifth Angel

> Revelation 9:1-12:
>
> *And the fifth Angel* (Samael) *sounded, and I saw a star fall from heaven unto the earth: and to him was given the key of the bottomless pit.*

Since the year 1950, a gigantic world has been approaching our planet Earth. This star has already fallen over the planet Earth, and to this star was given the key to the bottomless pit.

What we want to say with this is that the electro-magnetic waves of this gigantic star have already touched the axis of the Earth.

The key to the bottomless pit was given to this gigantic world.

The inferior animal psyche of this gigantic planetary bolder acts upon this terrestrial humanity by sucking, absorbing, attracting all of those billions of souls who do not have the sign of God on their foreheads.

This star acts from the bottom of the abyss, attracting billions of human beings.

The key to the bottomless pit was given to this star. Since the year 1950, billions of human souls have been entering into the abyss. The bottomless pit (the abyss) has been opened since the year 1950.

The symbol of that star is the radiant Cross! When the sheep become separated from the goats, then the Cross of the Redeemer will triumph.

This gigantic world will be visible for the whole world within a few years.

This star *"opened the bottomless pit; and there arose a smoke out of the pit, as the smoke of a great furnace; and the sun and the air were darkened by reason of the smoke of the pit."*

The Fifth Angel by Albrecht Dürer

And there came out of the smoke locusts upon the earth; and unto them was given power, as the scorpions of the earth have power.

And it was commanded them that they should not hurt the grass of the earth, neither any green thing, neither any tree; but only those men which have not the seal of God in their foreheads.

The locusts that come out of the smoke of the abyss are human demons, the psychological "I" of each human being. These human demons are the vultures of war, those potentates of gold and silver, the merchants of souls and bodies, perfumes and riches, as well as the lords of politics, the great diplomats, the materialistic scientists, the lords of the atomic bomb and of the hydrogen bomb, etc.

These human demons, with or without physical bodies, torment each other in the cities and within the abyss. *"And to them it was given that they should not kill them, but that they should be tormented five months: and their torment was as the torment of a scorpion, when he striketh a man."*

The number five is the number of rigor and of the Law, it is also the number of Mars and of war. Therefore, the two words "five months" are symbolic.

Presently, we are in the days of great affliction. Woe to the dwellers of the Earth, since the times of the end have arrived!

And in those days (these present days) *shall men seek death* (within the abyss), *and shall find it; and shall desire to die, and death shall flee from them.*

Life within the abyss is the same as this life which we have in the physical plane, but it is millions of times more horrible, more tenebrous, more materialistic, and more dense.

The human beings live within the abyss with their Astral Bodies. They torment each other and desire to die, but death flees from them.

Urban life in its entirety becomes millions of times more gross and terribly materialistic when it is transplanted into the abyss. Therefore, the human beings desire to die, but death flees from them.

And the shape of the locusts were like unto horses prepared unto battle; and on their heads were as it were crowns like gold, and their faces were as the faces of men.

Lo and behold, the psychological "I" of each human being: the vultures of war, the heads of states, the sly diplomats, the great generals.

And they had hair as the hair of women (filled with false sweetness and refined hypocrisy), *and their teeth were as the teeth of lions.*

And they had breastplates, as it were breastplates of iron; and the sound of their wings (airplanes) *was as the sound of chariots of many horses running to battle.*

And they had tails like unto scorpions, and there were stings in their tails (powerful armies which are armed with **stings**, atomic bombs, tele-electronically directed rockets, hydrogen bombs, etc.); *and their power was to hurt men five months."* Thus, this is how all nations will pay their karmic debts.

Thus, this is how the civil and military heads of states of the whole world, those diplomatic gentlemen, the great ones of the Earth, have *"tails like unto scorpions, and there were stings in their tails."*

Lo and behold the great military forces of the east and west, the military power, the heads of states, the great generals, the great diplomats, the powerful men of the Earth in this twentieth century, in this day and age.

*And they had a king over them, which is the Angel of the bottomless pit, whose name in the Hebrew tongue is **Abbadon**, but in the Greek tongue hath his name **Apollyon**.*

One woe is past; and behold, there come two woes more hereafter.

Chapter 20
The Sixth Trumpet

> Revelation 9:13-21:
>
> *And the sixth Angel sounded, and I heard a voice from the four horns of the golden altar which is before God.* This golden altar is the man, the woman, the fire, and the water: **Iod He Vau He**. The altar of God is Nature.
>
> *Saying to the sixth Angel* (Zachariel) *which had the trumpet, Loose the four Angels which are bound in the great river Euphrates.* These are the four Devarajas who govern the four winds.
>
> *And the four Angels were loosed, which were prepared for an hour, and a day, and a month, and a year, for to slay the third part of men.*

The four Angels of the four cardinal points of the Earth *"which were prepared for an hour, and a day, and a month, and a year"* will be let loose with the hydrogen bomb. Therefore, elements unknown to the human being will become unleashed and human science will not be able to control them.

The hydrogen bomb will be the **pandemonium**!

> *And the number of the army of the horsemen were two hundred thousand thousand: and I heard the number of them.*

The number 200,000,000 gives us the Second Arcanum of the Tarot, when its numbers are Kabbalisticaly added together. The Second Arcanum is the woman, the Priestess, occult science.

The number two is Nature, and this great Nature will be tremendously agitated by great cataclysms.

The dreadful and terrible cataclysms of the times of the end will be produced by atomic power and the hydrogen bomb. Unknown elements from nature will be released with the hydrogen bomb, and nobody will be capable of controlling them.

The Four Angels by Albrecht Dürer.

The human armies, armed with atomic power, tele-electronically controlled rockets, hydrogen bombs, etc. will wound this great Nature.

Therefore, woe to the dwellers of the Earth!

And thus I saw the horses in the vision, and them that sat on them having breastplates of fire, and of jacinth, and brimstone: and the heads of the horses were as the heads of lions; and out of their mouths issued fire and smoke and brimstone. These horses and they who sat on them are nations, crowds, and tongues.

Therefore, fire of passion, smoke of laziness, and brimstone of pain are issued out of the mouths of the dwellers of the Earth.

Rajas† and Tamas† brings sicknesses, pain, darkness, desperation, wars, famine, crowded hospitals, etc.

Rajas is emotion, passion. Tamas is inertia, laziness.

By these three was the third part of men killed, by the fire, and by the smoke, and by the brimstone, which issued out of their mouths.

Woe to the dwellers of the Earth! Woe to the scientists of the Antichrist! Woe to the vultures of war!

For their power is in their mouth, (which speaks blasphemies) *and in their tails: for their tails were like unto serpents, and had heads, and with them they do hurt.* These are the demons of this great Babylon: human-demons.

And the rest of the men which were not killed by these plagues yet repented not of the works of their hands, that they should not worship devils, and idols of gold, and silver, and brass, and stone, and of wood: which neither can see, nor hear, not walk:

Neither repented they of their murders, nor of their sorceries, nor of their fornication, nor of their thefts.

The times of the end have arrived and we are in them.

The day and hour of the times of the end are hidden within the Kabbalistic mystery of the Arcanum 2,500.

Oriphiel by Albrecht Dürer.

Chapter 21
The Seventh Trumpet

> Revelation 10:1-11:
>
> *And I saw another mighty Angel come down from heaven, clothed with a cloud; and a rainbow was upon his head, and his face was as it were the sun, and his feet as pillars of fire.* This Angel is Orifiel, the Genie of Saturn.
>
> *And he had in his hand a little book open: and he set his right foot upon the sea, and his left foot on the earth.*
>
> *And cried with a loud voice, as when a lion roareth: and when he had cried, seven thunders uttered their voices.* These seven thunders are the sublime voices of the seven Spirits before the throne, the seven Potencies of nature.
>
> *And when the seven thunders had uttered their voices, I was about to write: and I heard a voice from heaven saying unto me, Seal up those things which the seven thunders uttered, and write them not.*
>
> *And the Angel which I saw stand upon the sea and upon the earth lifted up his hand to heaven.*
>
> *And sware by him that liveth for ever and ever, who created heaven, and the things that therein are, and the earth, and the things that therein are, and the sea, and the things that are therein, that there should be time no longer:*
>
> *But in the days of the voice of the seventh Angel, when he shall begin to sound, the mystery of God should be finished, as he had declared to his servants the prophets.*

Orifiel, the Genie of Saturn, is the last, and is the one who harvests the life of human beings and nations with his scythe. *"Many are called and few are chosen."*

Really, the ones who will be victoriously seated at the table of the Lord will be few, because this tenebrous humanity has sunk within the abyss.

> *And the voice which I heard from heaven spake unto me again, and said, Go and take the little book which is open in the hand of the Angel which standeth upon the sea and upon the earth.*
>
> *And I went unto the Angel, and said unto him, Give me the little book. And he said unto me. Take it, and eat it up; and it shall make thy belly bitter, but it shall be in thy mouth sweet as honey.*
>
> *And I took the little book out of the Angel's hand, and ate it up; and it was in my mouth sweet as honey: and as soon as I had eaten it, my belly was bitter.*
>
> *And he said unto me, Thou must prophesy again before many peoples, and nations, and tongues, and kings.*

Certainly, in the days of the seventh Angel, the mystery of God will be finished, as he had declared to his servants, the prophets.

Let us now see what the sacred book the Koran says:

> *The heavenly wrath shall come. No one will able to stop it. The heavens shall shake violently and the mountains move and end crashing against the earth.*
>
> *Woe to them in that day, the ones who have accused the apostles of falsehood. Woe to those who have passed their lives in foolish and senseless arguments and discussions. Throw yourself into the fire, shall be commanded to them.*
>
> *Behold the fire of which reality thou denyest. Victims of the fire thou shall be, thou shall cry or curse or shout maledictions; or shall suffer with resignation; thy fate shall not change.*
>
> *Thou have only the just reward for thy actions.*
>
> Verses from Koran

Truly, the book of prophesy is sweet as honey in the mouth and bitter within the belly.

The "**Jinn**" paradises (the lands of the fourth dimension), where the divine humanity abides, will be opened in the days of the seventh Angel.

The Garden of Delights are the "**Jinn**" paradises; the just ones will abide in these lands.

> *These are they who are drawn nigh (to Allah),*
> *In the gardens of bliss.*
> *A numerous company from among the first,*
> *And a few from among the latter.*
> *On thrones decorated,*
> *Reclining on them, facing one another.*
> *Round about them shall go youths never altering in age,*
> *With goblets and ewers and a cup of pure drink* (the wine of light of the alchemist);
> *They shall not be affected with headache thereby, nor shall they get exhausted,*
> *And fruits such as they choose,*
> *And the flesh of fowl such as they desire.*
> *And pure, beautiful ones* (lovely maidens),
> *The like of the hidden pearls:*
> *A reward for what they used to do.*
> *They shall not hear therein vain or sinful discourse,*
> *Except the word peace, peace.*
> *And the companions of the right hand; how happy are the companions of the right hand!*
> *Amid thornless lote-trees,*
> *And banana-trees (with fruits), one above another.*
> *And extended shade,*
> *And water flowing constantly,*
> *And abundant fruit,*
> *Neither intercepted nor forbidden,*
> *And exalted thrones.*
> *Surely We have made them to grow into a (new) growth,*
> *Then We have made them virgins,*
> *Loving, equals in age...*
>
> Verses 11 to 36, chapter LVI of the Koran

In the days of the seventh Angel, the kingdom of God will be finished as He told his servants, the prophets. The "**Jinn**" paradises, where divine humanity dwells, will be opened.

> *The just shall be guests of the Mansion of Delights.*
> *Lying in their nuptial couches shall they direct their vision anywhere.*
> *In their foreheads shall shine their joy.*

They shall drink an exquisite sealed wine (the wine of light of the alchemist)
The seal shall be the Almizcle.
Whoever desires this happiness must strive to deserve it.
This wine will be mixed with the Tasnim's water.
Precious fountain where the ones that will be closer to the Eternal will quench their thirst.

Verses 22 to 28, chapter LXXXIII, Koran

This Almizcle, which is the origin of the seal of the great joy, is the semen. The wine of light of the alchemist is mixed with the Tasnim's water, and this pure water of life is the Christonic semen.

To transmute the water into wine is necessary. We must not spill these pure waters of life.

There must be sexual connection, but we have to withdraw before the spasm in order to avoid the seminal ejaculation. Thus, this is how we become Gods and enter into the Garden of Delights.

The semen is the precious fountain of life.

Precious fountain where the ones that will be closer to the Eternal will quench their thirst.

Really, this is why Mohammed with right justice said: *"The seal shall be the Almizcle, and who ever desires it shall strive to deserve it."* This striving is only possible with sexual magic. This is the Arcanum A.Z.F.

Those who desire to enter into the Garden of Delights must never ever in their life spill the semen.

The sacred phallus must enter to join the uterus, but the semen must not be spilled. *"Because strait is the gate, and narrow is the way, which leadeth unto life."* This is the clue in order to awake the Kundalini.

The Arcanum A.Z.F. is for the evil ones a stumbling stone, and a rock of offence.

We departed from the "**Jinn**" paradises through the door of sex, and only through this door can we return into the Garden of Delights.

In the days of the seventh Angel, only those who accept the Arcanum A.Z.F. will abide within the Garden of Delights. This is why Mohammed said the following:

> *The true servants of God enjoy the happiness. Will have chosen foods. And exquisite fruits. Shall be served with honor.*
>
> *The gardens of voluptuousness will be their home. Full of mutual blissfulness they shall repose in their nuptial couches.*
>
> *Cups of pure water will be offered to them. Clean and of a delicious flavor.* This pure water is the semen.
>
> *They shall not blush in their face nor shall be insensible. Beside them shall be intact virgins. And shall humbly lower their eyes.*
>
> Verses 39-47, Chapter XXXVII, Koran

Truly, God shines upon the perfect couple.

Man and woman were born to love each other.

Joyful are the beings who know how to love each other!

THE SIXTH ARCANUM

Thou art giving me labor, oh Lord, and fortitude with it.

Chapter 22
The Two Witnesses

> *And there was given me a reed like unto a rod* (the staff of Brahma, the rod of Aaron, symbol of the spinal medulla and of its marvellous medullar canal. The ascending flux of the creative energy of the Holy Spirit along the medullar canal converts us into Gods): *and the Angel stood saying, Rise, and measure the temple of God, and the altar, and them that worship therein.*
>
> Revelation 11:1-19

The human being is the temple of God and this temple has to be measured with a reed. If initiation is what you seek, then write this initiation upon a rod.

> *But the court which is without the temple leave out, and measure it not; for it is given unto the Gentiles: and the holy city shall they tread under foot forty and two months.*

Certainly, the court that is without the temple is the court of the profane people, the court of the fornicators. They will tread under foot the holy city for forty and two months; they profane the sacred city of nine doors.

This holy city is the human being, and the Ninth Sphere or the ninth door is the sex. The fornicators have tread under foot the holy city for forty and two months.

The science of the numbers show us that $4 + 2 = 6$. The Kabbalists know that the Sixth Arcanum of the Tarot is The Lover. Six is also the number of the great Harlot that is repeated three times: 666.

> *And I will give power unto my two witnesses, and they shall prophesy a thousand two hundred and threescore days, clothed in sackcloth.*

We write this quantity in the following way: 1,260, and if we make the Kabbalistic addition of the numbers among themselves, we have the following result: $1 + 2 + 6 + 0 = 9$. Nine is the Ninth Sphere. This Ninth Sphere is sex.

The great Master **Hilarion IX** said that in ancient times to descend into the Ninth Sphere was the maximum ordeal for the supreme dignity of the Hierophant. Hermes, Buddha, Jesus Christ, Dante, Zoroaster, Mohammed, Rama, Krishna, Pythagoras, Plato, and many others had to descend into the Ninth Sphere in order to work with the fire and the water, which is the origin of worlds, beasts, human beings, and Gods. Every authentic White Initiation begins here.

The fire and the water rise through two sympathetic cords that are entwined around the spinal medulla. In the East, these two witnesses are Ida and Pingala.

F + W = C. Fire plus water equals consciousness. The fire and the water produce the awakening of the cosmic consciousness. Thus, this is how we prophesy for a thousand two hundred and threescore days, clothed in sackcloth and doing much fasting and penance.

Through these two sympathetic cords, which are the two witnesses, is where the fire and the water of the sex ascend.

> *These are the two olive trees, and the two candlesticks standing before the God of the earth* (our **internal God**).
>
> *And if any man will hurt them, fire proceedeth out of their mouth, and devoureth their enemies: and if any man will hurt them, he must in this manner be killed.*

These two witnesses produce the awakening of the Kundalini. Then, we receive the flaming sword which threateningly turns every way to keep the way of the Tree of Life.

It was necessary for the Lord to be killed in this manner. Now we must resuscitate Him within ourselves. The two witnesses have the power to kill and give life.

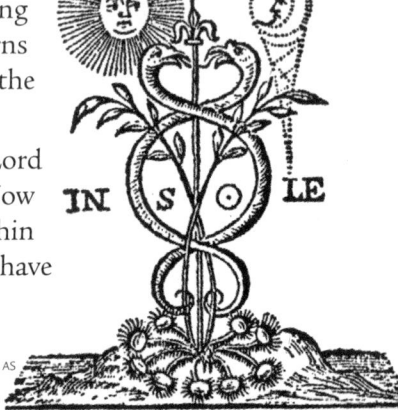

The Two Witnesses encircling the spinal column, as depicted in an Alchemical illustration.

> *These have power to shut heaven, that it rain not in the days of their prophesy: and have power over waters to turn them to blood, and to smite the earth with all plagues as often as they will.*

If the sacred serpent ascends, it opens heaven, but if it descends, it shuts heaven. The waters are turned to blood when we fornicate, and the affliction of the abyss is more terrible than death.

Fornication is the sin against the Holy Spirit. Whosoever fornicates sins against their own body. Thus, this is the way in which this fornicating humanity is often smitten with all plagues.

Whosoever spills the semen (reaches the orgasm) is a fornicator, even if they are officially married.

These two witnesses have the power of awakening the Kundalini (this is the fire of Pentecost).

> *And when they shall have finished their testimony, the beast that ascendeth out of the bottomless pit shall make war against them, and shall overcome them, and kill them.*
>
> *And their dead bodies shall lie in the street of the great city, which spiritually is called Sodom and Egypt, where also our Lord was crucified.*

The prophets prophesied in ancient times. Then, the two witnesses gave their testimony and they announced the times of the end. These two witnesses also gave testimony of the light, and this light came into the darkness, but the darkness knew it not.

The beast that ascended out of the bottomless pit, that Satan which everybody carries inside, made war against them, overcame them, and killed them, because this humanity delivered themselves to fornication.

The bodies of these two witnesses lay in the street of this great city which is "**Babylon the great, the mother of harlots and abominations of the earth,**" which is spiritually called Sodom and Egypt, where also our Lord was crucified. This is this valley of bitterness where this humanity (the great Harlot) lives.

And they of the people and kindreds and tongues and nations shall see their dead bodies three days and an half, and shall not suffer their dead bodies to be put in graves.

Jesus Christ, the great **Hierophant,** said:

I am able to destroy the temple of God, and to build it in three days. - Matthew 26:61

The body of the Savior of the world remained three days within its holy sepulchre. The prophet Jonah was three days inside the belly of the whale.

Actually, the bodies of the two witnesses still do not deserve to descend into the holy sepulchre, because they are filled with fornication. Since this humanity delivered themselves to fornication, their two witnesses are dead.

And they that dwell upon the earth shall rejoice over them, and make merry, and shall send gifts one to another; because these two prophets tormented them that dwelt on the earth.

The words of the prophets are a torment for the dwellers of the Earth.

And after three days and an half the spirit of life from God entered into them, and they stood upon their feet; and great fear fell upon them which saw them.

These three days symbolize the **Thrice-Spirit** of the human being, the perfect Holy Trinity. The resurrection of the dead comes after the third day.

We have suffered much for three days; now the two witnesses will resurrect.

And they heard a great voice from heaven saying unto them, Come up hither. And they ascended up to heaven in a cloud; and their enemies beheld them.

Now, these two witnesses are ascending with the Arcanum A.Z.F. because we are in the times of the end. This is the epoch of the accomplishment of this prophecy.

The resurrection of these two witnesses is absolutely a sexual problem.

These two witnesses resurrect when the man and the woman know how to withdraw from the sexual act without spilling the entity of semen (without reaching the orgasm). Thus, this is how the force of the Holy Spirit ascends inwards and upwards through these two witnesses.

So, these two witnesses are the two marvellous sympathetic canals of our creative energy.

The times of the end have arrived!

The divulging of the Great Arcanum, the resurrection of the two witnesses, and the final great cataclysm stamp with exactitude the end of this Aryan Root Race.

The human being who will not accept this scientific chastity will sink into the abyss.

A dreadful cataclysm will occur. However, not a single human being can know the date of that day and hour.

A planetary collision will occur, a collision of worlds, and only those who have made their two witnesses resurrect within themselves will be saved.

> *And the same hour was there a great earthquake, and the tenth part of the city fell, and in the earthquake were slain of men seven thousand: and the remnant were affrighted, and gave glory to the God of heaven.*

A tenth part of this great Babylon will fall. Thus, this is how the wheel of destiny will turn and this great harlot (humanity) will sink into the abyss

The number 10 is the wheel of destiny, the Tenth Arcanum of the Tarot.

"*...And in the earthquake were slain of men seven thousand.*" This is the Seventh Arcanum, which is expiation, karma, punishment.

Certainly, the great harlot will die, all lineages, nations, and tongues, as many as the sands of the sea.

The two witnesses will talk before the great cataclysm that is approaching.

Before the dreadful catastrophe that is approaching, the heavens will pass away with a great noise and the human multitudes from Mars, Mercury, Venus, and other planets will come in their cosmic ships to the planet Earth.

These brethren humanities from other planets will come in order to teach us law and order.

So, we will have the opportunity of listening to the words of the Son of Man.

Then... Woe to those who will abhor the Son of Man! Woe to those who abhor the Great Arcanum... Woe to those who will continue spilling the semen!

The human beings of this planet Earth have thrown themselves into the conquering of space, and soon they will knock upon the doors of other inhabited worlds with their ships.

The consequences of their audacity will be the answer of the Son of Man. Then, *"Behold, he cometh with clouds; and every eye shall see him."*

The Son of Man is the divine humanity. The Son of Man is represented by the superior multitudes of other inhabited worlds.

Every cosmic rocket launched up into space is placing us closer to this great cosmic event. Then, woe to those who will not accept the last words of the Son of Man!

Afterwards, the great cataclysm will occur!

The second woe is past; and behold, the third woe comes quickly.

And the seventh Angel sounded; and there were great voices in heaven, saying, The kingdoms of this world are become the kingdoms of our Lord, and of his Christ; and he shall reign for ever and ever.

And the four and twenty elders, which sat before God on their seats, fell upon their faces, and worshipped God,

Saying, we give thee thanks, O Lord God Almighty, which art, and wast, and art to come, because thou hast taken to thee thy great power, and hast reigned.

And the nations were angry, and the wrath is come, and the time of the dead, that they should be judge, and that shouldest give reward unto thy servants the prophets, and to the saints, and them that fear thy name, small and great; and shouldest destroy them which destroy the earth. These are the vultures of war and the scientists of the Antichrist.

The Final Judgement has already occurred. It took place on the 12th of April, 1950. Then, the Gods judged the great harlot (this humanity) and considered it unworthy.

The sentence of the Gods was: *To the abyss! To the abyss! To the abyss!*

This planet Earth will pass through a process of planetary disintegration and integration.

Nobody knows the day and the hour but the Father.

And the temple of God was opened in heaven, and there was seen in his temple the ark of his testament: and there were lightnings, and voices, and thunderings, and an earthquake, and great hail.

The Ark of His Testament is the sex. This Ark of His Testament is the Ark of Science, the Ark of Testimony, as well as the Ark of Alliance.

The Rod of Aaron, which is the symbol of the phallus, and the Cup of Omer filled with the manna, which is the symbol of the uterus, are inside the Ark of His Testament. (See Exodus 16: 31-36).

The key of all powers is found in the union of the phallus and the uterus. The tablets of the law are also inside the Ark of Science. Whosoever violates the divine Decalogue† will sink into the abyss.

To achieve the miracle of our salvation is only possible through the Ark of His Testament.

ENGRAVING BY ALBRECHT DÜRER

And there appeared a great wonder in heaven: a woman clothed with the sun, and the moon under her feet, and upon her head a crown of twelve stars: And she being with child cried, travailing in birth, and pained to be delivered.

Chapter 23
The Woman and the Dragon

> Revelation 12:1-17:
>
> *And there appeared a great wonder in heaven: a woman clothed with the sun, and the moon under her feet, and upon her head a crown of twelve stars:*
>
> *And she being with child cried, travailing in birth, and pained to be delivered.*

We, the brothers and sisters, teach to the human being how to build the temple with this great wonder that appeared in heaven in the times of the end.

This temple must be built upon the living rock, but this rock is filled with cactuses with sharp thorns that hurt the flesh.

The Son of Man is always born from the womb of a virgin.

Our adorable Savior bleeding upon his cross taught us the secret of the woman clothed with the sun, and the Venustic Initiation.

> *When Jesus therefore saw his mother, and the disciple standing by, whom he loved, he saith unto his mother, Woman, behold thy son!*
> John 19:26
>
> Then saith he to the disciple, *Behold thy mother! and from that hour that disciple took her unto his own home.*
> John 19:27

The name of this disciple was **John**, which is a name the sound of which must be divided into five vowels in the following way: **I.E.O.U.AN. John** is the **Word**; **John** is the son who is always born from the womb of a woman.

What we want to say with the former statement is that only by practicing sexual magic can we incarnate Christ within ourselves.

We will attain the Venustic Initiation only by working with the Arcanum A.Z.F.

The Word, Christ, is always born from immaculate conceptions. The Son of Man is always the son of a Virgin Mother.

This woman clothed with the sun, crowned with twelve stars, and the moon under her feet, is any woman who has reached the achievement of the secret degree of Virgin Mother. This is the Urania-Venus, the Queen of Heaven, who being with child cried, travailing in birth, and pained to be delivered.

And there appeared another wonder in heaven; and behold a great red dragon, having seven heads and ten horns, and seven crowns upon his heads.

This tenebrous dragon turns along with the wheel of the centuries. This dragon from darkness ascended from the abyss, and with the turn of the wheel this dragon will fall into the abyss.

This dragon from the abyss is the evil of the world, the Black Lodge, the secret enemy with his terrible evilness.

We will expiate our error with the number seven. The ten horns of the dragon are the symbol of the wheel of destiny. This wheel will turn and this beast will sink into the abyss.

The times of the end have arrived, and nobody knows with exactitude how many years these times of the end will endure.

This dragon of darkness is the prince of this world. This dragon of darkness is the psychological "I", the myself, the ego which all of us carry inside. In short, it is Satan.

And his tail drew the third part of the stars of heaven, and did cast them to the earth: and the dragon stood before the woman which was ready to be delivered, for to devour her child as soon as it was born.

Certainly, thousands of Bodhisattvas have fallen during this Age of Iron. So, the dragon of darkness stands before the woman in order to devour her child. The secret enemy wants to devour us.

Nirvana has epochs of activity and epochs of profound repose.

Since February 19, 1919, Nirvana entered into activity, because the times of the end have arrived and we need help.

On February 19, at 4:00 pm, the Virgins of Nirvana began to be born. Now, millions of Virgins from Nirvana are reincarnating in order to help us.

Now, it is amazing to contemplate these reincarnated Virgins who are living as simple maidens, as humble housemaids.

This is the great wonder which appeared in heaven; this is Venus-Urania, the woman clothed with the sun and the moon under her feet. She was born in order to be a Virgin Mother. This degree of Virgin is the Buddhic state.

This Virgin Mother, being with child, cried, travailing in birth, and pained to be delivered, and the dragon of darkness wants to devour her child in order to impede the incarnation of Christ within ourselves.

The Antichrist abhors the Arcanum A.Z.F., and he does not want the Christ to be born within us.

Many are called and few are chosen.

Christ is born within the heart of the human being in the long nights of winter.

The Savior is born in the manger of the world in nights of bitterness, darkness, and tears.

> *And she brought forth a man child, who was to rule all nations with a rod of iron: and her child was caught up unto God, and to his throne.*

This woman clothed with the sun, crowned with twelve stars, and the moon under her feet, always brings forth a man child, the Son of Man, who, in these times of the end, is very strong and must rule all nations with a rod of iron. Certainly, the Son of Man is caught up unto God and His throne.

> *And the woman fled into the wilderness, where she had a place prepared of God, that they should feed her there a thousand two hundred and threescore days.*

Every Virgin Mother lives in her own wilderness, far away from the world, the demon, and the flesh.

These Virgin Mothers create for themselves their own wilderness while they live in the world.

The Kabbalistic quantity 1,260 breaks down in this way: 1 + 2 + 6 + 0 = 9. Certainly, 9 is the Ninth Sphere, sex.

The Son of Man is born from within the fire and the water of the Ninth Sphere. It is here in this Ninth Sphere where every woman who has achieved the esoteric degree of Virgin is preserved for a thousand, two hundred and threescore days.

And there was war in heaven: Michael and his Angels fought against the dragon; and the dragon fought and his Angels.

So, Michael and all of us the brothers and sisters of the Ray of Strength fought against the dragon of darkness and against the tenebrous legions of the Black Lodge.

This fight against the dragon and his black Angels began precisely in the year 1950.

And prevailed not; neither was their place found any more in heaven.

These battles within the internal worlds between the legions of light and the legions of darkness have been terrible and dreadful.

And the great dragon was cast out, that old serpent called the Devil, and Satan, which deceiveth the whole world: he was cast out into the earth, and his Angels were cast out with him.

The great Black Lodge and all of its left-hand adepts normally abided within the distinct atomic regions of Nature.

As of the year 1950, the great battle between the White Lodge and the Black Lodge began.

So, since the year 1950, the henchmen of Lucifer and Ariman, the followers of the Bons† and Drukpas† (who are the enemies of the Fourth Path†), along with the Nicolaitans and the Tantric Anagarikas, have been entering into the abyss.

Certainly, the Avitchi of the Hindustani is the same abyss. This abyss is also the Klipoth of the Kabbalah. These Klipoth are atomic, tenebrous, and sublunar.

The antithesis of these Klipoth is a super-divine atom that is related with the church of Laodicea, or the lotus of one thousand petals.

We are this super-divine atom, when inwardly arriving to our final synthesis. The name of this atom is the "**Ain Soph**."

This Ain Soph is our atomic star. This star shines full with glory within the Abstract Absolute Space.

Kether, Chokmah, and Binah emanate from this star, that is to say, the Father, the Son, and the Holy Spirit of each human being emanate from this star.

The abyss is the antithesis of the "**Ain Soph**." The abyss is the fatal shadow of the Ain Soph. This Ain Soph is omniscience and happiness. [See illustration on page 164].

The tenebrous of the lunar path dwell within the abyss.

> *And I heard a loud voice saying in heaven, Now is come salvation, and strength, and the kingdom of our God, and the power of his Christ: for the accuser of our brethren is cast down, which accused them before God day and night.*

The accuser of our brethren is the black dragon. The accuser of our brethren stoned, poisoned, and crucified the prophets. The accuser of our brethren is the Black Lodge.

Now, the saints of the Lord will become victorious. They have defeated Satan.

> *And they overcame him by the blood of the Lamb, and by the word of their testimony; and they love not their lives unto the death.*

> *Therefore rejoice, ye heavens, and ye that dwell in them. Woe to the inhabiters of the earth and of the sea! for the devil is come down unto you, having great wrath, because he knoweth that he hath but a short time.*

Satan, full of anger, will bring the war between the east and the west.

Full of anger and knowing that he has but a short time, Satan will precipitate the atomic war.

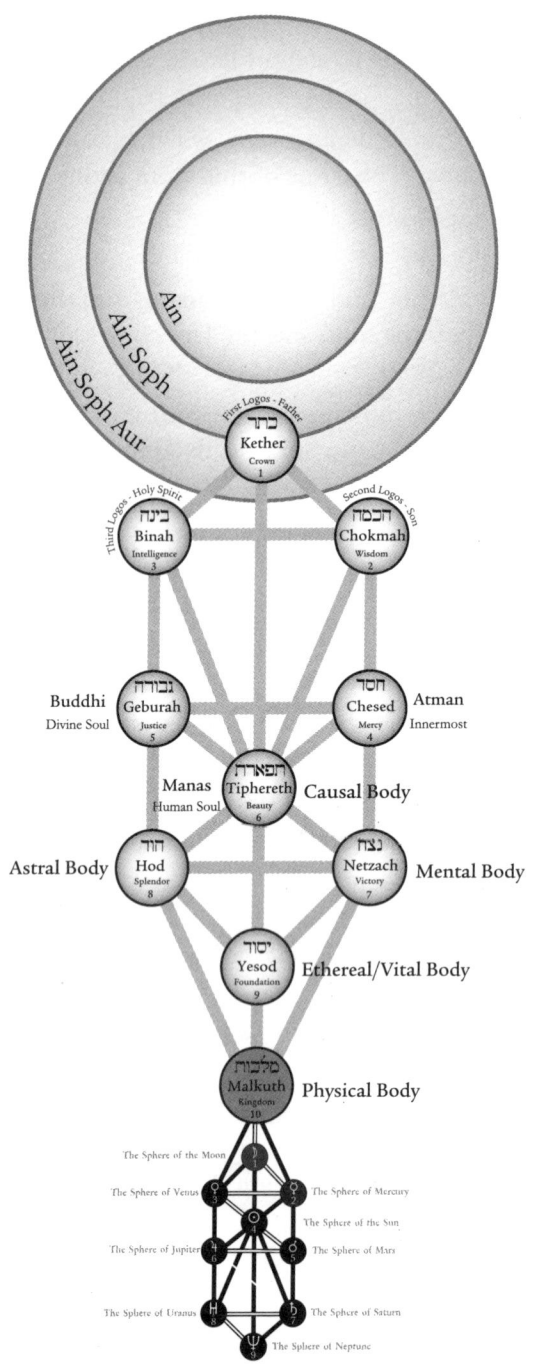

Wars of death and dreadful cataclysms will occur in this century.

> *And when the dragon saw that he was cast out into the earth* (and into the abyss), *he persecuted the woman which brought forth the man child.*
>
> *And to the woman were given two wings of a great eagle, that she might fly into the wilderness into her place, where she is nourished for a time, and times, and a half a time, from the face of the serpent.*

In these times of the end, the nirvanic women fly into the wilderness of their own life, far away from the face of the tempting serpent.

Many of these women become nuns for a while. The great majority of them are maids within family houses. Thus, this is how they earn their daily bread. Thus, this is how they serve with humbleness. They have the two wings of the great eagle of the Spirit and fly into the wilderness.

Certainly, these Virgin Mothers suffer the unspeakable, since for them, life in this world is a wilderness.

They complain because of lost time, since they do not find a man who wants to christify himself in this terrible wilderness.

So, they remain in their wilderness for a time, and times, and a half a time, that is to say, they remain in their job, their work, for a time (the routine of their job), and times (movements into other houses, offices, jobs) and half a time (the hour, the moment, when in the wilderness of their life, the man for whom they were waiting appears).

> *And the serpent cast out of his mouth water as flood after the woman, that he might cause her to be carried away of the flood.*
>
> *And the earth helped the woman, and the earth opened her mouth, and swallowed up the flood which the dragon cast out of his mouth.*

The tempting serpent of Eden tempts these women (who are symbols of the woman clothed with the sun) and try to make them sexually fall, but these Virgin Mothers transmute their creative energies and fly high with the two wings of the Spirit.

"The woman is the one who delivers the sword to man.
She is the Urania-Venus with the sword in her hand."

This philosophical earth, that is to say, this physical organism, swallows up the flood that the dragon casts out of his mouth, and transmutes this into light and fire.

This flood is the Universal Solvent of Alchemy, the Lapis Philosophorum, the pure gold or Summa Materia, which is also called Menstruum Universale.

This is the essence that the dragon casts out of his mouth that we must transmute in order to fly with the two wings of the Spirit as eagles of light.

Thus, this is how the Urania-Venus defends herself from the tempting serpent who made Eve-Venus sin.

There exist various types of women; let us know them:

The first, **Eve-Venus**, is the animalistic, instinctive, and brutish female.

The second, **Venus-Eve**, is the very human female, who loves when she finds a sexually passionate male who knows how to love her.

The third, **Venus-Urania**, is the very human, conscious woman filled with the deepest of both spiritual and human feelings.

The fourth, **Urania-Venus**, is the Mother of the Son of Man, the Virgins of Nirvana. This is the woman clothed with the sun and the moon under her feet. This woman is crowned with twelve stars, which are the symbol of the seven churches and the five senses, in other words, the twelve faculties.

Only the woman can establish justice upon the face of the Earth, because she has the power to awake the flaming fire within the man. The clue is found in the Arcanum A.Z.F.

The woman is the one who delivers the sword to man. She is the **Urania-Venus** with the sword in her hand.

She is before the Cosmic Scale in the Eighth Arcanum. She is the mother of the Son of Man.

She is the one who wants to bruise the head of the tempting serpent in order to tame it and raise it through the medullar canal.

Disgracefully, as Goethe said, "The law of the woeful and severe man inquires, fights, and agitates. What he needs the most is what he knows the least."

The man (human being) needs the Arcanum A.Z.F., but he does not know it. This is what he needs the most, but this is what he knows the least.

Now we, the brothers and sisters of the temple, teach this Arcanum, but the dwellers of the Earth abhor it.

Urania-Venus is tempted by the dragon, but the dragon is defeated.

> *And the dragon was wroth with the woman, and went to make war with the remnant of her seed, which keep the commandments of God, and have the testimony of Jesus Christ.*

Chapter 24
The Two Beasts

> Revelation 13:1-18:
>
> *And I stood upon the sand of the sea, and saw a beast rise up out of the sea, having seven heads and ten horns, and upon his horns ten crowns, and upon his heads the name of blasphemy.*

This beast with seven heads is this fornicating humanity. The ten horns are the wheel of destiny on which this beast rises up from the abyss and, turning, falls again into the abyss.

The ten crowns upon his seven heads signifies that this beast sovereignly reigns during this Age of Iron or Kali Yuga.

Nevertheless, when the wheel of destiny spins over its axis, this beast will tumble into the precipice.

> *And the beast which I saw was like unto a leopard, and his feet were as the feet of a bear, and his mouth as the mouth of a lion: and the dragon gave him his power, and his seat, and great authority.*
>
> *And I saw one of his heads as it were wounded to death; and his deadly wound was healed: and all the world wondered after the beast.*

We, the brothers and sisters of the temple, saw a new symbol when we examined this wounded head of the beast that was healed.

We saw a man like unto a gorilla, filled with a malignant intelligence. This dreadful and terrible gorilla-man was steering four beasts in front of him, he himself being the fifth. These four beasts were chained and he was steering them in front of him.

We understand with this symbol that the wounded head is the perverse human being of this fifth Root Race, the human beings of the present.

This malignant race launches a fratricide and barbarian war, and is healed after being mortally wounded. This is why all the world wonders after the beast.

Certainly, also the internal bodies are wounded in the battle. However, they are healed with the help of the Masters of Medicine.

And they worshipped the dragon (Satan) *which have power unto the beast: and they worshipped the beast, saying, Who is like unto the beast? Who is able to make war with him?*

Everybody in the world believes themselves to be civilized; they worship the beast. Everybody worships the "I," the myself, that Satan which all of us carry inside.

People live within evilness. Everybody loves the beast, and they wallow in the mud.

And there was given unto him a mouth speaking great things and blasphemies; and power was given unto him to continue forty and two months.

This beast has prominence during the whole Kali Yuga and is reigning with sovereignty. This beast is the great harlot whose reign is finishing.

And he opened his mouth in blasphemy against God, to blaspheme his name (with atheism), *and his tabernacle* (with fornication), *and them that dwell in heaven* (the Saints).

And it was given unto him to make war with the saints, and to overcome them (many initiates have fallen): *and power was given him over all kindreds, and tongues, and nations.*

This entire humanity capitulated before the great beast that rose up from the abyss and that is already falling into the abyss.

And all that dwell upon the earth shall worship him, whose names are not written in the book of life of the Lamb slain from the foundation of the world.

In the Koran, the Book of Life is called "Aliin," and this contains the conduct of the just ones and Angels.

The Book of the Lost Ones is called with the name of "Syyin" among the Mohammedans.

The good and evil deeds are weighed on the scale of the cosmic justice.

Those who are not written in the Book of Life are already sinking within the dreadful abyss.

Only the Gnostic faith can save the lost ones.

The Lamb has been slain from the foundation of the world because we committed fornication. Now we must resurrect the Lamb within ourselves with the Arcanum A.Z.F. This Arcanum is sexual magic.

If any man have an ear, let him hear.

He that leadeth into captivity shall go into captivity: he that killeth with the sword must be killed with the sword. Here is the patience and the faith of the saints.

The Law is the Law. Whatever we do we must pay for! The Saints know the Law, therefore they are patient.

Verily, verily, I say unto you, that the times of the end have arrived. So, he that leadeth into captivity shall go into captivity. He who killed with the sword must be killed with the sword.

We can be saved only by entering into the Ark of Science. We departed from Eden through the door of sex, and only through that door can we enter into Eden again. Eden is the same sex.

Nobody can enter into Eden through false doors. The Law is the Law. We came out through one door and only through that door can we enter again. This is the Law.

The Magnum Opus is the science of sexual transmutation. We must make the energy of the Third Logos (the Holy Spirit) return in ourselves inwardly and upwardly. Thus, this is how we convert ourselves into Gods.

In this great work of the alchemist, the water and the oil is necessary. We need half water and half oil.

Those who despise the water fail in the Great Work, because we can only illuminate ourselves with our own spiritual oil when we have pure waters of life (accumulated semen).

What be these two olive branches, which through the two golden pipes empty the golden oil out of themselves?

These are the two anointed ones that stand by the Lord of the whole earth. - Zachariah 4:12, 14

In synthesis, these are the two witnesses that are born from the lake. They emerge from the seminal vessels (testicles and ovaries).

The transmuted sexual energy, which is the pure golden oil, flows through these two olive branches.

Those who affirm that many paths leading to God exist and that sex is just one of them, really despise the pure waters of life. Therefore, they fail and sink into the abyss.

Verily, verily, I say unto you that in the whole of eternity, only and absolutely one strait gate and only one narrow and difficult way which leads unto light has been known. This gate and this way is sex.

Strive to enter in at the strait gate (sex); for many, I say unto you, will seek to enter in, and shall not be able. - Luke 13:24

Strait is the gate, and narrow is the way which leads unto light, and few are those who find it. Our adorable savior Jesus Christ never said that there were many ways; He clearly and without question spoke only of one gate and only of one way (sex). (See John 10:7-9; 14)

We, the brothers and sisters of the temple, invite you, beloved reader, to study the four Gospels. In these Gospels you will prove to yourself that only one strait gate and only one narrow and difficult way exists.

The preachers who affirm the existence of many ways leading unto God ignore that in the Great Work we need half oil and half water.

And I beheld another beast coming up out of the earth; and he had two horns like a lamb, and he spake as a dragon.

And he exerciseth all the power of the first beast before him, and causeth the earth and they which dwell therein to worship the first beast, whose deadly wound was healed.

And he doeth great wonders, so he maketh fire come down from heaven on the earth in the sight of men.

And deceiveth them that dwell on the earth by the means of those miracles which he had power to do in the sight of the beast; saying to them that dwell on the earth, that they should make an image to the beast, which had the wound by a sword, and did live.

This beast that has two horns like a lamb and that speaks as a dragon is the materialistic science of the dwellers of the earth.

Certainly, this great beast is double, because it has a mind that speaks of great wonders.

This materialistic science plays with what it ignores, and stumbles in the darkness.

This materialistic science deceives the dwellers of the Earth because of the miracles that it has power of performing in the sight of the beast (humanity). These miracles are: war missiles, space missiles, radio, television, ultra-modern airplanes, atomic bombs, hydrogen bombs which make fire come down from heaven over indefensible cities, atomic submarines, deadly rays, etc.

All of these inventions of this materialistic science, which is the beast with two horns, are the miracles with which it is deceiving all who dwell on the Earth.

Therefore, these deceived human beings worship the beast, and they say, "There is no one like unto the beast! Who is superior to this beast?"

And he had power to give life unto the image of the beast, that the image of the beast should both speak, and cause that as many as would not worship the image of the beast should be killed.

The followers of this materialistic science are poisoning the multitudes with their theories. Thus, this is how the image of the beast speaks.

Those Saints who do not worship the image (theories) of the beast are killed, incarcerated, and hated. Certainly, this beast with two horns is terrible.

And he causeth all, both small and great, rich and poor, free and bond, to receive a mark in their right hand, or in their foreheads:

And that no man might buy or sell, save he that had the mark, or the name of the beast, or the number of his name.

Here is wisdom. Let him that hath understanding count the number of the beast: for it is the number of a man; and his number is Six hundred threescore and six.

The mark of the beast is the two horns on the forehead. Millions and billions of human beings already have the mark of the beast on their foreheads and in their hands.

All of these souls with the mark of the beast are lost, and since the year 1950, they have been entering into the abyss. This human evolution totally failed.

Certainly, this world is already lost, because in the worldly trade, nobody can buy or sell, save those who have the mark of the beast on their forehead and in their hands. Thus, this is how worldly trade has become.

The number of the great beast is six hundred and sixty-six, and it is the number of a man, because this is a Kabbalistic number which is broken down as follows: 6 + 6 + 6 = 18. Then, when we make the addition of the number eighteen in itself, we have the following: 1 + 8 = 9.

Nine is sex. Nine is the human being, because the human being is the child of sex.

In summary, the Eighteenth and the Ninth Arcana are contained in the number 666. The Eighteenth Arcanum is the abyss, darkness. It is sexual temptations that the initiate must fight against. The Ninth Arcanum is the Ninth Sphere (initiation).

The Gods judged the great harlot whose number is 666.

The sentence of the Gods was: *To the abyss! To the abyss! To the abyss!*

THE LAMB IN SION. ENGRAVING BY ALBRECHT DÜRER

Chapter 25
The Lamb in Sion

> Revelation 14:1-20:
>
> *And I looked, and lo, a Lamb stood on the mount of Sion, and with him an hundred forty and four thousand, having his Father's name written in their foreheads.* The mount of Sion represents the superior worlds.

The number one hundred and forty-four thousand of those who have their Father's name written on their foreheads is a symbolic and Kabbalistic quantity. 144,000 is broken down in the following way:

1 + 4 + 4 = 9. This number nine is the Ninth Sphere (sex).

To receive the name of the Father on our foreheads and to be saved is only possible with the Great Arcanum.

The people of Sion are the people of Israel (spiritual people of God). These people are formed by all of those who practice sexual magic (they are chaste people).

> *And I heard a voice from heaven as the voice of many waters, and as the voice of a great thunder: and I heard the voice of harpers harping with their harps:*
>
> *And they sung as it were a new song before the throne, and before the four beasts* (of Alchemy), *and the elders: and no man could learn that song but the hundred and forty and four thousand, which were redeemed from the earth* (with a great sacrifice).
>
> *These are they which were not defiled with women; for they are virgins* (these are they who learned how to refrain the internal beast in order to avoid the ejaculation of the semen [orgasm]). *These are they which followed the Lamb whithersoever he goeth. These were redeemed from among men, being the firstfruits unto God and to the Lamb.*
>
> *And in their mouth was found no guile: for they are without fault before the throne of God.*

> *And I saw another Angel fly in the midst of heaven, having the everlasting gospel to preach unto them that dwell on the earth, and to every nation, and kindred, and tongue, and people,*
>
> *Saying with a loud voice, Fear God, and give glory to him; for the hour of his judgement is come: and worship him that made heaven and earth, and the sea, and the fountains of waters.*
>
> *And there followed another Angel, saying, Babylon is fallen, is fallen, that great city* (Paris, Rome, London, Berlin, cities of the United States, etc., in short, this present civilization), *because she made all nations drink of the wine of the wrath of her fornication.*
>
> *And the third Angel followed them, saying with a loud voice, if any man worship the beast and his name, and receive his mark in his forehead, or in his hand,*
>
> *The same shall drink of the wine of the wrath of God, which is poured out without mixture into the cup of his indignation; and he shall be tormented with fire and brimstone in the presence of the holy Angels, and in the presence of the Lamb.*

All of the people who worship the beast of their passions, and his image (intellectualism without spirituality) will be tormented with fire into the abyss, with the fire and brimstone of their own desires.

To pay the whole of our karma here in this very place, this physical plane, is preferable than to pay it within the internal worlds.

This nemesis, this karma, no matter how grave it might be in the physical plane, becomes very sweet if we compare it with the karma in the Astral Plane and within the abyss.

> *And the smoke of their torment ascendeth up for ever and ever: and they have no rest day nor night, who worship the beast and his image, and whosoever receiveth the mark of his name.*

The intellect is a very precious instrument for the Great Work of the Father when it is absolutely used for the pure service of the Spirit.

A mystic without intellect fails because of lack of culture. The intellect is satanic when it is used for the service of the internal beast.

The intellectual villains (cynics and skeptics) are the result of intellectualism without spirituality. These intellectual villains are the exact image of the beast.

The tenebrous ones torment each other within the abyss with their hatred, intrigue, calumny, anger, greed, lust, etc., and the smoke of their torment ascends for ever and ever.

The Saints know all of this. For this reason they are patient.

> *Here is the patience of the saints: here are they that keep the commandments of God, and the faith of Jesus.*
>
> *And I heard a voice from heaven saying unto me, Write, Blessed are the dead which die in the Lord from hence forth: Yea, saith the Spirit, that they may rest from their labours; and their works do follow them.*

Something continues to exist when the human being dies. This something is the thought of all our desires. The whole of our thoughts of desire continue, and this is already demonstrated. The sum of all those mental values continue.

The total addition of all of those values of desire constitute the "I," the myself, the ego, our false individuality. This "I" is the one that reincarnates in order to satisfy its desires.

Therefore, blessed are the dead who die in the Lord: they will enter Nirvana forever, for whosoever decapitates and dissolves the "I" dies in life, dies in the Lord.

The Truth cannot enter where the "I" abides. The Lord is the Truth.

The Lord Buddha taught us: one Essence, one Law, and one Goal.

The Essence is the Ens Seminis, the Law is the Arcanum A.Z.F., and the Goal is Nirvana. Thus, this is what the Buddha said:

If thou understand, O Kasyapa! that all beings are of the same essence (the Ens Seminis), *and that there is only one and unique truth* (the Christ), *and if thou lives in accordance with this comprehension, thou shall reach Nirvana.*

The Tathagata gives happiness and joy to the whole world, as the cloud that pours its waters (semen) *over the just ones and the sinners* (everybody receives it), *having the same feelings of compassion for the great and small; for the wise and for the ignorant; for the virtuous and for the sinner.*

The vast and swollen cloud impregnated with water pours into rain over pastures, thorny bushes, mountains, valleys, orchards and country fields. And all drink the water (semen) *of this rain which is the same one essence. And trees, and plants, and herbs, mix and flourish and fructify, each one in accordance to its kind and nature; rooted to the same earth. All of these plants in the field or in the orchard, receive the same water* (semen) *which vivifies and gives life to all.*

The Tathagata knows, O Kasyapa! the Law which virtue is the Knowledge and which goal is the peace of Nirvana (this law is the Arcanum A.Z.F.).

This law is the same for everybody but does not manifest itself in the same way for everyone, but in accordance with their needs. In the beginning the plenitude of this knowledge is not given equally, but in accordance with the predisposition of everyone. In ancient times, the Arcanum A.Z.F. was only taught in secrecy to the initiates.

Buddha taught this key unto his well-prepared disciples.

Whosoever wants to die in the Lord must wash their feet in the waters of renunciation. Thus, this is how the Lord Buddha taught chastity as a basic foundation of initiation.

Buddha asked his disciples the following:

Tell me, O disciples, when is a disciple no longer a disciple?

And Sariputra answered, "The good disciple must not break his vow of chastity. Whosoever breaks his vow of chastity is no longer a disciple of Sakyamuni."

This is textual from the gospel of the Lord Buddha, a transcription of the *Pitakas* or sacred scriptures of Buddhism. (See the book of Yogi Kharishnanda).

The Master Huiracocha gave the supreme key of chastity in Latin, as follows: "**Inmisio membri virili in vagina feminae sine ejeculatium seminis.**"

Whosoever wants to die in the Lord must practice the Ten Commandments for the new era:

First: Thou shalt love thy internal God, and thy neighbor as thy Self.

Second: Thou shalt study the secret doctrine of the Savior of the world.

Third: Thou shalt never slander thy neighbor, neither shalt thou utter immodest or vain words.

Fourth: Thou shalt sacrifice the self for the love of mankind and to love thy worst enemies.

Fifth: Thou shalt obey the will of the Father on Earth as it is in heaven.

Sixth: Thou shalt not commit fornication, neither adultery, in thy thought, words, and deeds.

Seventh: Thou shalt fight against the world, the demon, and the flesh.

Eighth: Thou shalt be infinitely patient and merciful.

Ninth: Thou shalt practice the Arcanum A.Z.F. with thy spouse.

Tenth: Thou shalt wash thy feet in the waters of renunciation.

You will die in the Lord with these Ten Commandments.

And I looked, and behold a white cloud, and upon the cloud one sat like unto the Son of Man, having on his head a golden crown, and in his hand a sharp sickle.

And another Angel came out of the temple, crying with a loud voice to him that sat on the cloud, Thrust in thy sickle, and reap:

> *for the time is come for thee to reap; for the harvest on the earth is ripe.* The time has arrived!
>
> *And he that sat on the cloud thrust in his sickle on the earth; and the earth was reaped.* The time for reaping has arrived!
>
> *And another Angel came out of the temple which is in heaven, he also having a sharp sickle.*
>
> *And another Angel came out from the altar, which had power over fire; and cried with a loud cry to him that had the sharp sickle, saying, Thrust in thy sharp sickle, and gather the clusters of the vine of the earth; for her grapes are fully ripe.*

The power of the fire lies in the sex. Angels and devils, Gods and beasts are born from sex.

Man is the priest and the woman the altar. Through sex we sow and through sex we harvest.

If the harvest is good, then we have a harvest of Gods.

If the harvest is evil, then the harvest is lost within the abyss.

The wise North American Kabbalist Manly P. Hall, who was cited by the great Master of the White Lodge, Dr. Francisco A. Propato, said in his book *Occult Anatomy of Man* the following: "Those who will be incapable of lifting the fire of the spinal medulla throughout their Shushumna canal, will be cast aside into a lateral kingdom, similar to that of the present apes (monkeys, chimpanzees, etc.)."

> *And the Angel thrust in his sickle into the earth, and gathered the vine of the earth, and cast it into the great winepress of the wrath of God.* The fulfilment of this nineteenth verse of the fourteenth chapter of Revelation is definitive.

The Angel cast the whole vine of the earth into the great winepress of the wrath of God. The great White Lodge knows that human evolution on earth is lost.

Human evolution totally failed and this humanity is sinking into the abyss.

And the winepress was trodden without the city, and blood came out of the winepress, even unto the horse bridles, by the space of a thousand and six hundred furlongs.

This Kabbalistic quantity is broken down as follows: 1 + 6 = 7.

This human race will expiate with supreme pain all of their evil deeds.

The three ineffable beings of this fourteenth chapter of Apocalypse, correspond to the three aspects of humanity: the world, family, and the human being.

These three Angels of the Most High are punishing countries, families, and human beings.

The Law is the Law and the Law is fulfilled. These three Angels obey the Son of Man.

The Lord of all powers is seated on a cloud of glory.

The Lord of all perfections has on his head a golden crown, and in his hand a sharp sickle.

VITRIOL, who is ruled by the Seven Angels.

VITRIOL means: Visitam Interiori Terra Rectifictur Invenian Ocultum Lapidum; Visit the interior of the earth, which by rectifying, you will find the occult stone.

Chapter 26
The Seven Angels with the Seven Vials

Revelation 15:1-8:

And I saw another sign in heaven, great and marvellous, seven Angels having the seven last plagues; for in them is filled up the wrath of God.

These seven Angels are Gabriel, Raphael, Uriel, Michael, Samael, Zachariel, Orifiel. Among these seven Angels, the fifth is the one who has suffered the most.

All of these seven Angels accomplish superior commands and they act in accordance with the law.

The Bodhisattva of the fifth Angel fell after the Atlantean catastrophe, but he arose again from the clay of the Earth after having suffered greatly. Now, this Bodhisattva has again returned to his God.

There is more happiness within the cathedral of the Soul for a sinner who is repented than for a thousand just ones who do not need repentance.

The fifth of the seven acquired the Elixir of Long Life in Lemuria about eighteen million years ago. Therefore, the fifth of the seven kept his Lemurian physical body during the entire Atlantean epoch and he was one of the wise spiritual guides who guided the destiny of millions of human beings from that submerged continent.

Then, after the submerging of Atlantis, this Master fell in love with a woman, and then with another. Thus, this is how he fell and lost his marvellous body and remained submitted to the terrible wheel of reincarnation and karma.

Eliphas Levi commits the mistake of commenting about an apocryphal document of Enoch† and falsely judging the twenty Egregores who descended upon Ardis, which is the top of the Mount Armon, and dogmatically condemning them by qualifying them as demons.

The teachings of Eliphas Levi are mixed with something impure.

Rudolf Steiner asseverates that Eliphas Levi was twice reincarnated as a priest in a Mexican tribe. This tribe, after having culminated in splendors of wisdom and glory, finally came to enter into decay and witchcraft.

So, this soul, who later in time was born with the name of Eliphas Levi, nourished himself in that Mexican epoch with that impure knowledge.

Thus, this is the only way for us to have a logical explanation of the great errors into which the Abbe Alphonse Louis Constant (Eliphas Levi) falls.

We clarify: we do not want to say that Eliphas Levi is a black magician, he is not, he is a Master, but what we affirm is that his books, in spite of having that seal of grandiosity, are mingled with a lot of impure knowledge. This is all.

Azasel is an Egregore who gave great assistance to humanity.

Azasel was the king Solomon. Actually, the Bodhisattva of Azasel is fallen, but it is logical that, in the close future, this Bodhisattva will rise from the clay of the Earth again.

All the Angels of families, Angels of countries, Angels of tribes, etc. are Egregores.

We find written in the Theosophical Glossary of H.P.B the following: "Egregores" from the Greek *Egregori*, "watcher."

Eliphas Levi calls them "the chiefs of the souls who are the spirits of energy and action," whatever that may or may not mean. The oriental occultists describe the Egregores as "beings whose bodies and essence is a tissue of the so-called Astral Light. They are the shadows (Bodhisattvas) of the higher Planetary Spirits whose bodies are of the essence of the higher divine light."

The Book of Enoch[†] gives the name Egregores to the Angels who married the daughters of Seth and who begot with them giants as children.

The names and symbols of the seven Angels of the Eternal One have also seven meanings, thus this is the reason why many esoteric students have become confused.

And I saw as if it was a sea of glass mingled with fire: and them that had gotten the victory over the beast, and over his image, and over his mark, and over the number of his name, stand on the sea of glass, having the harps of God.

This liquid, flexible, malleable glass is the Christonic semen. Certainly, the semen is the dwelling place of the fire.

This semen is the VITRIOL of the ancient medieval alchemists.

Those who have gained the victory over the beast walk happily on the sea of glass while uttering the lost word, uttering with the very pure rising of the divine and primogenitary language.

The larynx is the lyre of Orpheus. There is the need to learn how to play the lyre or Orpheus. There is the need to incarnate the Word.

We play the lyre of Orpheus and victoriously walk on the sea of glass when the Word is made flesh within us.

These are the victorious ones who have gained the victory over the beast, and over his image, and over the number of his name.

And they sing the song of Moses the servant of God, and the song of the Lamb, saying, Great and marvellous are thy works, Lord God Almighty; just and true are thy ways, thou King of saints.

Who shall not fear thee, O Lord, and glorify thy name? for thou only art holy: for all nations shall come and worship before thee; for thy judgements are made manifest.

And after that I looked, and, behold the temple of the tabernacle of the testimony in heaven was opened:

And the seven Angels came out of the temple, having the seven plagues, clothed in pure and white linen, and having their breasts girded with golden girdles.

And one of the four beasts gave unto the seven Angels seven golden vials full of the wrath of God, who liveth for ever and ever.

And the temple was filled with smoke from the glory of God, and from his power; and no man was able to enter into the temple, till the seven plagues of the seven Angels were fulfilled.

Chapter 27
The Seven Vials Are Poured

Revelation 16:1-21:

And I heard a great voice out of the temple saying to the seven Angels, Go your ways, and pour out the vials of the wrath of God upon the earth.

And the first (Angel Gabriel) *went, and poured out his vial upon the earth, and there fell a noisome and grievous sore upon the men which had the mark of the beast, and upon them which worshipped his image.*

This social demoralization with all of its vices, fornications, and shameful adulteries, is a noisome and grievous sore.

All of the human beings who have the mark of the beast and who worship his image have sinned against the Goddess-Moon.

The crimes that are committed against the Goddess-Moon are more bitter than death.

Everyone gathers the fruits of their evil deeds. Whosoever sows lightning will harvest tempests.

Abandoned women, men who were cheated by their adulterous wives, rapes, kidnapping, alcoholism, etc., are all together a noisome and grievous sore, and are what we gain because of the crimes committed against the Goddess-Moon.

Gabriel is the regent of the Moon. In these times of the end, only social degeneration exists, crimes against nature, incurable cancer, mothers abandoned with children, horrible adulteries, divorces by the millions, frightful diseases, uxoricides, etc.

All of these social maladies, all of these tears, all of these orphans, are what we have gained with our evil deeds. The whole of this is a noisome and grievous sore.

Thus, this is how Gabriel, the regent of the Moon, administers the law and punishes with his vial.

The present hour is grave and definitive. Therefore, the only way to be saved is by practicing the Eightfold Path taught by Buddha. This Eightfold Path is totally sexual.

The number eight represents the sign of infinity. The number eight symbolizes the two entwined serpents around the spinal medulla, the two witnesses and the caduceus of Mercury. Therefore, this Holy Eight is the path of the spinal medulla.

The middle path is in the dorsal spine. This is the path of the razor's edge.

The great Master Francisco A. Propato has said that within the sign of infinity, the brain, heart, and sex of the Genie of the Earth are symbolized.

The struggle is terrible: brain against sex, sex against brain, and heart against heart.

Hilarion IX said, "The fire of Phlegethon and the water of Acheron cross in the Ninth Sphere and form the sign of the infinite."

The eight steps of the Eightfold Path within the Ninth Sphere are as follows:

FIRST: Creative comprehension.

SECOND: Upright intentions.

THIRD: Upright words.

FOURTH: Absolute sacrifice.

FIFTH: Upright behavior.

SIXTH: Absolute chastity.

SEVENTH: Constant struggles against the black magicians.

EIGHTH: Supreme patience in all ordeals and sufferings.

The two witnesses that are entwined around the spinal medulla form the Holy Eight.

The sign of the infinite, the Holy Eight, is taught to the students in the Sacred Order of Tibet.

The number of the **Logos** is 888. If we multiply the number eight by three, then we have the 24 vowels of the great zodiacal lyre that are resounding in all of those who have incarnated the Cosmic Christ.

Therefore, the Eightfold Path taught by Buddha is absolutely sexual. Nevertheless, Buddha spoke in a concealed way, because in those times, to divulge the Great Arcanum was absolutely prohibited to the initiates.

The Eightfold Path is found in the central canal of our spinal medulla.

The Caduceus of Mercury has the form of an eight. Thus, the Caduceus is also the sign of the infinite. This Caduceus is the dorsal spine with its two sympathetic cords, Ida and Pingala. Thus, the eight steps of the Eightfold Path are within the spinal medulla.

We are in the times of the end, and if we want to depart from this valley of bitterness, we need to enter the Eightfold Path.

Four great Truths† exist which have the power to annihilate the prince of this world:

> **First Truth:** To have absolute consciousness of pain and bitterness.
>
> **Second Truth:** Pain is the child of fornication, and whosoever spills the semen (reaches the orgasm) is a fornicator. This is a tremendous Truth!
>
> **Third Truth:** We have an "I" that must be decapitated and dissolved in order to incarnate the Word, the Christ.
>
> **Fourth Truth:** We can only decapitate and dissolve the prince of this world, the "I," with the Arcanum A.Z.F.

Whosoever decapitates the "I" can incarnate the immolated Lamb. We need to incarnate the Word, the Christ, in order to be saved from the great cataclysm that will occur in these times of the end.

To comprehend the Four Truths is urgent. Whosoever walks on the Eightfold Path is converted into a Dragon of the Four Truths.

Every Dragon of the Four Truths is a Buddha. Listen to me, O Buddhas! You need to incarnate the Christ!

The Buddhas can incarnate the Christ only if they renounce Nirvana for the love of this humanity, and also by working with intensity in the flaming forge of Vulcan (sex).

Whosoever knows, the word gives power to. No one has uttered it, no one will utter it, except the one who has incarnated it. To incarnate the Word, the Verb, Christ, is necessary!

And the second Angel (Raphael) *poured out his vial upon the sea; and it became as a blood of a dead man: and every living soul died in the sea.*

When we, the brothers and sisters, investigated this second Angel whose name is Raphael, and this terrible verse, we then saw the present epoch with all of its horrors.

The sea of this verse are nations, crowds, and tongues. Everyone is inside the ship of their life, that is to say, everyone is within the arcanum of bitterness. Therefore, when the Angel poured out his vial upon the sea, the waters became as blood.

All the nations of the earth have become as blood. Rivers of blood are flowing through the mountains of pain. Dictatorships and persecutions are found everywhere. Revolution and death exist upon the whole surface of the earth. Some are against others and these others are against everyone.

Also in existence are coup d'etats everywhere, frightful Gestapos, fearful police, weeping, and supreme pain over all the lands. All the nations of the Earth are paying their own Nemesis, the karma of their own errors. All the nations of the earth have been called before the divine Tribunals. This is the Law. This is Karma.

The waters of life have become as blood, therefore this humanity has no relief. To send more prophets to the Earth is useless, since this humanity mortally hates the prophets.

Therefore, no one can save this humanity. No one can correct this humanity. This human evolution is a complete failure.

The waters have become as blood and only screams and supreme suffering are heard everywhere.

> *And the third Angel* (Uriel) *poured out his vial upon the rivers and fountains of waters; and they became blood.* Thus, this is how the constellation of Cancer will strike all the fornicators of the earth with its plague (cancer).
>
> *And I heard the Angels of the waters say, Thou art righteous, O Lord, which art, and wast, and shalt be, because thou hast judged thus.*
>
> *For they have shed the blood of saints and prophets, and thou hast given them blood to drink; for they are worthy.*

Therefore, numerous kinds of diseases will strike the human rivers and the sexual fountains of the human organism.

Radioactivity will produce unknown sicknesses, which science will be unable to cure.

> *And I heard another out of the altar say, Even so, Lord God Almighty, true and righteous are thy judgements.*
>
> *And the fourth Angel* (Michael) *poured out his vial upon the sun; and power was given unto him to scorch men with fire.*
>
> *And men were scorched with great heat, and blasphemed the name of God, which hath power over these plagues: and they repented not to give him glory.*

The fourth Angel Michael does not have a physical body in these times of the end.

The sun is the symbol of the Cosmic Christ. Christ is Love. Therefore, the antithesis of love is hatred.

Know ye, O nations, crowds and tongues, that hatred becomes that fire which burns! Therefore, there will be horrible atomic wars! This humanity will be burned with living fire!

The great cities will become ashes. Nonetheless, the human beings will blaspheme the name of God, who has power over these plagues; and they repented not, to give him glory.

Hear ye, O nations! Know, that the most terrible monster that exists upon the earth is hatred!

Since their own hatred will unleash all the wars, who can save this humanity? It is therefore already too late, there will be no relief. This humanity is a failure. Everyone for himself!

And the fifth Angel (Samael) *poured out his vial upon the seat of the beast; and his kingdom was full of darkness; and they gnawed their tongues for pain.*

And blasphemed the God of heaven because of their pains and their sores, and repented not of their deeds.

The fifth of the seven is the one who has suffered the most. He was a fallen Master, but now he is not. The fifth of the seven is now standing again.

The fifth of the seven poured out his vial upon the seat of the beast and his kingdom was full of darkness.

Millions of human beings already have the mark of the beast on their foreheads and in their hands.

Millions of human souls are already totally separated from their **Innermost** (Spirit).

Now, the urban life of all the cities of all nations of the world has been transplanted into the abyss.

In these submerged regions of the abyss, human beings continue to live this same urban life system, and they buy and sell *"the merchandise of gold, and silver, and precious stones, and of pearls, and fine linen, and purple, and silk, and scarlet, and all thyine wood, and all manner of vessels of ivory, and all manner of vessels of most precious wood, and of brass, and iron, and marble."*

The tenebrous live within the abyss with the same urban life that they are accustomed to. The abyss is more materialistic than the physical world.

Therefore, this kingdom of the abyss has now become more tenebrous than ever. Truly, almost the totality of this humanity has already entered into the abyss.

The fifth of the seven and his legions of Angels are collaborating with the plan of the Logos as they submerge the tenebrous into the abyss.

Millions of women and distinguished gentlemen, who are presently living on this world, do not have their Innermost (Spirit), and are therefore perverse demons, even though they still have physical bodies.

The planet Earth is a failed world. This civilization will be destroyed! Already, this humanity cannot be saved by anyone!

The fifth of the seven is watching over the tenebrous. Many have slandered the fifth of the seven just because he is a Watcher.

The tenebrous blasphemed against the God of heaven because of their pains and their sores, and they did not repent of their deeds.

The human being becomes a demon when the psychological "I" attains absolute control of the four bodies of sin (physical, ethereal, astral, and mental), then the **Innermost** (the Spirit) withdraws from him.

Millions of people who presently live on this world are already terribly perverse demons. Therefore, the kingdom of the beast is now more tenebrous than ever.

A divine ray exists within the human being. This divine ray wants to return towards its own star that has always been smiling upon it.

This star which guides our interior is a super-divine atom from the Abstract Absolute Space. The Kabbalistic name of this atom is the sacred Ain Soph.

Know, all of you, that the Ain Soph is secretly related with the lotus of one thousand petals.

This star which guides our interior (the Ain Soph) has sent its own ray into the world in order to build consciousness of its own happiness.

Happiness without consciousness of its own happiness is not absolute happiness. This is the reason why this ray had to have mineral, plant, and animal consciousness.

When this ray (the Spirit) incarnated for the first time into a savage and primitive human body, this ray awoke as a human being and had Self-consciousness of its own happiness. This ray could have returned towards its own star which guides its interior. But, disgracefully, within the profound bosom of the voracious and dense jungle, wild desire gave birth to the "I."

This is the way in which the instinctive forces of nature trapped the innocent mind of the human being. So, the false mirage of desire emerged, and the "I" continued reincarnating in order to satisfy its desires. Thus, we remained submitted to the law of evolution and karma.

Experiences and pain complicated the "I," for evolution is nothing more than a process of the complication of energy.

Therefore, the "I" became vigorous and complicated with experiences. Now it is too late, for millions of people are already converted into abominable demons.

Only a tremendous revolution can save us from the abyss. When the human being dissolves the "I," then there is a complete revolution.

The human being will stop suffering only when he is capable of dissolving the "I," since pain is nothing more than the result of our evil deeds. Thus, pain belongs to Satan (the "I") because he is the one who commits the evil deeds.

The Absolute Abstract Space, the Universal Spirit of Life, is absolute happiness, supreme peace, and abundance. Therefore, those who make a mysticism out of pain are masochists, since Satan (the "I") was and is the creator of pain.

The human being is corrupted because of pain, for pain is satanic. So, no one can be liberated with pain.

We need to be alchemists. Only with Alchemy can the "I" be dissolved. The root of the "I" is desire, and desire can be transmuted with Alchemy.

If you want to annihilate desire, then you must transmute it:

Sexual desire is transmuted into willpower, and willpower is fire.

Desire of accumulating (greed) is transmuted into altruism.

Anger, in other words, frustrated desire, is transmuted into sweetness.

Envy, which is also frustrated desire, is transmuted into happiness for our neighbor's good fortune.

All the words of desire can be transmuted into words of wisdom, etc.

Analyze all the human defects and you will see that they all have their foundation in desire.

So, you must transmute desire with Alchemy. Thus, this is the way for desire to be annihilated.

Whosoever annihilates desire dissolves the "I." Whosoever dissolves the "I" is saved from the abyss and returns towards his own interior star, which has always smiled unto him.

We can dissolve the "I" only with Holy Alchemy. The fundamental base of Alchemy is the Arcanum A.Z.F.

The Angels, Archangels, Seraphim, Potencies, Thrones, etc., are exactly the result of tremendous interior revolutions.

We have already passed through involution (descent of the Spirit into matter). We also suffered horribly in evolution (process of complication of the energy). Now, a complete revolution (dissolution of the "I") is urgent.

Only based on internal revolutions can we return, little by little, to our own super-divine atom. Thus, this is how we pass through Angelic, Archangelic, Seraphic and Logoic states, etc., until our ray finally becomes fused with its own happily shining star (the Ain Soph).

The abyss is terribly painful. The horrible antithesis of the Ain Soph is the abyss.

The fifth of the seven has poured out his vial upon the seat of the beast; and now his kingdom has become more tenebrous than ever. Woe to the dwellers of the Earth!

> *And the sixth Angel* (Zachariel) *poured out his vial upon the river Euphrates; and the water thereof was dried up, that the way of the kings of east might be prepared.*

The Euphrates river is one of the rivers of Eden. The first river corresponds to the element earth of the wise (the Tattva Prithvi). The second river corresponds to the element water (Tattva Apas). The third river corresponds to the element air (Tattva Vayu). The fourth river is the element fire (Tattva Tejas).

All the elements are integrated in the fire. Everything emerges from the fire and everything returns into the fire. The Euphrates river is the creative fire of the Holy Spirit.

Zachariel poured out his vial upon the Euphrates river and its waters dried up. Thus, this is how the Anglo-Saxon and French people are losing the power of procreation.

The waters of the Euphrates river are drying up and women are becoming sterile.

Now, the statistics are registering that in England and France the number of dead people is more and the number of births is less, because thousands of souls are entering into the abyss daily. No more physical bodies are given unto these souls.

Thus, this is why as a result we have a lesser number of births and a greater quantity of dead, since the waters of the Euphrates river are drying up, that the way of the kings of the Interior East might be prepared.

> *And I saw three unclean spirits like frogs came out of the mouth of the dragon, and out of the mouth of the beast, and out of the mouth of the false prophet.*
>
> *For they are the spirits of devils, working miracles, which go forth unto the kings of the earth, and of the whole world, to gather them to the battle of that great day of God Almighty.*

These three unclean frog-like spirits constitute the psychological "I" of every human being.

They are Core, Dathan, and Abiram. These are the three traitors, the three rebels, who we carry inside.

The first one is the rebel against Nature.

The second one is the rebel against divine Science.

The third one is the rebel against Truth.

The first is the Demon of Desire, the second is the Demon of the Mind, and the third is the Demon of Evil Will.

The first one is inside the Astral Body. The second one is inside the Mental Body. The third is inside the Body of Will (Causal Body).

All of these three together are the Black Dragon with three heads. They are also Sebal, Ortelut, and Stokin, the three traitors of Hiram Abif.

In short, these three unclean spirits are our psychological "I," the ego, the myself. These three unclean spirits are working miracles: hydrogen bombs, airplanes, cosmic rockets, mechanical marvels, in order to deceive people and to gather them to battle.

These three unclean spirits invented materialistic theory, the materialistic dialectic, historic materialism, etc.

These three unclean spirits are the erudites of materialistic science, and they laugh about everything that has a spiritual taste.

These three demons also perform marvels of chemistry, physics, medicine, and they deceive people with their miracles and false prodigies.

> *Behold, I come as a thief. Blessed is he that watcheth, and keepeth his garments, lest he walk naked, and they see his shame.*
>
> *And he gathered them together into a place called in the Hebrew tongue Armageddon.*

Armageddon is atomic war. Soon, human beings will use small pocket weapons armed with small atomic missiles in order to disintegrate the atomic bombs and the missiles in space charged with nuclear explosives.

The whole atmosphere will be filled with deadly radioactive particles.

Millions of flying cosmic ships that are occupied by other planetary humanities are watching us.

The day of this tremendous cataclysm is approaching and humanities of other planets are watching us!

And the seventh Angel (Orifiel) poured out his vial into the air; and there came a great voice out of the temple of heaven, from the throne, saying, it is done. The Angel of Saturn tosses his deadly scythe upon the surface of the Earth and everything is consummated.

A world is approaching the planet Earth, and when this world collides with the Earth, everything will be consummated. This collision of worlds will be cataclysmic in proportion.

And there were voices, and thunders, and lightnings; and there was a great earthquake, such as was not since men were upon the earth, so mighty an earthquake, and so great.

Now is the time when the true men will be known! Now is the time when we will know who is who!

Now, the learned ignoramuses will bite the dust. Those authoritative know-it-alls of some schools of villains (skeptics and cynics) will swallow mud.

Therefore, these false prophets will show their shame within the abyss among the failures.

Let the earth tremble! Let the wolf of the Law howl!

Now is the time when we will know the true men, and the time when we will see many crying like harlots!

The time for considerations has ended! Therefore, those who killed the prophets will find themselves naked. Those who were applauded by the great harlot will drink a very bitter bile.

These barbarians gave the Saints hemlock mingled with honey to drink. Now the Law will strike them with scorpions.

Let the catastrophe come! This is the time when we will know who is who! Now, the true men will be known!

And the great city was divided into three parts, and the cities of the nations fell: and great Babylon came in remembrance before God to give unto her the cup of the wine of the fierceness of his wrath.

And every island fled away, and the mountains were not found (because they were swallowed by the earth).

Thus, this is what the great harlot is worthy of! The Saints said what they had to say... now, let the tragedy come!

The hour of the great cataclysm has come! Let the Law come! Let the hurricane howl! Let the Earth tremble!

The time for waiting is over, it has already passed! Now... let tragedy come!

Thus, this is how the Avatar of Aquarius speaks...

Frankly, with sincerity I tell you, this time the just will not be punished because of the sinners. This happened once, but that time is already in the past.

The just will be secretly saved before the great cataclysm. Let us remember Lot who was taken from the damned city, also Elias who was taken into heaven in a chariot of fire.

Therefore, the just will be taken from great Babylon (this present civilization) before the great cataclysm.

Many cosmic ships will come to the planet Earth. Other planetary humanities are watching us; they know about the terrible time in which we live.

The just will be secretly helped before the final doom (the great cataclysm). They will be transported like Elias in a chariot of fire.

They will live on another planet. While the mountains will fly in the air broken into pieces, into dust, the Earth will vomit fire and water. The earth will become a mass of fire and water.

What will be the sign? When will be the day? When will be the hour? It will be when cosmic ships shall be built with the capability of reaching other planets.

It will be when these human beings of the Earth have prepared themselves in order to conquer and dominate other planetary humanities by force.

It will be when the time arrives that they want to repeat their own bloody historical conquerings on other planets. Then, you must be alert and vigilant.

Every step that human beings make towards conquering space places them closer and closer to the great cataclysm.

Frightful and terrible atomic wars of a great magnitude will occur before the great cataclysm.

> *And there fell upon men a great hail out of heaven, every stone about the weight of a talent: and men blasphemed God because of the plague of the hail; for the plague thereof was exceeding great.*

Chapter 28
The Whore and the Beast

Revelation 17:1-18:

And there came one of the seven Angels, which have the seven vials and talked with me, saying unto me, Come hither; I will shew unto thee the judgement of the great whore (this humanity) *that sitteth upon many waters:*

With whom the kings of the earth have committed fornication, and the inhabiters of the earth have been made drunk with the wine of her fornication.

So he carried me away in the spirit into the wilderness: and I saw a woman sit upon a scarlet colour beast (the great beast whose number is 666), *full of names of blasphemy, having seven heads and ten horns.* The seven heads of the beast are the seven capital sins. The ten horns signify that this beast ascends and will tumble into the abyss.

And the woman (the great whore [humanity]) *was arrayed in purple and scarlet colour* (this is how this humanity is symbolized in the internal worlds), *and decked with gold and precious stones and pearls, having a golden cup in her hand full of abominations and filthiness of her fornication:*

And upon her forehead was a name written, **Mystery, Babylon the great, the mother of harlots and abominations of the earth.**

And I saw the woman drunken with the blood of the saints, and with the blood of the martyrs of Jesus: and when I saw her, I wondered with great admiration.

And the Angel said unto me, Wherefore didst thou marvel? I will tell thee the mystery of the woman, and of the beast that carrieth her, which hath the seven heads and ten horns.

The beast that thou sawest was, and is not; and shall ascend out of the bottomless pit, and go into perdition: and they that dwell on the earth shall wonder, whose names were not written in the book

THE WHORE AND THE BEAST BY ALBRECHT DÜRER.

of life from the foundation of the world, when they behold the beast that was, and is not, and yet is.

And here is the mind which hath wisdom. The seven heads are seven mountains, on which the woman sitteth. The seven capital sins, **Anger, Greed, Lust, Envy, Pride, Laziness, Gluttony,** are related with the seven sub-planes or tenebrous regions of the abyss. These are the seven mountains on which the great whore is seated.

And there are seven kings (the seven kings of Edom): *five are fallen, and one is, and the other is not yet come; and when he cometh, he must continue a short space.*

The five inferior principles are: Soul, Mind, Astral Body, Ethereal Body, and Physical Body; these five principles are fallen, that is to say, the human being is fallen.

The sixth principle (Conscience Soul), or **Buddhi**, never falls. This principle will govern the sixth Root Race.

When the kingdom of the seventh principle comes, it will continue for a short space of time. During that period, a divine race will exist. This will be the seventh Root Race. The seventh principle is the **Innermost**.

And the beast that was, and is not, even he is the eight, and is of the seven, and goeth into perdition.

This beast that was, and is not, and that even he is the eight, is the shadow of the seven Sephiroth; this is the abyss.

And the ten horns which thou sawest are ten kings, which have received no kingdom as yet; but receive power as kings one hour with the beast.

The ten horns of the tragic wheel will ascend and will descend; they will rotate with the wheel of compensation. These ten horns ascend from the abyss, they impose themselves and command like ten kings, in order to tumble into the abyss when the wheel of nemesis (compensation or Samsara) is accomplishing its fatal rotation.

These (ten horns) *have one mind, and shall give their power and strength unto the beast.*

> *These shall make war with the Lamb, and the Lamb shall overcome them: for he is Lord of lords, and King of kings: and they that are with him are called, and chosen, and faithful.*
>
> *And he saith unto me, The waters which thou sawest, where the whore sitteth, are peoples, and multitudes, and nations, and tongues.*
>
> *And the ten horns which thou sawest upon the beast, these shall hate the whore, and shall make her desolate and naked, and shall eat her flesh, and burn her with fire.*

When the fatal wheel of compensation rotates, this whore (humanity) will be desolate and naked and the ten tragic horns will eat her flesh and burn her with the fire of their fornication, within the darkness of the abyss.

> *For God hath put in their hearts to fulfil his will, and to agree, and give their kingdom unto the beast, until the words of God shall be fulfilled.*
>
> *And the woman which thou sawest is that great city, which reigneth over the kings of the earth.*

This tragic, great city is **Babylon the great, the mother of harlots and abominations of the Earth,** that is to say, this perverse, modern civilization.

Woe to those who do not listen to the written words in this book!

Woe to the dwellers of the Earth!

Woe, woe, to those who betray the work of my Father!

Chapter 29
Babylon is Fallen

> Revelation 18:1-24:
>
> *And after these things I saw another Angel come down from heaven, having great power; and the earth was lightened with his glory.*
>
> *And he cried mightily with a great voice, saying, Babylon the great* (this perverse civilization from this Root Race) *is fallen, is fallen, and is become the habitation of devils, and the hold of every foul spirit, and a cage of every unclean and hateful bird.* This refers to human beings who are foul spirits of crime, vultures of war, unclean birds of prey and hatred, etc.
>
> *For all nations have drunk of the wine of the wrath of her fornication, and the kings of the earth* (the powerful men of the world) *have committed fornication with her, and the merchants of the earth are waxed rich through the abundance of her delicacies.*
>
> *And I heard another voice from heaven, saying, Come out of her, my people* (people who are initiated in the Christic mysteries), *that ye be not partakers of her sins, and that ye receive not of her plagues.*

Thus, this is the way in which the just will be secretly taken from within this great city (civilization) and they will be transported in interplanetary cosmic ships before the great cataclysm.

Therefore, these perverse dwellers of the Earth will perish. *For her sins have reached unto heaven, and God have remembered her iniquities.*

The just will live on another planet while the Earth passes through a great geological transformation. Afterwards, they will return to this world in order to form the sixth Root Race.

Therefore, Babylon the great, this civilization, will become ashes and blood.

BABYLON IS FALLEN BY GUSTAVE DORÉ.

"Babylon the great is fallen, is fallen, and is become the habitation of devils, and the hold of every foul spirit, and a cage of every unclean and hateful bird."

Reward her even as she rewarded you and double unto her double according to her works; in the cup which she hath filled fill to her double.

How much she hath glorified herself, and lived deliciously, so much torment and sorrow give her: for she saith in her heart, I sit queen, and am no widow, and shall see not sorrow.

Therefore shall her plagues come in one day, death, and mourning, and famine; and she shall be utterly burned with fire: for strong is the Lord God who judgeth her.

This civilization, the great whore, is collecting the fruits of its own evil deeds, since whosoever sows lightning will harvest tempests. This is the law. Therefore, this great whore will harvest the fruits of her evil deeds.

This civilization, the great whore, will be burned with the fire of the atomic war and with the cosmic fire that will emerge from the planetary collision. Thus, this is how this world will become a mass of fire and watery, cloud vapor.

The whole of this will be accomplished in the present Aquarian Age. Nonetheless, before the great cataclysm, you will see very frightful events. The Vatican will be destroyed, the great cities of the world will become ashes, blood, and ruins, money will become worthless, and human beings will kill each other just for a piece of bread.

This civilization, the great Babylon, will become dust.

And the kings of the earth (the potentates of gold and silver, the lords of the oil, men who are the vultures of war), *who have committed fornication and lived deliciously with her, shall bewail her, and lament for her, when they shall see the smoke of her burning.*

Standing afar off (trying to escape from the impeding doom) *for the fear of her torment, saying, Alas, alas, that great city Babylon, that mighty city!* (this modern civilization) *for in one hour is thy judgement come.*

And the merchants of the earth shall weep and mourn over her; for no man buyeth their merchandise anymore:

> *The merchandise of gold, and silver, and precious stones, and of pearls, and fine linen, and purple, and silk, and scarlet, and all thyine wood, and all manner of vessels of ivory, and all manner of vessel of most precious wood, and of brass, and iron, and marble.*
>
> *And cinnamon, and odours, and oiments, and frankincense, and wine, and oil, and fine flour, and wheat, and beasts, and sheep, and horses, and chariots, and slaves, and souls of men.* Even with souls of men these merchants of the Earth make business!
>
> *And the fruits that thy souls lusted after are departed from thee, and all things which were dainty and goodly are departed from thee, and thou shall find them no more at all.* The atomic war will terminate everything while the final impeding doom comes.
>
> *The merchants of these things which were made rich by her, shall stand afar off* (they will escape from the cities) *for the fear of her torment, weeping and wailing,*
>
> *And saying, Alas, alas, that great city* (this present modern civilization), *that was clothed in fine linen, and purple, and scarlet, and decked with gold, and precious stones, and pearls!*
>
> *For in one hour so great riches is come to nought. And every shipmaster, and all the company in ships, and sailors, and as many as trade by sea, stood afar off,*
>
> *And cried when they saw the smoke of her burning, saying, What city is like unto this great city!*
>
> *And they cast dust on their heads, and cried, weeping and wailing, saying, Alas, alas, that great city, wherein were made rich all that had ships in the sea by reason of her costliness! for in one hour* (the hour of karma and punishment) *is she made desolate.*
>
> *Rejoice over her, thou heaven, and ye holy apostles and prophets; for God hath avenged you on her.*

Thus, this is how the ray of the cosmic justice will fall upon this perverse civilization of vipers and there will be no relief.

> *And a mighty Angel took up a stone like a great millstone* (the Philosophical Stone), *and cast it into the sea* (the Christonic

semen), *saying* (thus sealing the prophecy), *Thus with violence shall that great city Babylon* (this present modern civilization) *be thrown down, and shall be found no more at all.*

And the voice of harpers, and musicians, and of pipers, and trumpeters, shall be heard no more at all in thee; and no craftsman of whatsoever craft he be, shall be found any more in thee; and the sound of a millstone shall be heard no more at all in thee:

And the light of a candle shall shine no more at all in thee; and the voice of the bridegroom and of the bride shall be heard no more at all in thee: for thy merchants were the great men of the earth (these are the great lords of business); *for by thy sorceries were all nations deceived.*

Sorcery is the golden calf, sorcery is idolatry, sorcery is the skepticism found in the dialectic of materialism. Sorcery is the exploitation of souls, sorcery is black magic, witchcraft, etc.

Therefore, because of all of these, **Babylon the great, the mother of harlots and abominations of the Earth** will be destroyed!

And in her was found the blood of prophets, and of saints, and of all that were slain upon the earth.

MAITREYA BODHISATTVA

Chapter 30
The Maitreya Buddha

Revelation 19:1-21:

And after these things I heard a great voice of much people in heaven, saying, Alleluia; Salvation, and glory, and honor, and power, unto the Lord our God:

For true and righteous are his judgements; for he hath judged the great whore, which did corrupt the earth with her fornication, and hath avenged the blood of his servants at her hand.

And again they said, Alleluia. And her smoke rose up for ever and ever.

And the four and twenty elders (from the zodiac) *and the four beasts* (of Sexual Alchemy) *fell down and worshipped God* (the Truth) *that sat on the* (internal) *throne, saying, Amen; Alleluia.*

And a voice came out of the throne (which we have within the profundities of our Being), *saying, Praise our* (internal) *God, all ye his servants, and ye that fear him, both small and great.*

And I heard as it were the voice of a great multitude, and as the voice of many waters (the seminal waters), *and as the voice of mighty thunderings* (the voice of the Gods), *saying, Alleluia: for the Lord God omnipotent reigneth* (God which we carry inside)

Let us be glad and rejoice, and give honour to him: for the marriage of the Lamb is come, and his wife (the soul) *hath made herself ready.*

And to her was granted that she should be arrayed in fine linen (the tunic of Masters), *clean and white: for the fine linen is the righteousness of saints.*

And he saith unto me, Write, Blessed are they which are called unto the marriage supper of the Lamb, and he saith unto me, These are the true sayings of God.

And I fell at his feet to worship him. And he said unto me, See thou do it not: I am thy fellowservant, and of thy brethren that have the testimony of Jesus: worship God (which is your internal God): *for the testimony of Jesus is the spirit of the prophesy.*

And I saw heaven opened, and behold a white horse; and he that sat upon him was called Faithful and True, and in righteousness he doth judge and make war. The one who writes this book gives testimony of this prophecy, because I am the servant or Bodhisattva of the fifth of the seven.

The Son speaks the word of the Father and he gives testimony of the Father. The Father is one with the Son; the Son is one with the Father.

The Son feels that he is unworthy to undo the buckles of the Father's shoes. Only the Father is perfect.

The Father is glorified in the Son and the Son is glorified in the Father.

The Maitreya Buddha Samael is the Kalki Avatar of the New Age; he is the one who sat upon the white horse. Nevertheless, his son, the poor servant who writes this *Aquarian Message*, really does not feel worthy of kissing the sacred feet of the Father.

Therefore, the Buddha Maitreya gloriously shines, but his son kneels before him.

His eyes were as a flame of fire, and on his head were many crowns; and he had a name written, that no man knew, but he himself. Because this name is written with characters of the language of light.

And he was clothed with a vesture dipped in blood (because of the battles against the Black Lodge within the suprasensible worlds); *and his name is called the Word of God*, because the Avatar of the new Aquarian Age is one Verb, Word (Christ).

And the armies which were in heaven followed him upon white horses (this is the cavalry of Nirvana), *clothed in fine linen, white and clean,"* because they are Masters.

The Maitreya Buddha

> *And out of his mouth goeth a sharp sword* (in order to wound the demons), *that with it* (the Word) *he should smite the nations: and he* (the Verb) *shall rule them with a rod of iron* (within the abyss): *and he treadeth the winepress of the fierceness and wrath of Almighty God.* The tenebrous have fought against this Word, but this Word is treading the winepress of the fierceness and wrath of the Almighty God and He threw them into the abyss.
>
> *And he hath on his vesture and on his thigh a name written (on a band with sacred characters),* **King of Kings, and Lord of Lords.**"

The power of the king is not on the forehead. The power of the king is in the sex.

The sceptre of the sacred kings, the two columns of the temple, and the Cross of the redeemer are made with the wood of the tree of good and evil. This is the Tree of Knowledge (sex).

When a man and a woman are sexually united, something is created.

We become Kings and Queens, Lords of Nature, when we receive the sacred fire of the Holy Spirit.

The Kundalini is the fire of the Holy Spirit.

The Kundalini develops, evolves, and progresses within the aura of the Mahachoan†. The Mahachoan is the Holy Spirit, the Third Logos we find in the flaming forge of Vulcan.

This flaming forge of Vulcan is sex. The Kundalini awakens only with the Arcanum A.Z.F.

The great German sage Krumm-Heller said the following in the eighth lesson of his *Zodiacal Course:*

> Instead of the coitus which reaches the orgasm, sweet caresses, amorous phrases and delicate touching should be lavished reflectively, keeping the mind constantly separated from animal sexuality, sustaining the purest spirituality as if the act were a true religious ceremony.
>
> Nevertheless, the man can and should introduce the penis and keep it in the vagina to bring about a divine

sensation upon both, full of joy, that can last for hours, withdrawing it at the moment the orgasm is near to avoid the ejaculation of semen. In this way, they will have a greater desire to caress each other each time.

This may be repeated as many times as desired without ever becoming tiresome. On the contrary, it is the Magic Key to daily rejuvenation, keeping the body healthy and prolonging life, because this constant magnetization is a fountain of health.

We know that in ordinary magnetism, the magnetizer communicates currents to the subject, and if the first has those forces developed, he can heal the second. The transmission of magnetic currents is ordinarily done through the hands or through the eyes, but it is necessary to say that there is no greater and more powerful conductor, a thousand times more powerful, a thousand times superior to others, than the virile member and the vulva as receiving organs.

If many persons practice this, they spread force and success in their surroundings for all those who come into commercial or social contact with them. But in the act of sublime, divine magnetization to which we are referring, both man and woman magnetize each other, the one being for the other as a musical instrument which, when plucked, gives off or emits prodigious sounds of mysterious and sweet harmonies. The strings of that instrument are spread all over the body, and the lips and fingers are its principal pluckers, on condition that the act be presided by the most absolute purity, which is what makes us magicians in that supreme moment.

The key in order to awaken the Kundalini is written in these former paragraphs of the Master Huiracocha. This is the Arcanum A.Z.F., this is the Great Arcanum.

When the great French poet Cazotte wrote his famous book entitled *The Loving Devil,* he was visited by a man who was covered with a cape. This mysterious personage was the Master **Zanoni**. The mysterious visitor made some mysterious secret salutations that Cazotte did not understand because he was not an initiate, but he became initiated by Zanoni.

The style in which the book *The Loving Devil* was written was very close to the Arcanum A.Z.F.

Therefore, in a whisper from the lips of Zanoni to the ears of this great French poet, the Great Arcanum was communicated.

We still remember the terrible prophecies of death made by Cazotte in his famous banquet.

Some initiates wanted to reveal the Great Arcanum, while others opposed. Then, Cazotte, while exulted with wisdom, prophesied exile for some of them, for others the deadly scaffold, suicide, the dagger, venom, and finally he prophesied his own death by the scaffold.

All the prophecies of Cazotte were accomplished with astonishing exactitude.

Another marvellous personage was the powerful and enigmatic Count Cagliostro. This man of indescribable age is a true Master who has the Elixir of Longevity.

No one can attain this elixir without having worked with the Arcanum A.Z.F. Cagliostro swallowed soil within his sepulchre and escaped from his sepulchre fossa due to the fact that he had received the Elixir of Longevity.

Cagliostro practised sexual magic intensely. Cagliostro was a disciple of Count St. Germain. Cagliostro was an alchemist; he transmuted the lead into gold and made genuine diamonds.

This Master was known in the distinct places of the world, under different names in different countries. He was known with the following names: Tis-chio, Milissa, Belonte, D'anna, Fenix, Pellegrini, Balsamo, Mesmer, Harut, and Cagliostro. This famous historical lineage was recorded by Alexandre Dumas in his work entitled, *The Queen's Necklace*.

Ragon commits the crime of slandering the Great Copto.

Eliphas Levi also slanders the Count Cagliostro by accusing him of being a black magician.

The Great Copto lived with the famous Schrader of Germany, and in England with the illustrious theosophist George Coston.

Cagliostro saved the life of the Cardinal Archbishop of Rohan with the science of the Philosophical Stone.

The Baroness of Oberkirch said the following of the Great Copto, "He was not absolutely beautiful but I never saw such equalled features. His sight, more than profound, was supernatural. The expression of his eyes was indescribable, with an equal quality of fire and ice, together influencing in an irresistible way, sometimes attracting, sometimes repelling."

Cagliostro had many alchemist disciples in Strasbourg. He was judged and persecuted by the Inquisition, sent into the bastille, and later into the fortress of Leone.

The Inquisition condemned him to death, but the enigmatic and powerful Count Cagliostro mysteriously disappeared from the prison. Death could not do anything to Cagliostro.

Cagliostro is still alive with the same physical body because when a Master has swallowed soil within his sepulchre, he is lord of the living and of the dead.

No one can reach this initiatic height without the secret practice of sexual magic. Therefore, whosoever rejects the Great Arcanum is surely a stubborn one.

The great initiates suffered a lot and many were they who perished in the secret trials when they were aspiring to know the supreme secret of the Great Arcanum.

Today we are publicly delivering the Arcanum A.Z.F. This Arcanum is written in this very book; whosoever rejects this precious treasure is an imbecile.

Another one that self-realized himself with sexual magic was the Count of St. Germain. The Count of St. Germain, Master of Cagliostro, rejuvenated himself at will and appeared and disappeared instantaneously when it was least expected. The Count of St. Germain even gave himself the luxury of passing as dead and, after entering into the sepulchre, was able to escape from it by placing his body into "**Jinn**" state.

Commonly, the Masters who have swallowed soil accomplish their mission in any given country, and afterward are able to pass themselves off as dead in order to close another chapter of their immortal life.

In accordance with the memories of a certain aristocratic lady, who was a contemporary of Louis XV, St. Germain appeared before her up to the year 1723, many years after his death, completely young again, in order to predict the French Revolution and the tragic death of Louis XVI. St. Germain pointed out the terrible work of the French ministers, and challenged their anger by making himself invisible and untouchable at will.

St. Germain was the rival of the musician Paganini. Paganini is a black magician.

St. Germain

St. Germain has the power of tongues. He speaks all the languages of the world fluently. This great Master was the advisor of Kings and wise men, and knew the contents of an enclosed scroll in his hand; he appeared and disappeared as lightning. He also transmuted lead into gold and made diamonds by vivifying carbon.

There exists the belief that he was born in Jerusalem and that he had an age of more than 2000 or 3000 years. We know that the Count of St. Germain lives with the same physical body. This great Master worked with the Arcanum A.Z.F., that is to say, he practised sexual magic intensely. Thus, this is the reason for his power. This is why he received the Elixir of Longevity.

St. Germain works with the ray of world politics. It is sad that Marie Antoinette did not listen to his advice.

Cagliostro was the best disciple of St. Germain. Cagliostro lived in the epoch of Jesus Christ. He was a friend of Cleopatra in Egypt. While he worked for Catalina de Medici, he was the Count Fenix. In short, Cagliostro, the disciple of Altotas, still lives with the same physical body, death being unable to cut the thread of his precious existence.

St. Germain was in Europe before the Second World War, after which time he returned to his sanctuary in Tibet. The king is not in the forehead but in the sex.

All the practices of Yoga, the whole knowledge of Kriya, always ends with the supreme secret of the Great Arcanum. When a Yogi is prepared, he receives from his Master's lips, whispered directly into his ears, the secret of the Arcanum A.Z.F.

The Secret Order of Tibet has the obligation of communicating the Great Arcanum to the Yogi from lips to ear. This order is formed by 201 members. The major rank is formed by 72 Brahmans.

Supreme meditation and absolute adoration takes us into ecstasy (Samadhi). Any Master of Samadhi is an illuminated one.

Nonetheless, we must know that illumination is one thing and that Self-realization is another very distinct matter. A Master of Samadhi (ecstasy) can disembottle the soul from the mind that is normally bottled up within the "I," during a state of supreme adoration to experience the Truth; but this does not signify the *incarnation* of the Truth.

After the ecstasy, the mind normally becomes bottled up within the "I," and the mystic is left with his same tragic and painful life. Only by *incarnating* the Truth is there a complete revolution within the human being.

Whosoever wants to incarnate the Truth needs to edify the temple upon the living rock. This living rock is the sex.

The temple of wisdom has seven columns. These are the seven degrees of the power of the fire. There are seven serpents: two groups of three, plus the coronation of the sublime seventh tongue of fire, which unites us with the One, with the Law, with the Father.

The first serpent belongs to the physical body, the second to the Vital Body, the third to the Astral Body, the fourth to the Mental Body, the fifth to the Body of Willpower, the sixth to the Buddhic Body, and the seventh to the Innermost.

These are the seven steps of knowledge. These seven serpents cannot be lifted up simultaneously. Since the Magistery of Fire is very difficult, one must advance by degrees.

Initially, it is necessary to raise the first serpent, then the second. Later on, the third can be raised, then the fourth, etc.

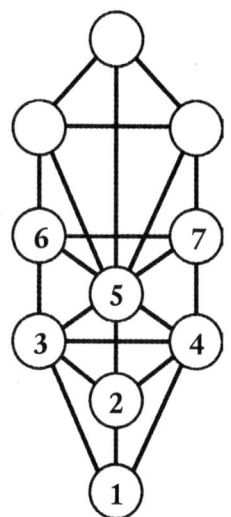

THE SEVEN BODIES ON THE TREE OF LIFE

The Yogi who does not practice with the Arcanum A.Z.F. is like a garden without water. Practice any Yoga, but work with the Great Arcanum in the Magisterium of Fire.

If you, beloved reader, suppose that some other way exists in order to attain the developmental evolution and progress of the Kundalini, I, Samael Aun Weor, the Maitreya Buddha of the new Age of Aquarius, solemnly swear unto you that you are absolutely mistaken.

Never in any school of mysteries on this Earth, or even on other planets of the infinite, has another path been known that is opposite to or distinct from the path of sex.

If you are already an elderly woman, if you can no longer have sexual contact, if you are already an old man, if you are sick, if you comprehend that your physical vehicle is no longer worthy in order to work with the Arcanum A.Z.F., then you must train yourself for Astral travel, that is to say, you must learn to consciously travel in the Astral Body.

So my child, prepare yourself with concentration, meditation, and adoration. Be chaste in thought, word, and deed. Comprehend your errors; annihilate not only desire, but even the very shadow of desire. Thus my child, prepare yourself with creative comprehension, and postpone your work with the Arcanum A.Z.F. for your future reincarnation.

Are you an old man? Are you an old woman? Are you an invalid? Then do not be disappointed, beloved child. Do not fill yourself with affliction, because in your future reincarnation you can work with the Arcanum A.Z.F., and you will convert yourselves into Gods.

Nevertheless, if you are full of youth, if you are not impotent, if you are a complete male or female and you reject the Great Arcanum in order to keep fornicating and you hide yourself within the speculations of your mind, then unhappiness to you, woe to you! Woe! Woe! Woe! It would be better for you not to have been born, because now you will inevitably tumble into the abyss.

That sophism that says that there are many paths to reach God is false. It is a complete falsity, because our adorable Savior taught us about only one narrow way and one straight gate. He said the following:

Luke 13:24-28:

> *Strive to enter in at the strait gate: for many, I say unto you, will seek to enter in, and shall not be able.*

> *Whence once the master of the house is risen up, and hath shut the door, and ye begin to stand without, and to knock at the door, saying, Lord, Lord, open unto us; and he shall answer and say unto you, I know you not whence ye are:*

> *Then shall ye begin to say, We have eaten and drunk in thy presence, and thou taught in our streets.*

> *But he shall say, I tell you, I know you not whence ye are; depart from me, all ye workers of iniquity.*

> *There shall be weeping and gnashing of teeth, when ye shall see Abraham, and Isaac, and Jacob, and all the prophets, in the kingdom of God, and you yourselves thrust out.*

Those who suppose that they can incarnate the Word, Christ, without the Arcanum A.Z.F. are ignorant.

The Akash is the vehicle of sound. The Kundalini is Akashic. Therefore, one cannot incarnate the Word without the Akash, since the Akash is the vehicle of sound.

This is why we need to raise the Akashic serpent in order to incarnate the Word, Christ.

The Kundalini (Akashic fire) becomes creative with the Word, because the Kundalini is the vehicle of the creative Word.

The creative energy of the Mahachoan is sexual and is uttered in the creative larynx. So, without the Arcanum A.Z.F. no one can incarnate the Word, Christ.

This is why the fifth of the seven, the Word of Aquarius, tells you: *"The king is not on the forehead. The king is in the sex."*

The Great Arcanum lies at the depth of all the schools of mysteries. If you reject the Great Arcanum, unhappiness to you! Woe! Woe! Woe!

If you have your mind filled with theories and throw this book aside saying, "It is just another book like the many that I have read," woe to you! Woe! Woe! Woe! because you have rejected the Word, you have insulted the Verb, in other words, you have signed your own death sentence and you will tumble into the abyss.

We are not threatening, beloved reader, we are warning you, because life has initiated its return towards the great Light, and the final judgment is already done. The times of the end have arrived.

Those who will be incapable of lifting the serpent through the medullar canal will be unable to ascend with the life which returns towards the Absolute. Therefore, these souls will sink into the abyss; they will become demons.

> *And I saw an Angel standing in the sun; and he cried with a loud voice, saying to all the fowls that fly in midst of heaven, Come and gather yourselves together unto the supper of the great God.*
>
> *That ye may eat the flesh of kings, and the flesh of captains, and the flesh of mighty men, and flesh of horses, and of them that sit*

> *on them, and the flesh of all men, both free and bond, both small and great.*

The atomic war and the great cataclysm which are approaching will terminate everyone, both free and bound, both small and great.

> *And I saw the beast, and the kings of the earth, and their armies, gathered together to make war against him that sat on the horse, and against his army.*

The tenebrous legions have started to enter into the Avitchi (abyss) after the Final Judgement which was made in 1950.

At that time, the great battles started in the Astral and Mental Worlds. So the beast and the tenebrous of the great Black Lodge were gathered together to make war against the One who was seated on the horse (the Word), and against His army.

The Bodhisattva who writes this very book gives testimony of the battles which the Black Lodge have cast against the one who is his Father in secret.

The Final Judgement and the entrance of the tenebrous into the abyss was urgent. These battles within the internal worlds will cause, as a repercussion, atomic wars and dreadful catastrophes in the physical world.

> *And the beast was taken* (into the abyss), *and with him the false prophet* (the materialistic intellectualism) *that wrought miracles before him* (these miracles and prodigies are hydrogen bombs, atomic bombs, astonishing inventions, and finally the tower of Babel), *with which he deceived them that had received the mark of the beast* (horns on the forehead), *and them that worshipped his image* (materialistic science). *These both were cast alive into a lake of fire burning with brimstone.* This lake of fire burning with brimstone is the fire of passion and desire, the abyss, the Avitchi, the eighth submerged sphere, that is to say the atomic infernos of Nature.

> *And the remnant were slain with the sword of him that sat upon the horse, which sword proceeded out of his mouth: and all the*

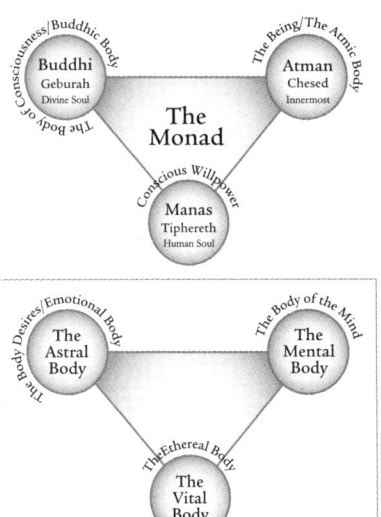

fowls were filled with their flesh. When somebody who has a physical body enters into the abyss, the Antakarana, which is the thread that connects the fourth and fifth human principles, is broken. Those inferior quaternaries which are separated from the spiritual triad become demons.

When a soul is very perverse, the Spirit abandons that soul. These people without Spirit are demons. Therefore, when the Spirit definitively abandons the body, the person passes through death, even though he may still be physically alive. Then, the name of this Spirit figures in the book of the deceased.

Presently, there are many people who already do not have the Spirit (the Innermost). Whosoever loses the Innermost becomes a demon, and every demon belongs to the abyss.

All of those who fight against the Word die by the terrible sword that he carries in his mouth. All of these tragedies, all of these catastrophes, all of these prophecies, all of these cataclysms, have a very solid foundation. This solid foundation is a return of life towards the Absolute.

Those who will not be capable of lifting up the serpent upon the staff will not be able to return into the Absolute, because this return is internal and its foundation lies on each step of the serpent.

This serpent must rise thirty-three degrees up through the spinal medulla. We have to return by climbing the seven steps of knowledge. We have to return through each one of the seven degrees of the power of the fire.

We cannot return with theories, because no one of us is a child of any theory. Each one of us is the child of a man and woman.

The question is sexual because we exist through sex. Those who commit the error of rejecting the Arcanum A.Z.F. will inevitably sink into the abyss.

Those who do not want to sink into the abyss must start by rising the septuple scale of burning fire.

You must remember that the abyss is filled with people of very good intentions. Remember that the abyss is filled with people that feel themselves to be perfect and holy. Thus, this is how many mystical fornicators will enter into the abyss.

Those who say: "I will not practice with the Arcanum A.Z.F., I keep my religion, my school is better, my system is superior, there exists other ways, etc," will sink into the abyss, because when they avoid the door of Eden (sex), they will find the door of the abyss.

We departed from Eden through the narrow door of sex, and only through that door can we return into Eden. Eden is the very same sex.

This return of life towards the Absolute signifies the fall of Babylon the great, the catastrophe, and the final disaster.

We, the brothers and sisters of the temple, delivered this Arcanum A.Z.F. in ancient times to the humanity of the ancient Earth-Moon. Those who then accepted the Great Arcanum elevated themselves to an Angelic state. In that epoch of the ancient Earth-Moon, we gave the same warnings.

This work was performed when the humanity of the Moon had reached the Age our present terrestrial humanity is in. This happens when life initiates its return towards the Absolute, and we, the brothers and sisters, always accomplish the duty of warning and teaching.

Those who in the ancient Earth-Moon rejected the Great Arcanum became terribly perverse lunar demons. Now these demons dwell within the abyss.

Some human beings of the fifth Root Race from the Earth-Moon came to accept the Great Arcanum too late, they are therefore now lifting themselves up into the Angelic state. A new dwelling was given unto this remnant group; this group now lives on another planet.

The brethren Max Heindel and Rudolf Steiner committed the mistake of supposing that the Moon is a piece of the planet Earth that was projected into space.

We, the ones who worked in ancient times with that humanity of the Moon, know very well that the Moon was a planet like the planet Earth within space, and is even more ancient than our planet Earth.

The Moon is the mother of the Earth, because the life that evolves today on our planet Earth was incarnated in ancient times within the Moon.

In ancient times, when life initiated its return towards the Absolute, there, in that ancient Earth-Moon, a tremendous apocalyptic event also took place.

Now, when this great life will completely abandon the Earth, this planet will become a new moon.

The sub-lunar spheres constitute the abyss. To name the Virgin within those tenebrous regions means to provoke the wrath of the demons.

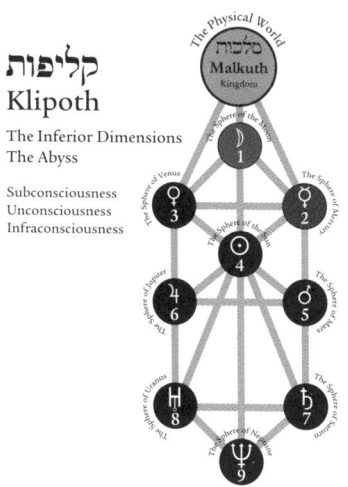

The tenebrous hate the Virgin and they furiously attack anyone who dares to name her in their regions.

The Virgin Mother of the world is the Kundalini. The tenebrous hate the great Mother, who when converted into a serpent of fire, rises through the medullar canal.

When the serpent descends from the coccyx downwards, then it becomes the tail of Satan. This descending serpent is the horrible tempting serpent of Eden.

This serpent victoriously rises through the medullar canal of Angels. This serpent is the tail of Satan in demons.

Chapter 31
The Millennium and the Judgement

Revelation 20:1-15:

And I saw an Angel come down from heaven, (the fifth of the seven) *having the key of the bottomless pit and a great chain in his hand.*

And he laid hold on the dragon, that old serpent, (Javhe) *which is the Devil, and Satan, and bound him a thousand years.*

In the year 1950, the genie of evil whose name is Javhe entered into the abyss. Javhe is paying a terrible karma. Javhe is a terribly perverse fallen Angel. This Javhe is the demon that tempted Jesus in the wilderness while saying "**Itababo.**"

Javhe is the supreme chief of the Black Lodge. Javhe is the secret author of the crucifixion of our Adorable Saviour. Javhe is the antithetic pole of Jesus.

The Roman soldiers who crucified the Adorable One were constituting the honorable guards of Javhe. Thus, this is why Javhe is now crucified within the abyss. This is his karma, the cross of the devil is inverted.

Therefore, Javhe is crucified with his head downwards and his feet upwards.

The Jewish people worship Javhe and they follow Javhe.

The fifth of the seven *"cast him into the bottomless pit, and shut him up, and set a seal upon him, that he should deceive the nations no more, till the thousand years should be fulfilled: and after that he must be loosed a little season."*

Javhe and his legions will remain in the abyss a whole Age. Afterward, it will be necessary that he be released for a short time.

It is necessary to give those that are lost the last opportunity to repent.

But the rest of the dead lived not again until the thousand years were finished. This is the first resurrection.

And when the thousand years are expired, Satan shall be loosed out of his prison.

And shall go out to deceive the nations which are in the four quarters of the earth, Gog and Magog, to gather them together to battle: the number of whom is as the sand of the sea.

And they went up one the breadth of the earth, and compassed the camp of the saints about, and beloved city: and fire came down from God out of heaven, and devoured them.

Woe! Woe! Woe! to those wretched ones that will not take advantage of this last and very short opportunity that is given unto the lost ones. They will sink eternally into the abyss.

And the devil that deceived them was cast into the lake of fire and brimstone, where the beast and the false prophet are, and shall be tormented day and night for ever and ever.

And I saw the dead, small and great stand before God; and the books (books of karma) *were opened: and another book was opened, which is the book of life: and the dead were judged out of those things which were written in the books, according to their works.*

Every human being has his own book, therefore, the deeds of each one are written in his or her book with sacred characters.

And the sea gave up the dead which were in it; and death and hell delivered up the dead which were in them: and they were judged every men according to their works.

And death and hell were cast into the lake of fire. This is the second death.

And whosoever was not found written in the book of life was cast into the lake of fire.

Life has initiated its return towards the great Light; the times of the end have arrived. Millions of human beings, as numerous as the sand of the sea, already have the horns on their forehead and the fatal mark in their hands.

Javhe was tied within the abyss, however the multitudes still worship him.

> *And I saw thrones, and they sat upon them, and judgement was given unto them: and I saw the souls of them that were beheaded for the witness of Jesus, and for the word of God, and that had not worshipped the beast, neither his image, neither had received his mark upon their foreheads, or in their hands; and they lived and reigned with Christ a thousand years* (a whole Age).

Since ancient times, those who accepted the Arcanum A.Z.F. transformed themselves into Kings and Queens, priests and priestesses of Nature.

They are the ones who will now govern under the orders of Christ in the new Age.

This is the first resurrection. Thus, this is how the divine Kings and divine Queens will reincarnate in order to govern.

> *Blessed and holy is he that hath part in the first resurrection: on such the second death hath no power, but they shall be priests of God and of Christ, and shall reign with him a thousand years* (a whole Age).

The Second Death is accomplished in a frightful and dreadfully great manner. The tenebrous will be slowly disintegrated until reaching death within the abyss. This is the Second Death.

Those who accept the Arcanum A.Z.F will save themselves from the abyss and the Second Death. They are the ones who will become gods and will be able to sing *Alleluia! Alleluia! Alleluia!*

The New Jerusalem by Albrecht Dürer.

PART THREE

The New Jerusalem

SICUT SUPERIUS SICUT QUOT INFERIUS

The New Jerusalem by Gustave Doré.

Chapter 32
The New Jerusalem

> Revelation 21:1-27:
>
> *And I saw a new heaven and a new earth* (this is the earth of the future, after the great cataclysm): *for the first heaven and the first earth* (this present one), *were past away; and there was no more sea.*
>
> *And I John saw the holy city, new Jerusalem* (the earth of the future sixth Root Race), *coming down from God out of heaven, prepared as a bride adorned for her husband* (the Christ).
>
> *And I heard a great voice out of heaven, saying, Behold the tabernacle of God is with men, and he will dwell with them, and they shall be his people, and* (this internal) *God himself shall be with them, and be their God.*
>
> *And God shall wipe away all tears from their eyes; and shall be no more death, neither sorrow, nor crying, neither shall there be any more pain: for the former things are passed away.*
>
> *And he that sat upon the throne* (the internal God) *said, Behold I make all things new. And he said unto me, Write: for these words are true and faithful.*
>
> *And he said unto me, It is done. I am Alpha and Omega, the beginning and the end. I will give unto him that is athirst of the fountain of the water of life freely.*

Certainly, He is the Alpha and the Omega, the beginning and the end of all things.

The human being has body, soul, and the Innermost. Beyond the Innermost every human being has three profundities: the first one is the origin of life, the second is the origin of the Word, and the third is the origin of the sexual force.

These three divine profundities of each human being constitute the resplendent Dragon of Wisdom. These three are the internal God and the Alpha and Omega, the beginning and the end. He is the internal Christ whom human beings need to incarnate within.

Whosoever is athirst, He will freely give unto them from the fountain of the water of life. Whosoever knows how to drink from these pure living waters is a glorified one, because he will never, ever be thirsty again (see John 4:14). This key is found in the Arcanum A.Z.F.

The fire (**I** = *ignis*) must fecundate the water (**A** = *aqua, water*) in order for the Spirit (**O** = *origo, principle, Spirit*) to be born.

Thus, this is why the Master Huiracocha has spoken extensively about the **I.A.O.** in his book entitled *Logos Mantra Magic*, as well as in his novel *Rosy-Cross*.

The mantra **I.A.O.** must be vocalized letter by letter. Each letter must be independently vocalized by prolonging its sound after a deep inhalation. All of these vowels are vocalized in succession and in the precise instant of being sexually connected with our spouse, that is to say, our priest or priestess spouse. Thus, this is how the sacred serpent awakens.

> *He that overcometh* (the sexual passion) *shall inherit all things; and I will be his God* (I will incarnate myself within him), *and he shall be my son* (because he is a Christified one),
>
> *But the fearful* (the tenebrous, cowards, unbelievers), *and unbelieving, and the abominable, and murderers, and whoremongers, and sorcerers, and idolaters, and all liars, shall have their part in the lake which burneth with fire and brimstone: which is the second death.*

This lake that burns with fire and brimstone is the lake of carnal passion. This lake is related with the lower animal depths of the human being and its atomic region is the abyss.

The tenebrous slowly disintegrate themselves within the abyss until they die. This is the Second Death.

> *And there came unto me one of the seven Angels which have the seven vials full of the seven last plagues, and talked with me, saying, Come hither, I will shew thee the bride, the Lamb's wife.*

The human being can travel to any place in the world or in the infernos with his Astral Body. The key in order to consciously travel with the Astral Body is the following: laying down on his bed, face up, the disciple must fall sleep while vocalizing the syllables **La Ra**.

The student will independently vocalize each syllable, that is to say, each syllable with a separate breath, as follows: *Lllllaaaaaaaaaaaaaaaaaaa Rrrrrrrraaaaaaaaaaaaaaaaaa.*

The vocalization of these two sacred syllables must be done mentally.

These two syllables have the power of making the sexual energy intensely vibrate. Thus, the disciple must fall asleep while vocalizing with tranquility in his bed. This is how the sexual energies, the creative energies of the Third Logos, begin to vibrate when the student vocalizes these two syllables.

These type of energies produce a sweet and subtle sound when they are intensely vibrating. This sound is similar to that of the cricket. The student must learn how to handle this sound, as this is the subtle voice which grants us the power to consciously travel with our Astral Body.

The student must arise from his bed in those precise instants in which he hears this mystical sound and direct himself to any place in the world. This is not a matter of performing it mentally. What we are teaching here must be performed in a factual action. The disciple, with his Astral Body, is actually detaching himself from the physical body. He then penetrates into the superior worlds in order to study the great mysteries of life and death.

Whosoever wants to learn how to sing these two sacred syllables should listen to Mozart's *Magic Flute*.

The Magic Flute is an opera which is related with an initiation that Mozart received in Egypt.

Thus, this is how John the prophet was taken from his physical body and while being in the spirit was carried away in order to see the heavenly Jerusalem.

> *And he carried me away in the spirit to a great and high mountain, and shew me that great city, the holy Jerusalem, descending out of heaven from God. Having the glory of God:*

and her light was like unto a stone most precious, even like a jasper stone, clear as crystal...

This most precious stone, which is even like a jasper stone, is the sexual organs of the Christified Ones. So, this stone is clear as crystal.

Let us remember the **Vitriol**, a liquid, flexible, and malleable crystal. This crystal is the Christonic semen. VITRIOL means: Visitam Interiori Terra Rectifictur Invenian Ocultum Lapidum; *Visit the interior of the earth, which by rectifying, you will find the occult stone.*

The occult stone is the Philosophical Stone. Therefore, to search within our philosophical earth is necessary, because by rectifying we will find this most precious stone, which is like a jasper stone and clear as crystal.

Inmisio Membri Virili In Vagina Feminae Sine Ejeculatium Seminis.

The sage Huiracocha said:

"Try to endure the described position for one hour and a comfortable ineffable sensation will be felt. Chest against chest, the two solar plexus in immediate contact, as well as all the astral centers placed together. This will permit an interchange of current in order to establish one just Androgyne."

Every initiate builds his own Jerusalem upon the living stone. This living stone is the sex.

The Jerusalem of the human being exists, as well as the Jerusalem from above and the Jerusalem from below.

Sicut superius, Sicut quot inferius.

The superior worlds are the Jerusalem from above.

The Earth of the future sixth Root Race is the Jerusalem from below.

The human Jerusalem is the human being with all of his Christified vehicles. The New Jerusalem gloriously shines.

And had a wall great and high, and had twelve gates (the twelve zodiacal gates in the universe and in the human being), *and at the gates twelve* (zodiacal) *Angels, and names written thereon, which are the names of the twelve tribes of the children of Israel,* which are the twelve fundamental tribes in which this humanity is divided in accordance with the twelve zodiacal signs.

"As above, so below." The human being has twelve faculties which are governed by twelve atomic Angels.

The twelve zodiacal signs exist within the starry space and within the human being.

It is necessary to transmute the sexual energy and make it pass through the twelve zodiacal gates of the human organism.

Thus, this is how the prophet continues speaking about the twelve zodiacal gates:

> *On the east three gates; on the north three gates; on the south three gates, and on the west three gates.*
>
> *And the wall of the city had twelve foundations, and in them the name of the twelve apostles of the Lamb.* These are the twelve zodiacal signs and the twelve energetic spheres which penetrate and co-penetrate without being confused.

Any solar humanity is completely Self-realized within the twelve planes. Therefore, the Twelfth Arcanum is the foundation of the Heavenly Jerusalem. This Twelfth Arcanum is the symbol of Sexual Alchemy.

The Twelfth Arcanum appears in the Tarot as follows: the Twelfth Arcanum represents a human being with his hands bound behind him, and suspended by one foot. His tied hands on his head force him to form a triangle with his arms, with

The Arcanum 12

TAU, THE 22ND HEBREW LETTER.

the vertex pointing downwards, and with his legs he forms a cross which is above the triangle. The gibbet is formed by the trunks of two trees, each with the stumps of six lopped branches, and by a cross-piece, thus completing the figure of the Hebrew Tau. Behold here the sacrifice and the performed work. This is what is called Sexual Alchemy.

Millions of books of Yoga, Occultism, Theosophy, Rosicrucianism, etc. exist, as well as thousands of schools, some of them with very ancient and very venerable traditions. Any student can submit himself to the most rigorous disciplines, practicing with the Kriya, visiting thousands of these schools, centers, lodges, acquiring titles, degrees, and even receiving from their instructors very beautiful and distinctive names, but if the student does not practice sexual magic, he will remain very venerable, learned, and even an erudite, but only for his people. Above in the superior worlds, he will remain just like an aficionado to these spiritual studies, he will be nothing but an ignorant disciple, a poor mystical shadow, profane, or even worse, he will be a very dangerous subject.

Therefore, to work with the gold and the silver, to work with the moon and the sun, is necessary in order to edify the heavenly Jerusalem within each human being.

The gold and the silver, the sun and the moon, are the sexual forces of man and woman.

The alchemist woman should never reach the physiological spasm either. Thus, this is how she will transmute her sexual energies and can awaken her serpent.

The highest degree that women can reach in this study is the degree of Virgin.

Sexual Alchemy is an hermetic art. The hermetic art is highly scientific, highly philosophical and highly mystical.

The whole science and philosophy of the Great Work is found enclosed within the Twelfth Arcanum.

The secret, living, and philosophical fire is hidden within the Christonic semen. The sexual alchemical mysticism is the mysticism of all the ancient initiates.

The philosophy of Sexual Alchemy has its principles in the school of the Essenes, in the school of Alexandria, in the teachings of Pythagoras, in the mysteries of Egypt, Troy, Rome, Carthage, Eleusis, as well as in the wisdom of the Aztecs and Mayas, etc.

The procedures of the science of Sexual Alchemy must be studied in the books of Paracelsus, Nicholas Flamel, Raymond Lully. We also find these procedures hidden within the veil of all symbols, in all the hieratic figures of ancient hieroglyphics of many ancient temples, as well as in the Greek and Egyptian myths.

To you that are searching for initiation, to you that read a lot, to you who hop from school to school, always searching, always hoping, always sighing, tell me with sincerity, have you awakened your Kundalini? Have you opened the seven churches of your spinal medulla? Have you incarnated the Lamb?

You who are searching, tell me, can you dominate earthquakes? Can you walk upon the water? Can you calm the tempest? Can you utter the golden language? Can you see the superior worlds and are you capable of studying the whole history of the Earth and of its races within the sealed records of Nature?

Answer me, beloved reader, be sincere with yourself: place your hand on your heart and answer me with sincerity. Have you Self-realized yourself? Are you sure that with your theories you will become a God? What did you achieve? What have you attained with your theories?

The poor servant who writes this book is an initiate of the Lemurian, Egyptian, Tibetan, etc., mysteries, and never knew in the history of the centuries one authentic Master who could Christify himself without practicing sexual magic.

Therefore, if you have hope of liberating yourself or reaching Self-realization or Christification without practicing sexual magic, then you are worthy of pity, you are worthy of compassion, you are an imbecile.

To transmute the lead of personality into the very pure gold of the Spirit is necessary.

In order to prepare the philosophical mercury (semen), the salt (matter) and the sulphur (fire) are urgent. This mercury must be transmuted and sublimated to the heart.

Christ is within the heart. It is in the heart where the forces which descend from above are mixed with those that arise from below. Thus, this is how that which is from below must be mixed with that which is from above in order for that which is from below to arise into the superior worlds of the great Light.

This is how we achieve the union of the cross with the triangle. The cross (human being) must be united with the triangle (Spirit) by means of the potable gold (the sacred fire of sex). These are the twelve foundations of the heavenly Jerusalem.

The human being who is formed within the maternal womb is the result of a sexual act, and certainly not the result of any theory, nor of any school. The human being is always the child of a male and a female.

In that conception, there were kisses, there was also love, there was a male and a female, and also there was a coitus in order to fertilize the egg, and finally the mother begat the child. Why are you forgetting this? Tell me with which theory were you engendered? Why now do you want to be born as a Master of the Great Day within the worlds of the light by excluding the phallus and the uterus?

What is natural is natural, beloved reader. Do not commit the error of wanting to be born of theories. Nobody can be born through the feet, neither can one eat with the knees. Everything must be in its own place. Everything works as it should.

What is natural is natural. The birth of the Son of Man is one hundred percent sexual. If in spite of everything that is said you still have hope of achieving the initiation with the famous "bellows system," which is based exclusively on respiratory exercises, then time and years will prove to you that you were mistaken and you will inevitably tumble into the abyss.

The bellows system, asanas, Kriyas, etc. are magnificent and marvellous exercises. We cannot disregard them. They help, they are worthwhile for the awakening of the chakras and the cleaning of the nervous canals, etc., but if the Yogi does not practice sexual magic, he will sink into the abyss, even when he is a fanatic of the "bellows system."

> *And he that talked with me had a golden reed to measure the city, and the gates thereof, and the wall thereof.* This golden reed is the dorsal spine of the human being.

The spinal fires ascend along the medullar canal. The development, ascension, and evolution of the Kundalini is very difficult. Each one of the thirty-three spinal vertebrae corresponds to the thirty-three sacred chambers of the temple.

The spinal fires are controlled by the fires of the heart. Thus, this is how the Kundalini ascends very slowly, based on sexual magic and sanctification.

Each vertebra has its virtues and its ordeals. To achieve the ascension to any vertebra without the permission of the cardiac fires is impossible. Therefore, the ascension of the Kundalini is controlled by the merits of our heart.

The guru who has not received the reed is not a true guru. Every initiate that raises the serpent upon the staff receives the reed.

This is how the city and the gates thereof and the wall thereof must be measured with the reed. The Jerusalem of every human being must be measured with the reed.

Therefore, the Master that still has not awakened the Kundalini is a false prophet.

Three vestibules exist: first, the vestibule of ignorance; second, the vestibule of study; third, the vestibule of wisdom.

The human multitudes live within the first vestibule. All theories, schools, lodges, orders, etc. are within the second vestibule. The third vestibule is that of wisdom. The Master and the internal God who guide us towards the great Light are found in this vestibule.

When we enter into the second vestibule, we are searching. We study Astrology, Yoga, Theosophy, etc. We visit different schools, hopping from flower to flower. Each flower is a sect, theory, school, lodge, etc. Thus, this is how many people pass through many reincarnations searching, hopping, reading here and there and everywhere.

When the student is tired of sighing and finally wants to know, this is when he enters through the straight, narrow, and difficult gate. This gate is sex. This is when we really enter into the third vestibule, the vestibule of wisdom.

We find the internal God and the Guru who lead us to the great reality within this vestibule. We need to edify the heavenly Jerusalem upon the living stone.

> *And the city lieth foursquare, and the length is as large as the breadth: and he measured the city with the reed, twelve thousand furlongs. The length and the breadth and the height of it are equal.*

We have reached the square of the circle and the perpetual movement. The city is situated and placed in a square. This reminds us of the holy and mysterious Tetragrammaton, the Holy Four.

If we profoundly explore the interior of our divine Being, then we find three profundities. These three profundities emerge from a mathematical point. It is urgent to know that this point is a super divine atom from the Abstract Absolute Space. The Kabbalistic name of this atom is the Ain Soph.

The three Christic profundities that we carry within emerge from the Ain Soph. This is the ternary emerging from this mathematical point.

3 + 1 = 4. Three plus one equals four. Behold here the holy Tetragrammaton, the Dragon of Wisdom (the internal Christ) which emanated from the Ain Soph and which will return into the Ain Soph.

This is why the city is shaped in a square because it is the perfect temple of the Lamb.

...and he measured the city with the reed, twelve thousand furlongs.

The number twelve thousand is Kabbalistically broken down as follows: 12,000 = 1 + 2 = 3. Behold here the ternary, which is the Lamb who emerged from the super divine atom.

The adorable One shines within the internal vehicles of each one who has Christified himself. This is love.

To edify the new Jerusalem without the Holy Four is impossible.

The name of the eternal One has four Hebrew letters: **Iod**, **He**, **Vau**, **He**.

The Tetragrammaton

These are the Four Winds. Certainly, there are few people who really know the right way in which to pronounce this name. Whosoever wants to edify the new Jerusalem must first awaken the sacred fire of Kundalini. This Pentecostal serpent is **Inri, Azoth**. The Sun is its father, the Moon its mother, the wind carries it in its belly, and the philosophical earth is its nurse.

The alchemist who wants to edify the new Jerusalem must work in his laboratory with the sulphur (fire), the Azoth (air), the mercury (water), and the earth.

The Great Work is symbolized by the lion (fire), the eagle (air), the man (water), and the bull (earth).

These four elements form the Cross of Initiation. You must know that the Cross of Initiation is received in the Heart Temple.

We must work with the elementals of fire, elementals of air, of the water, and of the earth while in the sacred mountain. This sacred mountain could either be the Himalayas or the Alps or of the Andes; these mountains always symbolize the spinal medulla with its thirty-three vertebrae.

We must be alchemists while in the sacred mountain. Thus, this is how we can receive the Initiation in the Heart Temple. We need to transmute led into gold in order to edify the new Jerusalem.

The salamanders light the fire and they fecundate the undines of the water in order for life to be born. The gnomes and pygmies which dwell within the great mountain transmute the lead into gold. The happy and playful sylphs vivify the fire in order for the Great Work to be performed. The receptacle must be hermetically closed in order to impede, at any cost, the spilling of the raw matter.

This is how the lead of personality is transmuted into the living gold of the Spirit. The receptacle must be animated by the fire of the salamanders (bake and re-bake and bake again, and do not be tired of baking). The sylphs of the air will animate the flames of thought. The gnomes will transmute the lead of your passions into the gold of the Spirit, and the undines, which are sometimes passionate, will joyfully move within the raw matter or universal sperm.

Therefore, the creatures of fire, air, water, and earth cannot be absent from the Great Work. We cannot transmute the lead into gold without the creatures of the four elements. The gnomes will not transmute lead into gold without water and without undines. The water and the undines must be fecundated and warmed by the burning fire of the salamanders. This is how it is possible to evaporate the waters and to transmute the lead of personality into the very pure gold of the Spirit.

The alchemist becomes disappointed and his Great Work fails without the mystic action of the sylphs. These creatures of the four elements are within ourselves here and now. Every Master of metallic transmutations edifies the heavenly Jerusalem.

> *And the city lieth foursquare, and the length is as large as the breadth.*

It is impossible to edify the new Jerusalem without the Holy Four.

Iod is the man, **He** is the woman, **Vau** is the phallus, **He** is the vulva.

All ineffable things are written with the holy name of the Eternal One. These four creatures were constantly moving back and forth. These four sacred letters are moving and combining in the whole of creation.

> And he measured the wall thereof a hundred and forty and four cubits, according to the measure of a man, that is, of the Angel.

144 = 1 + 4 + 4 = 9. This is the Ninth Sphere (sex). There is the need to descend into the Ninth Sphere (sex) in order to work with the fire and the water, which is the origin of worlds, beasts, human beings, and gods. Every authentic White Initiation starts here.

All of those who incarnated the Lamb, for example, Hermes, Jesus, Krishna, Rama, Buddha, Dante, Pythagoras, etc. descended into the Ninth Sphere.

Hilarion IX said that in the ancient mysteries the descent into the Ninth Sphere was the maximum ordeal for the supreme dignity of the Hierophant.

Nine is the measure of a man who is of the Angel, because we remain nine months within the maternal womb. The Son of Man can only be born within the Ninth Sphere. Never has it been known that an Angel was born without the Ninth Sphere.

Whosoever wants to cut off the head of Medusa (the psychological "I") must descend into the Ninth Sphere.

Whosoever wants to incarnate Christ must descend into the Ninth Sphere.

Whosoever wants to dissolve the "I" must descend into the Ninth Sphere.

The Ninth Sphere is the Sanctum Regnum of the divine omnipotence of the Third Logos (the Holy Spirit). It is here in the Ninth Sphere where we find the flaming forge of Vulcan.

Every fledgling who works in the Great Work must support himself on his staff, light himself with his own lamp, and cover himself with his sacred mantle. Every fledgling must be prudent.

If you want to incarnate Christ, you must obtain the characteristics of a lemon.

You must flee from lust and from alcohol. You must kill even the most intimate roots of desire.

> *And the building of the wall of it was of jasper: and the city was pure gold, like unto clear glass.*

To build the wall of the new Jerusalem is only possible with the Philosophical Stone (sex)... *and the city* (the internal vehicles of the human being) *was pure gold, like unto clear glass.* Lions of gold decorated the thrones of the divine kings.

The gold symbolizes the sexual fire of the Kundalini. The potable gold (Pentecostal fire) is similar to a liquid, flexible, and malleable glass. This glass is the Christonic semen.

The dorsal fires are Pentecostal fires, the fires of the heart are Christic, and in the forehead the rays of the Father flash magnificently.

> *And the foundations of the wall of the city were garnished with all manner of precious stones. The first foundation was jasper* (the Philosophical Stone); *the second, sapphire; the third, chalcedony; the fourth, an emerald.*
>
> *The fifth, sardonyx; the sixth, sardius; the seventh, chrysolite; the eighth, beryl; the ninth, a topaz; the tenth, a chrysoprasus; the eleventh, a jacinth; the twelfth, an amethyst.*

Each one of these stones represents determinate virtues. The sword of justice is adorned with all of these sacred stones.

Nine Initiations of Minor Mysteries and seven great Initiations of Major Mysteries exist. The **Innermost** is the one who receives all of these Initiations.

The Testament of Wisdom says:

> *Before the dawning of the false aurora upon the earth, the ones who survived the hurricane and the tempest were praising the* **Innermost**, *and the heralds of the aurora appeared unto them.*

The psychological "I" does not receives initiations. The human personality does not receive anything. Nonetheless, the "I" of some initiates becomes filled with pride when saying, "I am a Master, I have such initiations."

Thus, this is how the "I" believes itself to be an initiate and keeps reincarnating in order to "perfect itself," but the "I" never, ever perfects itself. The "I" only reincarnates in order to satisfy desires. That is all.

The experiences of every reincarnation make the "I" complicated and transforms it into a more perverse "I."

Evolution is a process of the complication of life. Therefore, we receive these precious stones in the manner that we dissolve the "I."

The **Innermost** is the one who receives His sacred stones within the superior worlds, as well as rings, chains, ineffable jewels which are adorned with these sacred stones, etc.

Any evil action is enough in order to lose certain sacred stones, that is to say, the loss of degrees.

An initiate who was forcing his physically ill wife to perform the sexual act was very close to losing a sapphire from his sword. Fortunately, this initiate knew how to obey when he was warned by the White Lodge.

The "I" is memory, a bunch of memories, the dust of centuries. Therefore, we receive degrees and the most precious stones according to how we dissolve it.

When the Dragon of Wisdom dissolves the "I," then the ten Sephiroth shine as precious stones in His ineffable, glorious body.

First, we must decapitate the "I" with the sword while in the flaming forge of Vulcan. Afterwards, we have to start slowly dying. (The "I" becomes dissolved based on Alchemy and a very rigorous comprehension. This is complete revolution).

And the twelve gates were twelve pearls; every several gate was of one pearl: and the street of the city was pure gold, as it were transparent glass.

The pearl is lunar. Sex is lunar. The twelve pearls symbolize the sexual fires of Pentecost that shine in the twelve faculties of the human being. The street of the heavenly Jerusalem is of pure gold as if it were transparent glass. As well, the human Jerusalem has twelve gates, that is to say, twelve vehicles.

The Theosophist brethren have studied the septenary of the human being. But every Christified one has twelve bodies, twelve vehicles that are connected to the great Reality. Twelve energetic spheres exist; a solar humanity lives and unfolds in these twelve energetic spheres. Therefore, the heavenly Jerusalem has twelve gates; in each gate is a pearl, a region, or world.

A zodiacal belt with twelve constellations also exists. The new Jerusalem, that is to say, the earth of the future sixth Root Race, is being gestated within the zodiacal womb.

Every evolution starts in Leo and ends in Leo. The street of the city is of pure gold (sacred fire) as if it were flexible, malleable glass, that is to say, Christonic semen. The Pentecostal fire rises from this liquid glass.

All of the twelve vehicles of the Christified one gloriously shines within the fire and the light of infinite space. These are the twelve pearls. This is the heavenly Jerusalem.

Therefore, each inhabitant of the new Jerusalem will be in themselves a true heavenly Jerusalem.

And I saw no temple therein; for the Lord God Almighty (the internal Being) *and the Lamb are the temple of it.*

This verse does not signify that the cosmic temples of internal instruction will cease to exist. The matter is more profound. In the new Jerusalem, the seven present religions and the five thousand sects will have no reason for existing, since the Lamb will be incarnated in every human being. This will be the Age of Christ.

And the city had no need of the (physical) *sun, neither of the* (physical) *moon to shine in it: for the glory of God did lighten it, and the Lamb is the light thereof.*

And the nations of them which are saved shall walk in the light of it: and the kings of the earth (the initiates) *do bring their glory and honour into it.*

And the gates of it shall not be shut at all by day: for there shall be no night there.

And they shall bring the glory and honor of the nations into it.

And there shall in no wise enter into it any thing that defileth, neither whatsoever worketh abomination, or maketh a lie: but they which are written in the Lamb's book of life.

Chapter 33
The Pure River of the Waters of Life

It is necessary that the students of the great, worldwide Gnostic movements (AGLA) receive initiation.

Imagination, Inspiration, and Intuition are the three obligatory ways for initiation.

Thought, feeling, and willpower must be totally liberated from the physical body.

To learn how to consciously travel in the Astral Body is indispensable.

First, the Gnostic student must elevate himself into Imaginative Knowledge.

Second, the student will acquire Inspirational Knowledge.

Third, the student will attain Intuitive Knowledge.

For some time the student will train with Imagination, afterwards with Inspiration, and later on with Intuition.

Practices for the Imagination

First: the syllables **Ma Ma**, **Pa Pa**, **Ba Ba** are the first syllables that we articulate in childhood. You can start the initiation with these syllables. You must sing these syllables while assuming an innocent and infantile attitude. You can learn the intonation of these sacred syllables when listening to *The Magic Flute* of Mozart.

Mozart placed these syllables in his marvellous opera. The disciple must fall asleep assuming an infantile attitude while remembering the first years of his childhood and then mentally singing the sacred syllables.

The word **Pa Pa** should be vocalized intoning the first syllable **Pa** in a high voice, then the second syllable **Pa** will be uttered in a lower voice. These two syllables should be pronounced many times. You must do the same thing with the syllable **Ma**.

Fall asleep while meditating on your childhood. Review with your imagination your whole childhood and mentally articulate the sacred syllables.

You must know that every child is clairvoyant until the age of four years. Afterwards, the innocent atoms of clairvoyance submerge themselves within the subconsciousness. Therefore, if you want to reconquer clairvoyance, meditate on your childhood and profoundly fall asleep while articulating the first syllable of the child, **Ma Ma**, **Pa Pa**, **Ba Ba**.

This type of meditation and the sacred syllables will awaken the infantile atoms of clairvoyance. Then you will elevate yourself into Imaginative Knowledge. You will learn to think with living images.

The present Root Race only thinks in concepts of ideas. These ideas are the result of desire.

Somebody thinks about conquering a woman, then an idea assaults his mind, etc. The ideas belong to the "I." Therefore, you must learn to think with living images. The infantile meditation and the sacred syllables will awaken the infantile atoms for new activity.

Imaginative Knowledge grants us the power to consciously and positively travel in the Ethereal Body. When the student has achieved Imaginative Knowledge, then he can start the exercises for Inspirational Knowledge.

We have given many clues in order to consciously travel with the Astral Body, so thousands of students have learned to travel in their Astral Body. However, we have seen in practice that those people who cannot quiet the mind, not even for an instant, who are accustomed to hopping from school to school, from lodge to lodge, always inquiring, always preoccupied, are not able to consciously Astral Travel.

Therefore, the clue in order to consciously travel in the Astral Body is to empty the mind.

Practice

While lying down with his body, the student will beg his internal God to take him out of his physical body. After this imploration the student must empty his mind, because for this practice it is useless to think. So, by comprehending the uselessness of thinking, the student will absolutely clear his mind and not think. Thus, by comprehending the uselessness of thinking, the mind will remain quiet and in silence for this practice.

Before anything else, comprehend that in order to consciously travel in the Astral Body, the process of thinking is an obstacle.

When we comprehend the uselessness of thinking during this practice, which will take us to Inspirational Knowledge, then the mind will naturally remain quiet and in silence.

There is the need to distinguish between a mind which is quiet and a mind which has to be forced to be quiet. There is the need to distinguish between a mind which is in silence and a mind which is silenced by force.

When the mind is quiet and silenced with violence, a secret struggle exists, and this mind is therefore not quiet, neither is it in silence.

Only when we have comprehended the uselessness of thinking during these practices, will the mind remain quiet and in silence by itself.

Afterwards, the student must tranquilly fall asleep. If the student achieves falling asleep without thinking, that is to say with his mind quiet and in silence, he will then consciously awaken out of his physical body, elevating himself into Inspirational Knowledge.

Therefore, it is indispensable for the dreamer to awaken, it is urgent to awaken the consciousness. All the human beings travel in the Astral Body during the hours of sleep, but they disgracefully live in the Astral Plane with the consciousness asleep. They are sleeping wanderers.

When the dreamer awakes from his dreams, then he elevates himself into Inspirational Knowledge. The Masters of the

White Lodge do not dream. They live at every hour with their consciousness awakened and in the state of vigil even when their physical bodies are sleeping within their beds.

The third step of knowledge is that of Intuitive Knowledge. In order to reach the ineffable summits of Intuitive Knowledge, there is the need to kiss the whip of the executioner and the hand of the one who strikes us. We must love and adore the whole of humanity, sacrificing ourselves for it, always ready to give even the last drop of our blood for the love of this poor, suffering humanity.

When any initiate who consciously moves in his Astral Body can provoke ecstasy by means of love, then this initiate escapes from the Astral Body and elevates himself into the worlds of Angels, Archangels, Seraphim, Potencies, Virtues, Thrones.

Thus, this is when we elevate ourselves into Intuitive Knowledge.

Whosoever reaches the ineffable summits of Intuition can contemplate the future heavenly Jerusalem.

Those that climb the three steps of Imagination, Inspiration, and Intuition can see the ancient Jerusalem (the ancient Earth) and the future Jerusalem (the future Earth that will come after the great cataclysm).

> *And I saw a new heaven and a new earth: for the first heaven and the first earth were past away; and there was no more sea.*
> Revelation 21:1

The inhabitants of the future Earth will be awakened citizens within the superior worlds. In the future Jerusalem, only happiness, peace, and love will exist.

Revelation 22:1-21:

> *And he shew me a pure river of water of life, clear as crystal, proceeding out of the throne of God and of the Lamb.*

This river of eternal water of life is the Christonic Semen. Those who long to rise through the three steps of imagination, inspiration, and intuition must wash their sins with the pure waters of life, because without chastity, nobody attains any progress in these studies.

> *In the midst of the street of it, and on either side of the river, was there the tree of life* (the ten Sephiroth), *which bare twelve manner of fruits* (twelve faculties), *and yielding her fruit every month: and the leaves of the tree were for the healing of the nations.*

Then, nobody will utilize their powers for evil doing. Whosoever has risen through the three steps of Imagination, Inspiration, and Intuition moves himself consciously in his internal vehicles, thus visiting the superior worlds.

The ten Sephiroth constitute the ten atomic surges of the great universal life. The initiate must consciously move within these ten surges of life.

A secret Sephira exists. This is the Ain Soph (the world of the Absolute Abstract Space). The fatal antithesis of the Ain Soph is the abyss. Therefore, the initiate that does evil with his twelve faculties becomes a black magician and falls into the abyss.

In the new Jerusalem, the leaves and the fruits of the Tree of Life will be for the healing of the nations.

> *And there shall be no more curse: but the throne of God and of the Lamb shall be in it; and his servants shall serve him.*
>
> *And they shall see his face; and his name shall be in their foreheads.*

Whosoever receives the name of the eternal One on his forehead will be saved from the abyss and from the Second Death.

No disbeliever or skeptic, no man without faith, can enter into the new Jerusalem. Those who doubt had better prepare themselves to enter into the abyss.

Those who ejaculate the semen, the sorcerers, the assassins, the liars, are people of the abyss. These people cannot receive the name of God on their foreheads.

In the new Jerusalem, only people filled with faith, love, chastity, and charity, etc., will live.

> *And there shall be no night there; and they need no candle, neither light of the* (physical) *sun; for the* (internal) *Lord God giveth them light: and they shall reign for ever and ever.*
>
> *And he said unto me, These sayings are faithful and true: and the Lord God of the holy prophets sent his Angel to shew unto his servants the things which must shortly be done.*

Whosoever has risen through the three steps of Imagination, Inspiration, and Intuition has awakened in the internal worlds. Every initiate, while out of his physical body, can ask his Master to show him the future Jerusalem and the things which must shortly be done.

What is necessary is to abandon laziness and to perform the practices of Imagination, Inspiration, and Intuition which take us towards initiation.

> *Behold, I come quickly; blessed is he that keepeth the sayings of the prophesy of this book.*

This is the Aquarian message; this is the book for the new Age.

This is the secret doctrine of the Savior of the world.

So, the seer of the Book of Apocalypse (who, by the way, is not incarnated today) continues to literally say the following:

> *And I John saw these things, and heard them. And when I had heard and seen, I fell down to worship before the feet of the Angel which shewed me these things.*
>
> *Then saith he unto me, See thou do it not: for I am thy fellow servant, and of thy brethren the prophets, and of them which keep the sayings of this book: worship God.*

This Angel did not allow himself to be praised. Nonetheless, thousands of disciples enjoy being praised by people. They are the ones who say, "I am a great seer, nothing is hidden for me, I do not ignore anything. I am a great initiate, I am a Master, I know everything etc." Thus, this is how Satan enjoys his self-praise. The psychological "I" is Satan. He is the one that says "I am the reincarnation of a great Master," or of a great man.

The truly humble Bodhisattva never praises himself. The humble Bodhisattva says, "I am just a miserable slug from the mud of the earth, I am a nobody. My person has no value. The work is what is worthy."

The Bodhisattva is the human soul of a Master. The Master is the internal God.

The temple of the Milky Way is marvellous. A great bolder closes the entrance to the profane. Inside this temple, we find thousands of Bodhisattvas from the Milky Way. They look like illiterate peasants. However, the internal God of each one of them governs constellations and worlds. When we cast ourselves to their feet in order to worship them, they say, "I am a nobody, I do not know anything, I have no value."

See thou do it not: for I am thy fellow servant, and of thy brethren the prophets.

The human being in himself is nothing but a sinning shadow. Only the Seer of the seer, that is to say the Father who is in secret, is perfect.

And he saith unto me, Seal not the sayings of the prophecy of this book: for the time is at hand.

In that epoch of John, one could still say, *"He that is unjust, let him be unjust still: and he which is filthy, let him be filthy still: and he that is righteous, let him be righteous still; and he that is holy, let him be holy still."*

Today, we can not say this because the times of the end have arrived.

We are in the precise instant in which we have to define ourselves as eagles or reptiles, as Angels or demons.

And behold, I come quickly: and my reward is with me, to give every man according as his work shall be.

I am Alpha and Omega, the beginning and the end, the first and the last.

The Lamb is the Alpha and the Omega, the beginning and the end, the first and the last. The Beloved One enters into the soul in order to reward each one according to his work.

> *Blessed are they that do his commandments, that they may have right to the tree of life* (the ten Sephiroth), *and may enter in through the gates* (of sex) *into the city* (the New Jerusalem).
>
> *For without are dogs,* (the false prophets, those who are founders of evil schools in order to exploit the souls, the fornicators, etc. will be out) *and sorcerers, and whoremongers, and murderers, and idolaters, and whosoever loveth and maketh a lie.*
>
> *I, Jesus have sent mine Angel to testify unto you these things in the churches.*

And Jesus, the one who received the Venustic Initiation exclaims the following:

> *I am the root and the offspring of David, and the bright and morning star.*

Christ is the Star of Dawn. Christ enters into the soul when the soul receives the Venustic Initiation.

> *And the Spirit* (the Christ) *and the bride* (the soul) *say, Come. And let him that heareth say, Come. And let him that is thirst come. And whosoever will, let him take the water of life freely.* Only by taking the pure waters of life, will you attain the Venustic Initiation.

Whosoever drinks from these pure waters of life will never be thirsty, that is to say, whosoever works with the Arcanum A.Z.F. will lift up the Son of Man within themselves and never by thirsty.

> *For I testify unto every man that heareth the words of the prophecy of the book, if any man shall add unto these things, God shall add unto him the plagues that are written in this book:*
>
> *And if any man shall take away from the words of the book of this prophecy, God shall take away his part out of the book of life, and out of the holy city, and from the things which are written in this book".*

Whosoever wants to reproduce this book can do it with entire liberty. Nevertheless, those persons who for false pudency take from this book the secrets of the Arcanum A.Z.F., woe of them! God shall take away his part out of the Book of Life and out of the holy city, and from the things which are written in this book.

You can reproduce this book with the goal that the Aquarian message will reach all of the nations of the world, but woe! woe! woe! to those who add to it or take the words from the book of this prophecy, because truly, truly, I tell you, God shall add unto him the plagues that are written in this book.

He which testifieth these things saith, *Surely I come quickly. Amen, Even so, come, Lord Jesus.*

The grace of our Lord Jesus Christ be with you all. Amen.

THE END

Epilogue: About Alcyone
FROM THE YEAR 1977, NINETEEN YEARS AFTER THE
WRITING OF THE *AQUARIAN MESSAGE*.

Since the year 1962, the 4th of February, between two and three in the afternoon, the Age of Aquarius or the Age of the Water Carrier began.

There occurred an event that you might have recorded within your memories. I am referring to a congress of worlds or planets, which was gathered precisely under the constellation of Aquarius.

Truly, this was a heavenly traffic jam. This was an encounter of worlds.

There were two eclipses: one of the Sun, and the other of the Moon.

Many years before, we addressed such a cosmic event, and even gave the hour in which it would occur. We judiciously asserted that such a cosmic event was going to take place on the 4th of February, 1962, between two and three in the afternoon (this is a concrete fact that actually occurred).

For twenty years we repeated the same facts. So, when the event finally came to pass, when this cosmic phenomena occurred, none of the sisters or brothers of the International Gnostic Movement found this to be something new. They only came to corroborate what we had addressed with much anticipation.

A congress of worlds such as the one that took place in that year, day, and hour does not happen every day, but only when a new era begins. Therefore, facts are facts, and we have to surrender before these factual events.

But, this is not all: from the date already mentioned, something else is going to occur.

We already know that Aquarius is an era governed by Saturn and Uranus and this is completely revolutionary...

In Alchemy, Saturn is allegorized by the black crow, that is to say, "the return into the original, primeval chaos."

In regard to Uranus, it is perfectly demonstrated that it is one hundred percent revolutionary, catastrophic.

In relation to the stars, there are events, there are phenomena, that are worth knowing about.

Much has been said about **Alcyone**, and this invites us to reflect. Once, while in the superior dimensions, I had to converse extensively with him. I then verified that he is truly an Adept of the great White Fraternity.

He greatly mentioned the star Alcyone, and also referred to Krishnamurti. In some way, he associated K.M. with that star. This is profoundly significant.

The star Alcyone is a very fascinating sun. Many other suns rotate around that sun.

We have been told that the Sun that shines upon us is the seventh sun that rotates around this star Alcyone. Naturally, this would not be admitted by the wise men of official science, but we, the esoterists, do not ignore the reality concerning the significance of that great sun.

A great organization of worlds exist around Alcyone. There are seven suns and each one of them shines and gives life to its own planets and its satellites (which rotate in their respective orbits around each one of these suns). We cannot deny that our Sun has its own group of worlds or planets that it shines upon and gives life to.

When one comprehends the form in which these system of suns are organized and how they rotate around their gravitational centers, one then advances greatly in the field of knowledge.

The Pleiades have been cited by the sacred scriptures, by the Bible, and by many esoteric teachings. Alcyone is precisely the principal sun of the Pleiades, and around it seven suns gravitate (our sun being the seventh one which rotates around Alcyone).

Each sun is the center of a solar system, and Alcyone is the center of seven solar systems.

This invites us to a brief reflection.

Let us remember Saturn with its rings of stones, meteoric sand, or rocks, etc. Those rings are limited exclusively to Saturn. But, it is good to know that Alcyone also has rings. These rings are larger than those of Saturn. Rather than being made up of rocks, meteoric stones, and other distinctive materials such as the rings of Saturn, Alcyone's rings undoubtedly form one sole thing and are radioactive. These rings are constituted of radiation.

But what type of radiation am I referring to? Simply, to that radiation that is the result of the fractionation of an electron. The fractionated electrons liberate energy, a type of energy that some authors call "**manasic**." This term is Sanskrit and in some way is related to the Inferior Manas (inferior mind) and with the Superior Manas (superior mind; Manas is the Sanskrit word for mind).

So, these electrons liberate a type of unknown energy.

Obviously, if the intellectual animal (mistakenly called human) could disintegrate the electrons as he disintegrates the atoms, then a catastrophe would be provoked, that not only could affect the tridimensional world of Euclid, but moreover, could affect the Sephirothic regions of **Hod** (the world of emotions), or **Netzach** (the world of the mind), and perhaps even **Tiphereth** (the world of natural causes). Thus, these regions could suffer great damage.

If any foolish terrestrial scientist could disintegrate the electron, then he would obtain a different type of energy, different from that which results from the fractionation of the atom; it is an eneregy more terrible than the energy of the H-bomb or any other deadly element.

Fortunately, scientists are not capable of fractionating the electron in order to take advantage of the energy enclosed within it.

On Alcyone, the cases of fractionation (the destruction of electrons) does take place. This phenomena liberates a type of unknown energy, an energy different from cathodic rays, x-rays, or N-rays.

It was in the year 1974 when three astronauts (who were gravitating around the earth) reported a type of radiation or a type of unknown energy, unsuspected by official science.

Obviously, since 1962, specifically since the 4th of February of the cited year, our planet Earth (and the whole solar system in general) has been in the momentum of entering within the astonishing rings of Alcyone. Such rings extend themselves across many light years; they are immensely huge.

So, in a given moment, our solar system will enter within Alcyone's rings. Very few are they who suspect what will happen.

Paul Otto Hess states that if the Earth enters into the rings first, it will appear as if it were a great bonfire, like a pictorial light of firecrackers.

But, if the Sun is the first to enter (which the calculations that are being made seem to indicate), such radiation will interfere with the solar rays and as a result darkness will endure for 110 hours; after this, everything will resume normally. The difference between the second aspect from the first of this phenomena is that instead of everything appearing like a great bonfire, what will occur is that the whole Earth will be covered in darkness, but in reality it will not be darkness, for everything will be saturated with lights.

For example, it is like a meteor shower (shooting stars) upon the face of the Earth; after its conclusion, everything resumes as normal.

Nonetheless, the Earth, already within the rings of Alcyone, will be submitted to a very special vibration.

The molecules, whether they are of iron, phosphorus, calcium, copper, nitrogen, carbon, starch, etc., would be completely modified due to this radiation. This signifies, as you can see, a change in matter.

The men of science believe that they know matter, but in reality they do not.

The concept that they have about matter is nothing more than a concept.

Matter as **substance** is unknown to physicists.

I am not saying that merely physical matter cannot be destroyed, but the substance itself, that famous Iliaster that reposes within the profound darkness of the abyss or bottomless space during the great cosmic night, is indestructible. This is unknown to modern scientists.

Atoms offer many surprises that the men of science, of nuclear physics, do not even remotely suspect.

Within their interior, the atoms carry that which the Hebrews call "igneous particles," "hashim" or "igneous souls." These igneous souls are formidable. Without these igneous souls, atoms cannot process themselves within the living constitution of matter.

Therefore, in reality, no one truly knows the power, for instance, of a few grains of sand. We can be sure that nobody knows the power that is enclosed there, or what it is capable of doing.

The hashim or igneous souls are enclosed within each atom. The great magicians of the east know how to work with these igneous particles of the atoms. In any case, the atoms are impelled by these igneous particles, which are obviously suspected by modern scientists.

Therefore, do not take this following assertion as a strange statement: the igneous radiations or vivifying radiations of the atoms of Alcyone will come to alter the molecules of nature.

Once this radiation envelops the Earth, it will be tremendous, so tremendous that there will be no night for a duration of two thousand years. The whole Earth will be enveloped by this radiation, and in order to see, the light of the Sun will not be necessary. This radiation will illuminate even the deepest caverns, and for two thousand years there will be no night, but only one complete day without night.

Thus, this is how it is written, and the best wise men agree with this.

Obviously, what we are emphatically affirming today will not be accepted by the men of science. In no way will they accept this statement, simply because this does not commune with their scientific talents. But, this is a reality.

The organisms of all beings will be modified, plants, animals, etc., etc., etc.

Many plants that do not exist today, many species of animals whose germs are latent in the bottom of the ocean or in the rocks or in the most remote mountains, will be vivified by this radiation, and will consequently come into existence.

This event happens every ten thousand years. It happened before, and will happen again, because this phenomena obeys heavenly transit. Our solar system has to forcedly pass through the rings of Alcyone.

Some people might say that Alcyone is very far, that it is related to the Pleiades and that it has nothing to do with our solar system. It is very appealing to speak in this ignorant manner.

The reality is that the Sun that shines over us forms part of Alcyone; it is the seventh one. It is a sun related to a system of suns which rotate around Alcyone.

This formerly cited event will process or will endure for two thousand years.

The radiation of Alcyone's rings exercises a specific influence upon the rotation of our planet. This signifies that the velocity of rotation over its axis will be slower, and as a consequence or corollary, our world will continue to rotate around the Sun in a wider orbit.

The planet Earth will become a little more distant from the solar center.

The verticality of the axis of our planet with respect to the elliptic will be a concrete fact.

The poles are melting due to the deviation of the axis of the Earth. This has already been demonstrated. Today, the magnetic pole no longer coincides with the geographical pole.

The deviation of the poles will be precipitated with the tremendous radiation of Alcyone.

The Count of Saint Germain said, "The seasons of spring and summer will be the first to be altered." This spring (1977) has everything, but nothing that belongs to spring. We have to tolerate cold weather while in spring. Also summers have not been the same; it seems that these seasons are going to disappear.

The poles are melting, and with the radiation of Alcyone, this melt down will be precipitated. The ice will invade the whole north and south; only the equatorial zone will be tolerable.

A new glaciation is coming!

The Earth has already suffered from previous glaciations, and a new one is coming.

The cold weather that occurred in the United States a while ago was like nothing experienced before.

When is our planet Earth, or better if we say our solar system, going to penetrate within the tremendous rings of Alcyone?

When will we start passing through this ring, which every 10,000 years we have to pass through?

Not a single scientist can predict this. Really, it is unpredictable. But since the year 1962, we are in the momentum of penetrating within it. So, do not be astonished if from one moment to the next we will penetrate into the rings of Alcyone.

I point to the facts: the astronauts who in 1974 were in orbit around the Earth are the ones that gave us the information about a strange type of radiation.

A terrible change in Nature will come, this is obvious: the submergence of the present continents and the emergence of new ones, etc.

But the limit of limits will happen with the arrival of **Hercolubus**.

The event of Hercolubus is preceded by the entrance of our planet Earth into the rings of Alcyone. This is when we will comprehend that physical nature is not always the same.

If you believe that physical matter, the matter that compounds our world, existed always with the same mathematical formulae, then you are completely mistaken. Matter was distinct in the Polar, Hyperborean, Lemurian, and Atlantean epochs. Now, when we cross through the rings of Alcyone, the mathematical formulae will completely change.

Example: as a result of this radiation, the elements that today are working for medicine will become obsolete.

The formulae for animals will be out of order.

The knowledge of contemporaneous physics will be the laughing stock of all the world.

Everything that is being taught in modern chemistry will become useless, because chemistry will change its formulae within a few years, upon the entrance into the radiation of Alcyone.

Once again we will evidence the Law of the Pendulum.

We are starting the new cycle of transformations that was initiated on the 4th of February, 1962, between two and three in the afternoon, in spite of what the stubborn people might say. But we always refer to the facts.

There has never been a more grandiose concentration in heaven like the one on the 4th of February, 1962.

Let us then not be surprised that from one moment to the next our solar system will enter within the rings of Alcyone. We must prepare ourselves now.

Many will not resist the radiation and will die!

Physical matter will become more radioactive, more fluorescent, and this will in some way be helpful for our spiritual work.

It is clear that we must review our daily conduct. We must become more reflective, more careful with our critical judgements, and especially very careful with our **negative emotions**.

When we are in the very field of psychology, we find many disorders within people.

Everyone is being dragged down by negative emotions, and this is very grave.

There is nothing more harmful for profound internal development than negative emotions.

When you are assaulted by a negative emotion, you must express the best that is possible within you during that event. If a negative emotion has arrived, for instance, a negative emotion of envy that is eating you up, down to the very marrow of your bones, then try and display a very harmonious behavior, not in favor of envy, of course, but in favor of your neighbor's good.

If an emotion of anger is shaking us up, then speak with an extraordinary sweetness, and instead of being upset with the one that has hurt us, speak well of this one who has offended us. Thus, we will not be hurt internally.

It is not an easy task to express good when one is feeling a negative emotion. But it is only this way that it must be.

If we have an emotion of resentment because someone has been bothering us, then let us speak with love and in favor of the one who has bothered us.

It is clear that we must not remain on the surface. We must eliminate those undesirable psychological elements that from moment to moment produce within us negative emotions of anger, envy, hatred, lust, pride, etc., etc. At the very least, we must eliminate the psychological aggregates that have produced these negative emotions. Thus, we will not be hurt.

Unquestionably, this physical world of forty-eight laws is in the momentum of entering into the rings of Alcyone. So, everyone is being shaken up by negative emotions and nothing could be more contagious than these emotions.

There exist bacteria and viruses, there is no doubt of this.

Bacteria originate many types of sicknesses. This has already been demonstrated in the test tubes of the laboratories.

In regard to pathogenic viruses, these are infinitely small and therefore more dangerous. Let us observe, for instance, the virus of cancer. Even though some might think that its isolation has still not been achieved, we have to inform you that in **Israel** the virus has already been isolated. We do not know with which name this virus was baptized.

We baptized this virus with the name "Cancro" and we have spoken about this extensively before.* It is so tiny that a powerful electronic microscope is necessary in order to study it.

Regardless of the fact that these viruses are so tiny, they become more dangerous and more contagious.

Nonetheless, negative people, victims of negative emotions, become more contagious than viruses and bacteria.

Grouchy people, who are always filled with envy, who are always obnoxious at any given moment, people who are filled with morbid minds at any given time, people who suffer deliriums of persecution, who say they are bewitched, who say that are hated by everybody, are negative and infect the groups; they infect others.

In our work, we isolate such people. If they do not comprehend, if they feel upset and think that we do not love them, they are mistaken: we love them, and through this way we are insinuating that they must become positive, amicable, and magnetic. We offer them the opportunity to study our wisdom, but we isolate them in a certain way because they are dangerous for the groups.

A negative person can infect other negative people, and if this person dictates a lecture, then he infects thousands of people. They are more dangerous, thousand of times more dangerous, than viruses and bacteria.

There is the need to specify who the negative people are and which are the negative emotions.

It is not enough to say that such a fellow is negative or that the other fellow is not. There is the need to specify who are the negative people.

If a person is screaming, grouchy, and complaining all day, is this person positive or negative?

If a person is tremendously lustful and his life is processed by virtue of lust, if this person is full of frightful emotions and

---

* Editor: See *Occult Medicine and Practical Magic* by the author.

sees in each person of the opposite sex a sexual opportunity, what would we say about this person? If just a look from the opposite sex agitates him and that look is enough for him to be constantly with lust, what can we think of him? Obviously, he is a negative person, and of course this person comes to infect other people.

If a person goes everywhere from instant to instant with negative emotions, this person infects the whole world.

The angry ones who at any time are thundering and lightning infect other people with their anger.

It comes into my memory the case of a friend of mine who had the custom of placing his hands under the belt of his pants. So one day, a man approached him with a gun in his hand and asked him, "What's the matter with you? Do you want to start something with me?"

Then my friend answered, "No!"

"So then why do you have your hands like that?"

My friend then answered, "It is a custom that I have, sir."

The other person then said, "Ah well, excuse me, what happened is that I am enraged (with anger)."

Thus, this is an example of someone negative infecting the whole world.

People like this have to be isolated from groups; they do not understand or they do not comprehend that they are negative. They think that we do not love them, but we love them; what occurs is that they are infected people that interrupt the interior, profound development of the Being.

Behold, this is the grave part of this matter. Therefore, from a psychological point of view, it is necessary that we do not allow ourselves to be pulled in by negative emotions.

We have the longing of visiting or entering within the Sephirothic regions of space. One thing is to grasp a Sephira and another thing is to penetrate within it. Obviously, the Sephiroth are atomic and we, the Gnostics, must penetrate within the Tree of Life.

We must know that there are many Sephirothic regions within space; to penetrate within them is marvellous.

How are we going to penetrate into the Kabbalistic region of **Hod** if we do not have a psychological body? There exist psychological projections (Astral projections). The diverse psychological aggregates can, at any given moment, integrate themselves in order to penetrate within the Sephira **Hod** (Astral World, or First Heaven). But this would only be a subjective entrance; this would not have objectivity as when the second body (Astral Body) has been created. This body has to be created in order to handle the emotions of this region. What type of emotions am I referring to? I am referring to **superior emotions**. The inferior emotions are an obstacle for experiencing what is Reality (**God**), and for the psychological development of the Being.

If we want to be born again, to create a second body, in order to penetrate into the Sephirotic region of **Hod** (the kingdom of heaven), then it is obvious that we should not torpidly waste our energies by letting ourselves be pulled in by negative emotions, such as violence, hatred, jealousy, pride, etc.

If the energies are wasted by inferior emotions, then with what energy are we going to create a psychological body? How is this going to be achieved if we are wasting the energies?

In order to create a psychological body (to be born again) it is necessary to save our energies.

In order to explore the regions of **Hod** (according to what has been taught, these immense regions are governed by ineffable beings, by solar beings, example: the Beni-Elohim or the Children of God who dwell within those profound regions) only the one who saves energies can penetrate into the profundities of **Hod**.

It would be impossible to penetrate or to have access to the mysteries of life and death without the Kabbalistic body of **Hod**. This is obvious.

Therefore, let us begin to save our energies. When a negative emotion is shaking us up, then it is worth knowing which psychological aggregate produced it. After having observed this aggregate (sin) in action, we must submit it to the technique of **meditation**, in order to comprehend and disintegrate it. Otherwise, how else are we going to do it?

What is most terrible is that negative emotions transform the human being into a **liar**. The liar produces a mistaken connection, because the energy of the Elder of Days (our Father who is in heaven, the Truth) flows harmoniously and perfectly throughout the ten Sephiroth of the Hebraic Kabbalah until reaching Malkuth (or the Kingdom), the physical person, or psycho-physical person. The liar connects himself in a wrong way; he intentionally, with his negative emotions, produces a dislocation of his mind, and consequently, a lie emerges, which is a mistaken connection.

One can be a liar due to a negative emotion that transforms us into slanderers and liars, or one can be consciously and by will a liar. In any case, these are negative connections of the mind with the superior centers of the Being. A dislocation of the mind with the superior centers of the Being is produced (therefore, we do not perceive things in their true sense).

We have to say the truth always, at any cost, and no matter what. To say the truth and nothing else but the truth is the crude fact of this matter.

So, negative emotions transform people into liars.

The karma of liars is monstrosity: children who are born with two heads, deformed children, are like that because they have been connected in the wrong way with the superior centers of the Being. These souls were intentionally and continuously lying in their past life. Therefore, they come into their new existence with a deformed body. Behold here what a lie is.

We must pay much attention to this matter.

When one has created a second psychological body, which permits us to enter within the Sephirothic regions of **Hod,** one can evidence by oneself what a lie is, falseness.

Michael is the one who is the regent of such a Sephira, and it is obvious that He marvellously shines within this region.

So, how are we going to explore those regions if we are liars, if we are victims of negative emotions? It is obvious that we cannot.

How are we going to explore the regions of **Netzach** if we do not correctly connect ourselves with the superior centers of the Being?

It is necessary to create a psychological Mental Body in order to explore the regions of **Netzach** (Mental World), otherwise it is impossible.

No one can create a psychological Mental Body if they allow themselves to be pulled in by negative emotions. There will not be enough energies in order to create this individual mind, which would permit us to explore the psychological regions of the universal mind.

So, in order to explore the regions of **Hod** and **Netzach**, it is necessary to utter the truth and nothing but the truth, and no person can say the truth if they are being pulled by negative emotions.

We need to obey the Father who is in heaven, and those who let themselves be pulled by negative emotions are not obeying the Father. The Father is the Truth and nothing but the Truth. So, in order to obey the Father who is in heaven, the psychological connections must be perfect. One must harmoniously and correctly learn to connect oneself with the Father who is in heaven.

The one who has also has created a body of Conscious Will has done so by having learned to obey the Father.

All of us have the Elder of Days within our depths, mentions the great Kabbalist **Schimeon Ben Jochai,** but few are those who know how to obey the Elder of Days.

One cannot obey the Elder of Days if one does not do the will of the Father. One does not do the will of the Father who is in heaven when one lies. The will of God the Father is not fulfilled when one allows oneself to be pulled by negative emotions.

Therefore, beloved readers, it is necessary to learn to live wisely. It is necessary to self-explore, to observe ourselves better.

So, we are now going to enter into an extraordinary epoch. The great selection has begun. Not all of this humanity who populate the face of the Earth will serve as a seed bed for the coming sixth Root Race, which will populate the future world.

Once this planet Earth is within the rings of Alcyone, then all we the workers of the Great Work have been stating will become evident.

The Tree of Life is the spinal medulla. This Tree of Wisdom is also the ten Sephiroth, the twenty-two creative Major Arcana, letters, sounds, and numbers, with which the Logos (God) created the Universe.

Glossary

Androgynous: (Greek) Gk. androgynos, "male and female in one," from andros "male" + genika "female", meaning: having male and female sexual polarities or characteristics. A sexless being capable of reproducing its own species by means of asexual reproduction, in other words, a living species that without having evident sexual organs is capable of reproducing its own species (i.e. fissiparous "Tending to break up into parts or break away from an androgynous body").

Angel: "The whole cosmos is directed, watched, and animated by a series of almost interminable hierarchies of conscious beings. Each one of them (whether they are called by one name or another, such as Dhyan Chohans, Angels, or Devas, etc.) have a mission to accomplish, and are messengers only in the sense that they are agents of the Karmic and Cosmic Laws. They vary in their respective degrees of consciousness and intelligence infinitely. All of them are perfect humans in the most complete sense of the word. Multiple angelical services characterize divine love. Each Elohim works within his specialty. We can and must appeal for angelical protection." - The Three Mountains

Army of the Voice: A reference to Elohim Sabbaoth (Hebrew), the army or host of gods and goddesses.

Aryan Race: Quoted from Webster's Revised Unabridged Dictionary: "From Sanskrit [=a]rya excellent, honorable; akin to the name of the country Iran, and perh. to Erin, Ireland, and the early name of this people, at least in Asia. 1. One of a primitive people supposed to have lived in prehistoric times, in Central Asia, east of the Caspian Sea, and north of the Hindoo Koosh and Paropamisan Mountains, and to have been the stock from which sprang the Hindoo, Persian, Greek, Latin, Celtic, Teutonic, Slavonic, and other races; one of that ethnological division of mankind called also Indo-European or Indo-Germanic." In Universal Gnosticism, this term refers to the vast majority of the popluation of this planet, and is noted for its close relationship with Ares or Mars, the God of War. Compare with "AquAryan" and "barbAryan." The Aryan race, the fifth great race to exist on this planet, is under the guidance of Ares, Mars, the Fifth of the "Seven Spirits before the Throne of God."

Bodhisattva: (Sanskrit) Literally, Bodhi means "enlightenment" or "wisdom." Sattva means "essence" or "goodness," therefore the term Bodhisattva literally means "essence of wisdom." In the esoteric or secret teachings of Tibet and Gnosticism, a Bodhisattva is a human being who has reached the Fifth Initiation of Fire (Tiphereth) and has chosen to continue working by means of the Straight Path, renouncing the easier Spiral Path (in Nirvana), and returning instead to help suffering humanity. By means of this sacrifice, this individual incarnates the Christ (Avalokiteshvara), thereby embodying the supreme source of wisdom and compassion. Interestingly, the Christ in Hebrew is called Chokmah, which means "wisdom," and in Sanskrit the same is Vishnu, the root of the word "wisdom." It is Vishnu who sent his Avatars into the world in order to guide humanity. These avatars were Krishna, Buddha, Rama, and the Avatar of this age: the Avatar Kalki. "The truly humble Bodhisattva never praises himself. The humble Bodhisattva says, 'I am just a miserable slug from the mud of the earth, I am a nobody. My person has no value. The work is what is worthy.' The Bodhisattva is the human soul of a Master. The Master is the internal God." - The Aquarian Message

Bons: The oldest religion in Tibet. It was largely overshadowed (some say persecuted) by the arrival of Buddhism. Samael Aun Weor had accepted the statements of earlier investigators which described the Bon religion as essentially Black; but upon further investigation he discovered that they are not necessarily Black, just extreme in some practices.

Book of Enoch: Quoted from Blavatsky's *The Secret Doctrine*: "The history of the evolution of the Satanic myth would not be complete if we omitted to notice the character of the mysterious and Cosmopolitan Enoch, variously called Enos, Hanoch, and finally Enoichion by the Greeks. It is from his Book that the first notions of the Fallen Angels were taken by the early Christian writers. The "Book of Enoch" is declared apocryphal. But what is an Apocrypha? The very etymology of the term shows that it is simply a secret book, i.e., one that belonged to the catalogue of temple libraries under the guardianship of the Hierophants and initiated priests, and was never meant for the profane. Apocrypha comes from the verb Crypto, [[krupto]], "to hide." For ages the Enoichion (the Book of the SEER) was preserved in the "city of letters" and secret works -- the ancient Kirjath-Sepher, later on, Debir (see Joshua xv., 15)... The Book of Enoch, in short, is a resume, a compound of the main features of the History of the Third, Fourth and Fifth Races; a very few prophecies from the present age of the world; a long retrospective, introspective and prophetic summary of universal and quite historical events -- geological, ethnological, astronomical, and psychic -- with a touch of theogony out of the antediluvian records. The Book of this mysterious personage is referred to and quoted copiously in the Pistis Sophia, and also in the Zoharand its most ancient Midrashim. Origen and Clement of Alexandria held it in the highest esteem. To say, therefore, that it is a post-Christian forgery is to utter an absurdity and to become guilty of an anachronism, since Origen, among others, lived in the second century of the Christian era, yet he mentions it as an ancient and venerable work. The secret and sacred name and its potency are well and clearly though allegorically described in the old volume. From the XVIIIth to the Lth chapter, the Visions of Enoch are all descriptive of the Mysteries of Initiation, one of which is the Burning Valley of the "Fallen Angels." Perhaps St. Augustine was quite right in saying that the Church rejected the BOOK OF ENOCH out of her canon owing to its too great antiquity, ob nimiam antiquitatem. There was no room for the events noticed in it within the limit of the 4004 years B.C. assigned to the world from its "creation"!

Causa causorum: (Latin) "Cause of Causes."

Collyrium: A solution to wash the eye. Related to Alchemy, one finds the following quote from Basil Valentine (Triumphant Chariot Of Antimony): "You titular Doctors, you I speak to, who write long Scroles of Receipts: you Apothecaries, who with your Decoctions fill Pots, no less than Those (in Prince Courst) in which Meat is boiled for the sustentation of some hundreds of men: you, I say, who hitherto have been blind, suffer a Collyrium to be poured into your Eyes, and permit them to be anointed with Balsom, that the most thick skin of Blindness may fall from your Sight, and you behold the Truth, as in a most clear Glass. GOD grant you Grace, that you may know his wonderful Works, and the Love of your Neighbour be rooted in you, that you may search out true Medicine, which the Ruler of the Heavens hath, by his own omnipotent hand, and his ineffable and eternal Wisdom, from above infused in, impressed on, and communicated to his Noble Creatures, for the Good of Mankind; whence man may find help in his greatest Necessity, and Counsel for Health in his Diseases.

Why do you, miserable Worm of the Earth, and food of Worms, look so intently on the Rind or Shell, and neglect the Kernel, being unmindful of your Creator, who formed you according to his Image; when as you ought to give thanks to him, and with diligent Study to search out his Works, exceeding Nature herself? Return and look into your self, there behold the Image of your own ingratitude, that you may be ashamed of yourself, especially because you have not search out those things, which the most wise GOD, for the good of Mortals; hath infused in his Creatures; by knowing which, you might have offered unto him the most acceptable Sacrifice of Praise and Gratitude."

Consciousness: From various dictionaries: 1. The state of being conscious; knowledge of one's own existence, condition, sensations, mental operations, acts, etc. 2. Immediate knowledge or perception of the presence of any object, state, or sensation. 3. An alert cognitive state in which you are aware of yourself and your situation. In Universal Gnosticism, the range of potential consciousness is allegorized in the Ladder of Jacob, upon which the angels ascend and descend. Thus there are higher and lower levels of consciousness, from the level of demons at the bottom, to highly realized angels in the heights.

"Wherever there is life, there exists the Consciousness. Consciousness is inherent to life as humidity is inherent to water." - *Fundamental Notions of Endocrinology and Criminology*

"It is vital to understand and develop the conviction that consciousness has the potential to increase to an infinite degree." - the 14th Dalai Lama. See also: Level of Being.

"Light and consciousness are two phenomena of the same thing; to a lesser degree of consciousness, corresponds a lesser degree of light; to a greater degree of consciousness, a greater degree of light." - *The Esoteric Treatise of Hermetic Astrology*

"Wherever there is light, there is consciousness." - *The Great Rebellion*

Cteis: The Cteis was a circular and concave pedestal, or receptacle, on which the Phallus, or column [obelisk] rested. The union of these two, as the generative and producing principles of nature, in one compound figure, was the most usual mode of representation. Here we find the origin of the point within a circle, a symbol which was first adopted by the old sun worshipers. The Compass arranged above the Square symbolizes the (male) Sun, impregnating the passive (female) Earth with its life-producing rays. The true meanings, then are two-fold: the earthly (human) representations are of the man and his phallus, and the woman with her receptive cteis (vagina). The male female divinities were commonly symbolized by the generative parts of man and woman... The Phallus and Cteis (vagina), emblems of generation and production, and which, as such, appeared in the Mysteries. The Indian Lingam was the union of both, as were the Boat and Mast, and the Point within the Circle. The Cteis was symbolized as the moon. The female personification of the productive principle. It generally accompanied the Phallus... and as a symbol of the prolific powers of nature, and was extensively venerated by the nations of antiquity.

Decalogue: (Greek deka, "ten" and logos, "word") The Ten Commandments.

Digerere: (Latin) to bear, carry, wear.

Dugpas: (Also known variously as Druk-pa, Dugpa, Brugpa, Dag dugpa or Dad dugpa) A large sect which broke from the Kagyug-pa "the Ones of the Oral Tradition." They considered themselves as the heirs of the indian Gurus: their teaching, which goes back to Vajradhara, was conveyed through Dakini, from Naropa to Marpa and then to the ascetic and mystic poet Milarepa. Later on, Milarepa's disciples founded new monasteries, and new threads appeared, among which are the Karmapa and the Drukpa. All those schools form the Kagyug-pa order, in spite of episodic internal quarrels and extreme differences in practice. The Drukpa sect is recognized by their ceremonial large red hats, but it should be known that they are not the only "Red Hat" group (the Nyingmas also use red hats). Samael Aun Weor wrote repeatedly in many books that the Drukpas practice and teach Black Tantrism, by means of the expelling of the sexual energy.

Ego: Defined by Universal Gnosticism, "ego" indicates either 1. any particular psychological aggregate or "I," or 2. their collection as a whole. Each person carries millions of such "I's" that constantly surge and struggle for dominance over the person. Each ego has its own thoughts, feelings and actions (will). Thus each person is a multiplicity of "I's" or competing wills. Egos are understood to be organized by three (in Three Brains: thought, emotion and action), by seven (the seven captial sins: avarice, laziness, lust, pride, anger, envy and gluttony) and legion: the incredible variety of manifestations they may take. The goal of every true religion is the removal of these egos, thereby freeing the Essence (the consciousness) from suffering, and reuniting it with it's origin (thereby establishing religare, or "reunion" with the divine).

Egregores: (Greek, "to watch over")

Eightfold Path: The Buddha Shakyamuni taught that the path to the freedom from suffering was accomplished by following eight fundamental steps:
1. Right view or understanding;
2. Right intention or motivation;
3. Right speech or communication;
4. Right action or conduct;
5. Right vocation or livelihood;
6. Right effort;
7. Right attention or mindfulness;
8. Right presence or concentration.

Elixir of Long Life: "When the Adept renounces the supreme bliss of Nirvana, the Adept then may ask for the Elixir of Long Life. The blessed ones who receive this marvelous Elixir die but do not die. On the third day they are raised. This has already been demonstrated by the Adorable one." The Perfect Matrimony

Elohim: (Hebrew) From NHVKT, or the letters aleph, lamed, he, yod, and mem. It carries many meanings. Fundamental are its components: El means "God," Eloah means "Goddess," so Elohim can be read both as a plural word for "Gods and Goddesses" and as a descriptive term for a single androgynous being. The term is commonly used as a reference to the Cosmocreator Archangels, the "seven spirits before the Throne."

Ens Seminis: (Latin) Literally, "the entity of semen." A term used by Paracelsus.

Ens Virtutis: (Latin) Literally, "army; host; mighty works (pl.); strength/power; courage/bravery; worth/manliness/virtue/character/excellence." Paracelsus stated that the ens virtutis must be extracted from the ens seminis, thus saying that all virtue and excellence is developed from the force within the sexual waters.

Evolution: In Universal Gnosticism, the term evolution refers to the birth, growth and development of any cosmic manifesation from an atom to a sun. Evolution is always followed by devolution, or decay and death.

Four Noble Truths: Legend has it that the first teaching of the Buddha Shakyamuni revealed Four Truths to humanity. He said, "It is through not understanding, not realizing four things, that I,

Disciples, as well as you, had to wander so long through this round of rebirths. And what are these four things? They are the Noble Truth of Suffering, the Noble Truth of the Origin of Suffering, the Noble Truth of the Extinction of Suffering, the Noble Truth of the Path that leads to the Extinction of Suffering." Vast teachings have been given expressing the nature of these Four Noble Truths; but perhaps none have been as direct as this short expression from *The Aquarian Message* by Samael Aun Weor:

First Truth: To have absolute consciousness of pain and bitterness

Second Truth: Pain is the child of fornication, and whosoever spills the semen (reaches the orgasm) is a fornicator. This is a tremendous Truth!

Third Truth: We have an "I" that must be decapitated and dissolved in order to incarnate the Verb, the Christ.

Fourth Truth: We can only decapitate and dissolve the prince of this world, the "I," with the Arcanum A.Z.F.(White Tantrism).

Fourth Path: There are four basic divisions amongst spiritual schools:

1. The path of the Fakir: those who seek union with God through willpower; this includes those who practice Hatha Yoga, physical austerities (tapas), etc.

2. The path of the Monk : those who seek union with God through emotion; this includes those who practice Bhakti Yoga, whose religion is prayer, or music or devotional practices.

3. The path of the Yogi: those who seek union with God through the intellect; this includes those who practice Jnana Yoga, who study and memorize theories and doctrines, or through various forms of meditation.

4. The path of the well-balanced human being: includes those schools and religions which unify all three paths in one, under the equilibriating influence of chastity, and guided by the Three Factors: birth, death and sacrifice.

Gemmation: (ATMS) The formation of a new individual, either animal or vegetable, by a process of budding; an asexual method of reproduction; gemmulation; gemmiparity.

Hanasmuss: (plural: Hanasmussen) "The Twice Born who does not reduce his Lunar Ego to cosmic dust converts himself into an abortion of the Cosmic Mother. He becomes a Marut, and there exist thousands of types of Maruts. Certain oriental sects and some Muslim tribes commit the lamentable error of rendering cult to all of those families of Maruts. Every Marut, every Hanasmuss has in fact two personalities: one White and another Black (one Solar and another Lunar). The Innermost, the Being dressed with the Solar Electronic Bodies, is the White Personality of the Hanasmuss, and the pluralized "I" dressed with the Protoplasmic Lunar Bodies is the Hanasmuss' Black Personality. Therefore, these Maruts have a double center of gravity." In synthesis, everyone who has ego is a Hanasmuss. For more information, see the lecture entitled "The Master Key," available in the Thelema Press edition of Didactic Self-knowledge.

Hermaphrodite: A Hermaphrodite is a Human Being who physically produces sperms and ova within their own masculine and feminine sexual genitalia. In order to create they fecundate themselves; they physically unite the outcome of their own two sexual polarities (sperm and ovum) by means of willpower.

Hiram: A biblical personage; a skillful builder and architect whom King Solomon procured from Tyre for the purpose of supervising the construction of the Temple. According to the Masonic story, Hiram Abiff was murdered by three traitors who were subsequently found by twenty-seven Master Masons.

Homo Nosce Te Ipsum: Latin for the Greek phrase *gnothi seauton:* "Know thyself," a precept inscribed in gold letters over the portico of the temple at Delphi. Its authorship has been ascribed to Pythagoras, to several of the wise men of Greece, and to Phemonoe, a mythical Greek poetess. According to Juvenal, this precept descended from heaven.

Human Being: According to Gnostic anthropology, a true Human Being is an individual who has conquered the animal nature within and has thus created the Soul, the Mercabah of the Kabbalists, the Sahu of the Egyptians, the To Soma Heliakon of the Greeks: this is "the Body of Gold of the Solar Man." A true Human Being is one with the Monad, the Inner Spirit. A true Human Being has reconquered the innocence and perfection of Eden, and has become what Adam was intended to be: a King of Nature, having power of Nature. The Intellectual Animal, however, is controlled by nature, and thus is not a true Human Being. Examples of true Human Beings are all those great saints of all ages and cultures: Jesus, Moses, Mohammed, Krishna, and many others whose names were never known by the public.

Hydrogens: "The scientist Prout admitted in his time that the different elements of nature are condensations formed by the most simple of elements, Hydrogen. There exist twelve fundamental types of Hydrogen; they correspond to twelve categories of matter that are contained in the universe from the Absolute down to the Infernal Worlds." - Samael Aun Weor, from The Doomed Aryan Race, ch. 5. In Universal Gnosticism, the term Hydrogen refers to fundamental matter, the varying levels of which are distinguished by their atomic weight. The most elevated forms of matter are the simplest while the most dense are the most complex.

Hyperboreans: A nation mentioned in Greek mythology. The name means "beyond the North Wind," thus they are supposed to have been somewhere north of Greece, but the name also means "beyond the mountains" and "those who carry (merchandise) across." Apollo was said to spend the winter months among them, and his mother Leto was presumed to have been born in their land. Perseus went there seraching for the Gorgon, and Heracles chased the Cerynitian hind to their country. The writer Pindar represented them as a blessed people untouched by human afflictions. H. P. Blavatsky places their country around the North Pole, saying it was "The Land of the Eternal Sun," beyond Boreas, the God of Winter. She asserts that this land was of a near tropical climate.

Illiaster: The primordial seed of creation.

Intellectual Animal: When the Intelligent Principle, the Monad, sends its spark of consciousness into Nature, that spark enters into manifestation as a simple mineral. Gradually, over millions of years, that spark gathers experience and evolves up the chain of life until it perfects itself in the level of the mineral kingdom. It then graduates into the plant kingdom, and subsequently into the animal kingdom. With each ascension the spark receives new capacities and higher grades of complexity. In the animal kingdom it learns procreation by ejaculation. When that animal intelligence enters into the human kingdom, it receives a new capacity: reasoning, the intellect; it is now an animal with intellect: an Intellectual Animal. That spark must then perfect itself in the human kingdom in order to become a complete and perfect Human Being, an entity that has conquered and transcended everything that belongs to the lower kingdoms. Unfortunately, very few Intellectual Animals perfect themselves; most remain enslaved by their animal nature, and thus are reabsorbed by Nature, a process belonging to the Devolving side of life and called by all the great religions Hell or the Second Death.

Kali Yuga: (Sanskrit) The fourth, the black or Iron Age, our present period.

Kalki Avatar: (Sanskrit) According to the prophesies of India, in his tenth and final incarnation Lord Vishnu will incarnate himself as the Avatar Kalki, who will come riding his white horse and with his blazing sword in his hands. At the end of Kali Yuga (the present eon) He will punish all evil doers in this world, destroy this world, and recreate a golden age again. As it says in the ancient *Vishnu Purana:*

> When the practices taught by the Vedas and the institutes of law shall nearly have ceased, and the close of the Kali age shall be nigh, a portion of that Divine Being who exists of his own spiritual nature in the character of Brahma, and who is the beginning and the end and who comprehends all things shall descend upon the earth. He will be born as Kalki in the family of an eminent brahmin, of Sambhala village, endowed with the eight superhuman faculties. By his irresistible might, He will destroy all the barbarians and thieves, and all whose minds are devoted to iniquity. He will then reestablish righteousness upon earth, and the minds of those who live at the end of the Kali age shall be awakened and shall be as pellucid as crystal. The men who are thus changed by virtue of that peculiar time shall be as the seeds of human beings and shall give birth to a race who shall follow the laws of the Krita Age, the Age of Purity. - Vishnu Purana 4.24

This is the Buddha Maitreya of the Mahayana Buddhists, Sosiosh of the Zoroastrians, and "The Faithful and True" of the book of The Revelations of St. John 19:

> And I saw heaven opened, and behold a white horse; and he that sat upon him was called Faithful and True, and in righteousness he doth judge and make war. His eyes were as a flame of fire, and on his head were many crowns; and he had a name written, that no man knew, but he himself. And he was clothed with a vesture dipped in blood: and his name is called The Word of God. And the armies which were in heaven followed him upon white horses, clothed in fine linen, white and clean (without ego). And out of his mouth goeth a sharp sword (the Word, the

knowledge), that with it he should smite the nations: and he shall rule them with a rod of iron (Iron is the metal of Mars, of Samael): and he treadeth the winepress of the fierceness and wrath of Almighty God. And he hath on his vesture and on his thigh (next to the phallus) a name written, KING OF KINGS, AND LORD OF LORDS.

Krumm-Heller, Dr. Arnold (Huiracocha): Arnold Krumm-Heller was born Arnold Krumm on April 15, 1876. At the age of sixteen, he left to meet some family in South America for work. There he traveled extensively, where he supposedly learned healing methods and medicinal techniques from the native Indians in Argentina, Chile and so on. In his early twenties, he went back to Germany where he entered into the initiatic fraternity of the "Rose Cross." Later, he returned to Latin America and established various initiatic institutions called "Fraternatis Rosicruciana Antiqua" (The Ancient Rosecrucian Fraternity). He established himself in Mexico City where he made the center of his initiatic fraternity. He was made the Dean of Linguistics at the University of Mexico City, was of high rank in the Mexican Army, and was also made a Doctor of Medicine at the University of Berlin. He was known by his Inner Name, Huiracocha, who is one of the Venerable Masters of the Ray of Medicine and Science. Samael Aun Weor, as a young man, was trained in the initiatic institution set up by Huiracocha (as described in The Three Mountains). Arnold Krumm-Heller (Heller was his mother's maiden name, hyphenated as is the custom in Mexico) wrote many books on esotericism and the Rosecrucian Brotherhood. One of his best known works was "Iglesia Gnostica" (in English:"Gnostic Church"). Krumm-Heller expressed his disgust for the "dead teachings" of the esoteric institutions that were springing up in the first part of the 20th century. He exclaimed that a living teaching had been preserved by certain small groups of Indians in Peru, Colombia and other places in Latin America. Rather than just read about mystics in far off places, he said that the real knowledge was accessible to anyone who sought for it. He said that he never ran off to India to eat roots and wear rags (as many Theosophists of his time were doing). Rather, he exclaimed that the true teachings can be accessible to anyone who put into practice certain esoteric exercises and seek for the Truth Within.

Kundabuffer organ: "In ancient times (due to a certain mistake performed by some Sacred Individuals) humanity developed the negative side of the Sexual Center, its Tenebrous Luciferic Aspect.

When the Electronic Sexual Fire is directed downwards into the Atomic Infernos of the human being, it becomes the Abominable Kundabuffer Organ, the Tail of Satan. Fortunately, after its development, such Luciferic Organ vanished from humanity; nevertheless, its fatal consequences still remain. It is urgent to know that the disastrous consequences of the abominable Kundabuffer Organ remained deposited within the five cylinders of the Human Machine. It is indispensable to know that the evil consequences of the Abominable Kundabuffer Organ constitute the Lunar Ego, the Pluralized I." - Samael Aun Weor, from The Doomed Aryan Race, ch. 10. For a full explanation, see The Elimination of Satan's Tail by the same author.

Level of Being: "The level of Being of the drunkard is different from that of the abstemious one, and the level of Being of the prostitute is different from that of the virgin... If we imagine the numerous rungs of a ladder which extends itself upwards, vertically... Unquestionably, we find ourselves on any one of those rungs. On lower rungs will be people worse than us, and on the higher rungs persons better than us will be found." See Revolutionary Psychology by the same author.

Loedere: (Latin) To hurt, to damage, to bruise, to break, etc. The word carries in itself the idea of a sudden violent action due to an exterior agent: a wound because of a hit, a fall, a crash, a cut, a burn.

Logos: (Greek, "word") In Greek and Hebrew metaphysics, the unifying principle of the world. The central idea of the Logos is that it links God and man, hence any system in which the Logos plays a part is monistic. The Logos is the manifested deity of every nation and people; the outward expression or the effect of the cause which is ever concealed. Thus, speech is the Logos of thought; hence it is aptly translated as the Verb, the Word. The First Logos is the Father, the sephiroth Kether; the Second Logos is the Son, the sephiroth Chochmah, and the Third Logos is the Holy Spirit, the sephiroth Binah. These three are one; the tri-unity.

Macrocosmos: (Greek) Macro means "great, large." Cosmos means "order, harmony, the world (from its perfect order and arrangement)." In Universal Gnosticism, the term macrocosmos can refer to the universe in general, or specifically to a galaxy, which is one of seven levels of the whole creation.

Mahachoan: (Sanskrit) Maha means "great," Chohan means "lord." A Great Lord, or ruler of a cosmic heirarchy.

Mahamanvantara: (Sanskrit) "Great Cosmic Day." A period of activity, as opposed to a Mahapralaya, a cosmic night or period of rest.

Manu: (Sanskrit) From Hindu mythology, the progenitor and lawgiver of the human race. From H.P. Blavatsky: "Who was Manu, the son of Swayambhuva? The secret doctrine tells us that this Manu was no man, but the representation of the first human races evolved with the help of the Dhyan-Chohans (Devas, Elohim) at the beginning of the first round. But we are told in his Laws (Book I. 80) that there are fourteen Manus for every Kalpa -- or interval from creation to creation -- and that in the present divine age, there have been as yet seven Manus... We are told in the Sacred Hindu scriptures that the first Manu produced six other Manus (seven primary Manus in all), and these produced in their turn each seven other Manus (Bhrigu I, 61-63) -- the production of the latter standing in the occult treatises as 7 x 7. Just as each planetary Round commences with the appearance of a 'Root Manu' (Dhyan Chohan) and closes with a 'Seed-Manu,' so a Root and a Seed Manu appear respectively at the beginning and the termination of the human period on any particular planet."

Master atom: "The mental body has an atomic nucleus which serves as its base. This nucleus is the Master Atom of the mind. This Master Atom contains the whole wisdom of Nature. Whosoever learns how to be in communication with this atom through meditation will be taught and instructed in the cosmic wisdom, since this atom is a sage. This Master Atom resides in our seminal system. By practicing Sexual Magic, this atom rises towards our head and then illuminates us in the world of the mind." - from The Revolution of Beelzebub

Materialist: In the esoteric sciences, a "materialist" is one who only believes in what his five senses can tell him, thus he relies exclusively on the data of the sensory, third dimensional world. This type of person has no understanding of the superior senses or the superior dimensions, and thus is limited to what he can perceive physically. As C.W. Leadbeter said, "It is one of the commonest of mistakes to consider that the limit of our power of perception is also the limit of all there is to see."

Microcosmos: (Greek) Micro means "small, little, trivial, slight." Cosmos means "order, harmony, the world (from its perfect order and arrangement)." In Universal Gnosticism, the term microcosmos refers to the human being, who is a universe in minature.

Monad: (Latin) From monas, "unity; a unit, monad." "(The number) one is the Monad, the Unity, Iod-Heve or Jehovah, the Father who is in secret. It is the Divine Triad that is not incarnated within a Master who has not killed the ego. He is Osiris, the same God, the Word." - Tarot and Kabbalah "When spoken of, the Monad is referred to as Osiris. He is the one that has to Self-realize Himself... Our own particular Monad needs us and we need it. Once, while speaking with my Monad, my Monad told me, 'I am self-realizing Thee; what I am doing, I am doing for Thee.' Otherwise, why are we living? The Monad wants to Self-realize and that is why we are here. This is our objective."

Noah: See Vaivasvata Manu.

Oviparous: (Latin; oviparus; ovum egg + parere to bring forth) Producing young from eggs; as, an oviparous animal, in which the egg is generally separated from the animal, and hatched after exclusion. Quoted from Webster's Revised Unabridged Dictionary

Pralaya: (Sanskrit) A period of repose or rest.

Protoplasmatic: (from protoplasm - the living substance of a cell)

Rajas: One of the three Gunas, or primordial qualities. From the Mahabarata:

> Brahma said: I shall now declare to you accurately what the quality of Passion (Rajas) is. Injuring others, beauty, toil, pleasure and pain, cold and heat, lordship (or power), war, peace, arguments, dissatisfaction, endurance, might, valour, pride, wrath, exertion, quarrel, jealousy, desire, malice, battle, the sense of meum or mineness, protection of others, slaughter, bonds, and affliction, buying and selling, lopping off, cutting, piercing and cutting off the coat of mail that another has worn, fierceness, cruelty, vilifying, pointing out the faults of others, thoughts entirely devoted to worldly affairs, anxiety, animosity, reviling of others, false speech, false or vain gifts, hesitancy or doubts, boastfulness of speech, praise and criticisms, laudation, prowess, defiance, attendance (as on the weak and the sick), obedience (to the commands of preceptors and parents), service or ministrations, harbouring of thirst or desire, cleverness or dexterity of conduct, policy heedlessness, contumely, possessions, and diverse decorations that prevail in the world among men, women, animals, inanimate things, houses, grief,

incredulousness, vows and regulations, actions with expectation (of good result), diverse acts of public charity, the rites in respect of Swaha salutations, rites of Swadha and Vashat, officiating at the sacrifices of others, imparting of instruction, performance of sacrifices, study, making of gifts, acceptance of gifts, rites of expiation, auspicious acts, the wish to have this and that, affection generated by the merits of the object for which or whom it is felt, treachery, deception, disrespect and respect, theft, killing, desire of concealment, vexation, wakefulness, ostentation, haughtiness, attachment, devotion, contentment, exultation, gambling, indulgence in scandal, all relations arising out of women, attachment to dancing, instrumental music and songs – all these qualities have been said to belong to the quality of Passion (Rajas).

Samadhi: (Sanskrit) Literally means "union" or "combination" and it's Tibetan equivilent means "adhering to that which is profound and definitive." Related terms include satori, ecstasy, manteia, etc. Samadhi is a state of consciousness. In the west, the term is used to describe an ecstatic state of consciousness in which the Essence escapes the painful limitations of the mind (the "I") and therefore experiences what is real: the Being, the Great Reality. There are many levels of Samadhi. In the sutras and tantras the term Samadhi has a much broader application whose precise interpretation depends upon which school and teaching which is using it.

Sensual Mind: From Gnostic Psychology, one of the three types of mind. "Unquestionably, the Sensual Mind develops its basic concepts via external sensory perceptions. Under these conditions the Sensual Mind is terribly crude and materialistic. It cannot accept anything which has not been physically demonstrated. Since the fundamental concepts of the Sensual Mind are based on external sensory data, undoubtedly it can know nothing about what is real, about the truth, about the mysteries of life and death, about the Soul and the Spirit, etc. For the rogues of the intellect, totally trapped by their external senses and incarcerated within the basic concepts of the Sensual Mind, our esoteric studies are lunacy." - Samael Aun Weor, The Great Rebellion, ch. 12

Staurus: A cross in the shape of an X, related to the Hebrew letter Tav.

Tamas: One of the three Gunas, or primordial qualities. From the Mahabarata:

Complete delusion, ignorance, illiberality, indecision in respect of action, sleep, haughtiness, fear, cupidity, grief, censure of good acts, loss of memory, unripeness of judgment, absence of faith, violation of all rules of conduct, want of discrimination, blindness, vileness of behaviour, boastful assertions of performance when there has been no performance, presumption of knowledge in ignorance, unfriendliness (or hostility), evilness of disposition, absence of faith, stupid reasoning, crookedness, incapacity for association, sinful action, senselessness, stolidity, lassitude, absence of self-control, degradation, - all these qualities are known as belonging to Darkness (Tamas).

Whatever other states of mind connected with delusion exist in the world, all appertain to Darkness. Frequent ill-speaking of other people, censuring the deities and the Brahmanas (priests), illiberality, vanity, delusion, wrath, unforgiveness, hostility towards all creatures, are regarded as the characteristics of Darkness. Whatever undertakings exist that are unmeritorious (in consequence of their being vain or useless), what gifts there are that are unmeritorious (in consequence of the unworthiness of the donee, the unseasonableness of the time, the impropriety of the object, etc.), vain eating, - these also appertain to Darknesss (Tamas).

Indulgence in calumny, unforgiveness, animosity, vanity, and absence of faith are also said to be characteristics of Darkness. Whatever men there are in this world who are characterised by these and other faults of a similar kind, and who break through the restraints provided by the scriptures, are all regarded as belonging to the quality of Darkness.

Thelema: (Greek) Willpower.

Theosophical septenary: "The different pseudo-esoteric and pseudo-occult schools affirm emphatically that the human being possess seven bodies:

1. The first one is called physical body, it is the famous Stula-Sarira of the Oriental theosophists.

2. The second one in Orient is called Linga-Sarira or Vital body and is the base of the organic life, the tetra-dimensional part of the physical body.

3. The third body is Kamas, the principle of desire, the famous Astral body cited by the medieval alchemists.

4. The fourth body is called the Mental body by the Hindustani and Inferior Manas in Sanskrit.

5. The fifth vehicle is the Causal body or Arupic as is called by the theosophists.

6. The sixth body is the Buddhic or Intuitional, the Superlative Consciousness of the Being.

7. The seventh is called Atman the Ineffable by the Hindustani... the Innermost. Certainly, the ancient wisdom says: "Before that the false aurora ..... It is necessary to adore and worship the Innermost." - Samael Aun Weor

Three-brained biped: Gnostic Psychology recognizes that humanoids actually have three centers of intelligence within: an intellectual brain, an emotional brain, and a motor/instinctive/sexual brain. These are not physical brains; they are divisions of organized activity. Each one functions and operates independent of the others, and each one has a host of jobs and duties that only it can accomplish. Of course, in modern humanity the three brains are grossly out of balance and used incorrectly. See Revolutionary Psychology by the author.

Universal Flood: The story of the Flood is present in histories and mythologies around the world.

Vaivasvata Manu: From *The Secret Doctrine* by H. P. Blavatsky: "In one case it has reference to that mystery when mankind was saved from utter destruction, by the mortal woman being made the receptacle of the human seed at the end of the Third Race, and in the other to the real and historical Atlantean submersion. In both cases the "Host" — or the Manu which saved the seed — is called Vaivasvata Manu. Hence the diversity between the Puranic and other versions; while in the Sathapatha Brahmana, Vaivasvata produces a daughter and begets from her the race of Manu; which is a reference to the first human Manushyas, who had to create women by will (Kriyasakti), before they were naturally born from the hermaphrodites as an independent sex, and who were, therefore, regarded as their creator's daughters. The Purânic accounts make of her (Ida or Ila) the wife of Buddha (Wisdom), the latter version referring to the events of the Atlantean flood, when Vaivasvata, the great Sage on Earth, saved the Fifth Root-race from being destroyed along with the remnants of the Fourth. This is shown very clearly in the Bhagavad Gitâ, where Krishna is made to say: — "The Seven great Rishis, the four preceding Manus, partaking of my essence, were born from my mind: from them sprung (were born) the human races and the world." (Chapter X., verse 6). Here the four preceding "Manus," out of the seven, are the four Races which have already lived, since Krishna belongs to the Fifth Race, his death having inaugurated the Kali Yuga. Vaivasvata Manu, the son of Surya (the Sun), and the saviour of our Race, is connected with the Seed of Life, both physically and spiritually."

Glossary

Aaron 50, 151, 157
Abbadon 140
Abbe Alphonse Louis Constant 186
Abif 199, 286
Abiram 199
Abortion 286
Abraham 222
Abraxas 72, 105
Absolute 35, 37, 41, 65, 83, 94, 122-123, 163, 190-191, 195-196, 216, 220, 223, 225-227, 245, 257, 285, 287
Absolute Abstract Space 196, 257
Absolute Space 163, 195, 245
Abstemious 290
Abstract 163, 195-196, 245, 257
Abyss 58, 61-62, 66, 71, 84, 90, 105, 118, 122, 137, 139, 145, 153, 155, 157, 160, 162-163, 165, 169-172, 174-175, 178-179, 182, 194-198, 200, 203, 205-206, 215, 222-231, 236, 244, 257, 267
Acheron 190
Action 19, 24, 26, 186, 237, 247, 250, 275, 283-284, 290, 294
Actions 17, 146, 283, 293
Activity 40, 160-161, 254, 291, 295
Actors 107
Acts 51, 58, 84, 96, 137, 282, 293-294
Adam 14, 131, 286
Adept 264, 284
Adepts 162
Adoration 32, 34-35, 122, 220-221
Adore 107, 123, 256, 295
Adulterated 17
Adulteries 189
Adulterous 189
Adultery 70-72, 97, 107, 132, 134, 181
Advent 49
Affirm 16, 79, 111, 172, 186, 294
Affirmation 121

Affirmations 109
Affliction 139, 153, 222, 292
Afflictions 287
Africa 17
African 114
Age of Iron 1-2, 18, 160, 169
Age of Purity 288
Ages 1-2, 17-18, 26, 73, 280, 287
Aggregate 275, 283
Aggregates 271, 274
AGLA 23, 26, 253
Agni 63
Ain 163, 195, 197, 245, 257
Ain Soph 163, 195, 197, 245, 257
Air 3, 42, 81, 94-95, 104, 137, 198, 200-201, 246-247
Airplanes 140, 173, 199
Akash 75, 223
Akashic 223
Alchemical 34, 152, 242
Alchemist 147-148, 171, 217-218, 241, 246-247
Alchemists 187, 196, 247, 294
Alchemy 39, 65, 89, 104, 109, 121, 124, 167, 177, 196-197, 213, 239, 241-242, 250, 264, 281
Alcohol 249
Alcoholism 189
Alcyone 264-271, 277
Aleph 284
Alert 76, 202, 282
Alexandre Dumas 217
Alexandria 242, 281
Aliin 170
Allah 147
Allegorically 281
Allegorized 264, 282
Alleluia 213, 231
Alliance 21, 157
Almighty 33, 90, 104, 122, 157, 187, 193, 198, 215, 251, 289
Almighty God 215, 289
Almizcle 148
Alpha 33-34, 235, 259

Alphonse 186
Alps 246
Altar 58, 67, 79, 104-105, 115, 129, 131, 141, 151, 182, 193
Altotas 220
Altruism 197
Amen 33, 45, 91, 109, 126, 213, 261
America 8-9, 13, 15, 113, 289
American 24, 26, 182
American Gnostic Liberation Action 26
Americans 8
Amethyst 249
Anagarikas 162
Analyze 64, 197
Anatomy 47, 182
Andes 246
Androgyne 238
Androgynos 279
Androgynous 13, 279, 284
Androids 3, 5
Andros 279
Angel Harpocrates 95
Angelic 197, 226-227
Angelical 279
Anger 115, 163, 179, 197, 205, 219, 271, 273, 283
Anglo-Saxon 7, 198
Angry 157, 273
Anguish 119
Anguished 33-34, 107
Anima 94-95
Animal 16, 51, 105, 137, 196, 215, 236, 265, 285-288, 292
Animalistic 167
Animals 16-17, 94, 104, 268, 270, 288, 292
Anna 217
Annihilate 191, 197, 221
Annihilated 11, 64, 68, 90-91, 197
Annihilates 197
Annihilation 62, 90
Anoint 91
Anointed 46, 50, 172, 281
Antakarana 225
Antediluvian 281
Anthropology 286

Anthropophagi 4
Antichrist 20, 132, 143, 157, 161
Antimony 281
Antipas 65
Antiqua 289
Antiquitatem 281
Antiquity 281, 283
Antithesis 163, 193, 197, 257
Antithetic 229
Antoinette 219
Anus 57
Anxiety 292
Apas 59, 198
Ape 116
Apes 11, 13, 182
Apocalypse 19, 23, 25, 30, 45, 98, 183, 258
Apocalyptic 4, 23-24, 33, 107, 129, 227
Apocrypha 280
Apocryphal 185, 280
Apollo 287
Apollonius of Tyana 94
Apollyon 140
Apostle 19, 43
Apostles 40, 57, 146, 210, 239
Apostolic College 135
Apothecaries 281
Apples 17
April 157, 289
Aqua 236
Aquarian 24, 30-31, 101, 117, 135, 209, 214, 233, 258, 261, 263, 280, 285
Aquarian Age 24, 30, 117, 135, 209, 214
Aquarian Message 30-31, 101, 214, 233, 258, 261, 263, 280, 285
Aquarius 1, 9, 25, 108, 135, 201, 221, 223, 263
Arab 114
Araucans 8
Arcadia 82
Arcana 175, 277
Arcanum 38-39, 51, 80, 84, 104-105, 113-114, 123-126, 141, 143, 148-151, 154-156, 159, 161,

167-168, 171, 175, 177, 179-181, 191-192, 197, 215-223, 226-227, 231, 236, 239, 241, 260, 285
Arcanum A. Z. F. 51, 80, 84, 123-124, 126, 148-149, 154, 159, 161, 167-168, 171, 179-181, 191, 197, 215-223, 226, 231, 236, 260, 285
Archaic 39
Archangelic 197
Archangels 2, 197, 256, 284
Archbishop 218
Architect 286
Archivists 120
Ardis 185
Ares 279-280
Argentina 289
Argona 27
Ariman 162
Aristocratic 219
Ark 50, 84, 119, 157, 171
Ark of Alliance 157
Ark of Science 84, 119, 157, 171
Ark of Testimony 157
Armageddon 199
Armed 90, 114, 140, 143, 199
Armies 140, 143, 214, 224, 288
Armon 185
Arms 28, 124, 129, 239
Army 23, 26, 35, 43, 74, 77, 114, 141, 224, 279, 284, 289
Arnold Krumm-Heller 289
Arrogance 117
Arrow 51
Artist 41
Arupic 295
Aryabarta 24, 26
Aryan 1, 7-9, 17, 135, 155, 279, 287, 290
Aryan Race 1, 279, 287, 290
Aryan Root Race 7-9, 17, 135, 155
Asanas 244
Ascend 79, 81, 116, 152, 203, 205, 223, 244, 282
Ascended 81, 129, 153-154, 160
Ascendeth 153, 178

Ascending 120, 151, 154
Ascends 75, 125, 153, 155, 179, 203, 244
Ascension 85, 244, 287
Ascetic 283
Aser 124
Asexual 279, 285
Ashamed 282
Ashes 19, 82, 193, 207, 209
Ashrama 26
Asia 3, 7, 20, 279
Asleep 28, 54, 95, 237, 253-255
Aspirant 87, 89
Aspire 68, 87, 89-90
Aspiring 218
Assassinated 65, 120
Assassination 65
Assassins 45, 257
Assisi 94
Astral 40, 45, 47, 81-82, 117, 139, 178, 186, 195, 199, 205, 221, 224, 236-238, 253-256, 274, 294
Astral Bodies 40, 117, 139
Astral Body 40, 45, 47, 81-82, 199, 205, 221, 236-237, 253-256, 274, 294
Astral Light 186
Astral Plane 178, 255
Astral Travel 221, 254
Astral World 274
Astrologers 9
Astrologist 17
Astrology 245, 282
Astronauts 266, 269
Astronomers 9, 11
Astronomical 281
Atheism 170
Atheistic 131
Atheists 116, 129, 131
Atlantean 1-5, 11, 113, 185, 270, 295
Atlanteans 1-4
Atlantic 7, 15
Atlantic Ocean 7
Atlantis 1, 3-4, 7-8, 11, 15, 20, 185
Atman 295
Atmic 37

Atmosphere 16, 115, 117, 134-135, 200
Atom 65, 87-89, 93-95, 163, 195, 197, 245-246, 265, 267, 284, 291
Atomic 2-4, 20, 24, 43, 45, 57-58, 60, 64-65, 70, 77, 79, 84, 87-88, 91, 103, 106, 113, 115, 118, 134, 139-141, 143, 162-163, 173, 193, 199, 202, 209-210, 224, 236, 239, 257, 273, 287, 290-291
Atoms 49, 79-80, 86-87, 89, 110, 254, 265, 267
Atrophied 4, 14
Attached 39, 90
Attachment 90, 293
Augeias 113
Augoeides 35, 111
August 24, 59
Augustine 281
Aun Weor 21, 30, 221, 280, 283, 285, 287, 289-290, 293, 295
Aura 88-89, 215
Auras 88
Aureole 103
Aurora 250, 295
Auspicious 293
Austere 39
Austerities 285
Austral 1
Australia 11
Autumn 1-2
Avalokiteshvara 37, 280
Avarice 283
Avatar 30, 42, 201, 214, 280, 288
Avatar Kalki 30, 280, 288
Avatars 280
Avitchi 162, 224
Awake 55, 75, 148, 167
Awaken 46, 53, 75, 82, 216, 241, 246, 254-255
Awakened 55, 242, 244, 256, 258, 288
Awakening 47, 54, 57, 79, 152-153, 244
Awakens 46, 50, 54, 57, 59, 79, 83, 85, 215, 236
Awakes 59, 255
Aware 75, 282
Awareness 54
Azasel 186
Azoth 131, 246
Aztec Calendar 11-12
Aztecs 8, 12, 242
B. C. 281
Ba Ba 253-254
Babaji 42
Babel 116-117, 224
Babylon 19, 116-117, 121, 135-136, 143, 153, 155, 178, 201, 203, 206-209, 211, 226
Bacteria 271-272
Balaam 65
Balac 65
Balsam 76, 281
Balsamo 217
Banana trees 147
Banquet 35, 37, 61, 76, 217
Baptized 272
Barbarian 170
Barbarians 200, 288
Barbaryan 279
Barley 114
Barnard 11
Baroness of Oberkirch 218
Barquisimeto 23
Basil Valentine 281
Bastille 218
Battle 20, 27, 140, 162, 170, 198-199, 230, 292
Battles 27, 162, 214, 224
Bautista 32
Beast 18-20, 49, 100, 104, 113-114, 122, 153, 160, 169-170, 172-174, 177-179, 187, 189, 194-195, 198, 203-206, 224, 230-231
Beasts 18, 49, 98, 104-105, 108-109, 113-114, 123, 126, 152, 169, 171, 173, 175, 177, 182, 188, 210, 213, 248
Beatitude 55, 80, 83

Beautiful 4, 8, 17, 46, 63, 75-76, 107, 119, 127, 147, 218, 241
Beauty 47, 73, 292
Bed 54, 70-71, 73, 95, 237, 277
Bedroom 95
Beds 4, 97, 107, 256
Beelzebub 291
Beethoven 69
Beheaded 231
Being 1-2, 9-10, 16-17, 27-28, 34-35, 43, 45, 49, 58, 61, 63, 68, 75, 78-79, 84, 87-88, 92-93, 95, 97-99, 103-107, 109-111, 113, 116, 124, 126-127, 132-133, 139-141, 151, 154-155, 158-161, 163, 168-170, 175, 177, 179, 183, 195-196, 198, 205, 213, 216-217, 220, 230, 235-239, 241, 243-245, 249, 251, 258-259, 264-266, 270-271, 273-276, 279-280, 282, 284-288, 290, 292-295
Belief 219
Beliefs 67
Believe 5, 11, 20, 27, 29, 109, 119, 266, 270
Believes 170, 250, 291
Bell 34, 68
Bellows 243-244
Belly 49, 64, 127, 146, 154, 246
Belonte 217
Beloved 26, 33-35, 43, 45, 54, 58-59,
Benares 94-95
Beni-Elohim 274
Benjamin 58, 124
Berlin 178, 289
Beryl 249
Betray 206
Betrayed 58
Betraying 64
Betrays 123
Bewitched 272
Bhagavad Gitâ 295
Bhakti Yoga 285
Bheri 68
Bhrigu 291
Bible 14, 264

Biblical 5, 23, 286
Bile 200
Billions 87, 132-133, 137, 174
Binah 36, 61, 163, 290
Biped 295
Bird 82, 207-208
Birds 11, 15, 99, 207
Birth 158-161, 196, 243, 284-285, 288
Births 198
Bitterness 35, 51, 119, 133, 153, 161, 191-192, 285
Black 2, 4, 45, 65, 69-70, 84, 107, 113-115, 120-123, 131, 134, 160, 162-163, 186, 190, 199, 211, 214, 217, 219, 224, 229, 257, 264, 280, 283, 286, 288
Black Age 2
Black Dragon 45, 163, 199
Black Lodge 120-121, 160, 162-163, 214, 224, 229
Black Tantrism 65, 283
Blaspheme 170, 193
Blasphemed 193-195, 202
Blasphemies 115, 143, 170
Blasphemy 60, 100, 169-170, 203
Blavatsky 280, 287, 291, 295
Bleed 73, 88
Bleeding 80, 159
Bless 123
Blessed 14, 33, 39, 41-42, 58, 63, 67-69, 179, 199, 213, 231, 258, 260, 284, 287
Blessed One 33, 39, 41, 67
Blessing 109, 111, 126
Blind 91, 281
Blindness 281, 294
Bliss 54, 147, 284
Blissfulness 149
Blond 113
Bloody 71, 202
Blue 27, 33
Bodhi 280
Bodhisattva 110, 120, 133, 185-186, 212, 214, 224, 259, 280
Bodhisattvas 160, 186, 259

Bodies 1-2, 13, 19, 26, 40, 54, 85, 93, 117, 126, 139, 153-154, 170, 186, 195, 198, 221, 251, 256, 286, 294
Body 14, 26, 29, 34, 39-42, 45, 47, 54, 68, 70, 75, 81-82, 92-95, 97, 107, 120, 153-154, 185, 193, 196, 199, 205, 216, 218-221, 225, 235-237, 250, 253-256, 258, 274-276, 279, 286, 291, 294-295
Body of Will 199
Bolivia 15
Bomb 139, 141
Bombs 11, 24, 140, 143, 173, 199, 224
Bon 280
Bond 174, 224
Bondman 117
Bonds 292
Bone 26, 50
Bones 19, 42, 271
Bonfire 20, 266
Bons 162, 280
Book 23, 25-27, 29-30, 42, 45, 78, 80, 101, 107-109, 111, 145-146, 170-171, 181-182, 186, 203, 206, 214, 216-218, 223-225, 230, 236, 242, 252, 258-261, 280-281, 288, 291
Book of Enoch 186, 280-281
Book of Life 78, 80, 170-171, 230, 252, 260
Books 75, 132, 186, 230, 241-242, 283, 289
Brahma 88, 151, 288, 292
Brahmana 295
Brahmanadi 46
Brahmanas 294
Brahmans 220
Brahmin 288
Brain 2, 46, 49, 51, 79, 87, 89, 106, 190, 295
Brains 2, 283, 295
Brass 43, 48, 70-71, 143, 194, 210
Brave 113
Bravery 284

Brazen 105
Bread 68, 114, 165, 209
Breastplates 140, 143
Breasts 14, 187
Breath 35, 61, 237
Breathes 59
Breeze 33, 42, 122
Brethren 115, 156, 163, 214, 227, 251, 258-259
Bride 85, 211, 235-236, 260
Bridegroom 211
Bridles 183
Brimstone 143, 178, 224, 230, 236
Brother 23, 68, 89
Brotherhood 23, 289
Brothers 5, 23, 26, 64, 95, 107, 119, 159, 162, 168-169, 172, 192, 226, 263
Brugpa 283
Buddha 30, 60, 152, 179-181, 190-192, 213-215, 217, 219, 221, 223, 225, 227, 248, 280, 284, 288
Buddha Shakyamuni 284
Buddhas 192
Buddhi 205
Buddhic 161, 221, 295
Buddhic Body 221
Buddhism 181, 280
Buddhists 288
Burn 117, 206, 290
Burned 19, 43, 63, 95, 135, 193, 209
Burneth 236
Burning 103, 132-133, 209-210, 224, 226, 247, 281
Burning Valley 281
Burns 64, 193, 236
Burnt 131-132
Business 122, 210-211
But 2-3, 5, 7, 11, 13-15, 17-18, 26,
Cactuses 159
Cadavers 87
Caduceus 132, 190-191
Cage 207-208
Cagliostro 217-218, 220
Caiaphas 45
Calcium 266

Calculations 132-133, 266
Calendar 11-13
Calf 104, 211
Calumniate 85
Calumniating 85
Calumniator 83
Calumny 179, 294
Calvary 73
Cana 49
Canaanites 58
Canal 46, 49-50, 87, 104-105, 151, 168, 182, 191, 223, 228, 244
Canalis 46
Canals 46, 51, 79, 155, 244
Cancer 189, 193, 271
Cancerous 129
Cancro 272
Candelabra 46, 57
Candle 211, 258
Candlelights 99
Candlestick 46, 50-51, 58, 114
Candlesticks 43, 57, 152
Cannabalism 4
Cannons 27-28
Cape 216
Capital 203, 205
Captain 28
Captains 117, 223
Carbon 219, 266
Cardiac 244
Cardinal 141, 218
Cardinal Archbishop of Rohan 218
Caribbean Islands 11
Casay 27
Case 20, 94, 267, 273, 275, 295
Cases 265, 295
Caspian Sea 279
Cataclysm 78, 108, 117, 125, 132, 135, 155-156, 191, 200-202, 207, 209, 224, 235, 256
Cataclysmic 200
Cataclysms 23, 25, 115, 141, 165, 225
Catalina de Medici 220
Catastrophe 5, 11, 16, 19-20, 25, 129, 132-133, 156, 185, 200, 226, 265

Catastrophes 224-225
Catastrophic 5, 7, 16, 33, 264
Cathedral 45-46, 185
Cathodic 266
Cattle 49
Causal 199, 295
Causal Body 199, 295
Cause 15-16, 79, 165, 173, 224, 281, 290
Cause of Causes 281
Cavalry 214
Cavernous 83
Caverns 2-3, 39, 267
Cavities 81, 87
Cazotte 216-217
Cellular 13
Celtic 279
Censer 129, 131
Censure 294
Censuring 294
Center 51, 89, 264, 268, 286, 289
Centers 54, 67, 238, 241, 264, 275-276, 295
Centimeters 15
Central 7-8, 20, 37, 49, 191, 279, 290
Central Asia 279
Centralis 46
Centuries 2-3, 20, 29, 39, 41, 59, 121, 127, 160, 242, 250
Century 113, 120, 140, 165, 281, 289
Cerebral 89
Ceremonial 283
Ceremony 215
Cerynitian 287
Ch 287, 290, 293
Chain 229, 287
Chained 169
Chains 96-97, 250
Chakras 43, 46-47, 71, 81-82, 244
Chalcedony 249
Chaldea 7
Chalice 46, 51, 58, 68
Challenged 219
Chamber 50, 73
Chambers 119, 244
Change 10, 95, 146, 266, 269-270
Changed 288

Chaos 77, 264
Chariot 201, 281
Chariots 140, 210
Charitable 67
Charity 67, 70, 89, 97, 257, 293
Chased 287
Chaste 49, 64, 66, 85, 177, 221
Chasten 91
Chastity 65-66, 71, 91, 94, 97, 122-123, 155, 180-181, 190, 256-257, 285
Chemical 16
Chemistry 199, 270
Cherubim 50, 119
Chibchas 8
Chickens 129
Chief 26, 41, 117, 135, 229
Chiefs 186
Child 14, 28, 35, 71, 80, 107, 127, 134, 158-161, 165, 175, 191, 221-222, 226, 243, 254, 285
Childhood 253-254
Childlike 28, 83
Children 3-5, 11-15, 33, 65, 71, 84, 103, 122-123, 128-129, 132, 186, 189, 239, 274-275
Children of God 274
Chile 11, 23, 289
Chimpanzee 116
Chimpanzees 182
China 7, 114
Chinese 114
Chini-Chini 68
Chitra 46
Chohan 290-291
Chohans 279
Choir 34, 77
Chokmah 36, 61, 163, 280
Choral 41
Chotaban 69
Christian 67, 280-281
Christianity 2
Christic 66, 94, 207, 245, 249
Christification 26, 30, 94, 122, 242
Christified 84, 88, 90, 93, 98, 123, 236, 238, 246, 251
Christified Ones 84, 88, 238

Christify 165, 242
Christonic 64, 148, 187, 210, 238, 242, 249, 251, 256
Christonic Semen 64, 148, 187, 210, 238, 242, 249, 251, 256
Chrysolite 249
Chrysoprasus 249
Chur 34
Church 45, 57, 59-61, 63-67, 69-71, 73, 75-77, 79, 81, 83-85, 87, 89, 91, 118, 131, 163, 281, 289
Church of Laodicea 45, 87, 89, 91, 163
Church of Sardis 75-77, 79, 81
Church of Thyatira 67, 69-71, 73
Cinnamon 210
Circle 245, 282-283
Cities 4, 7, 15-16, 19, 58, 127, 134, 139, 173, 178, 193-194, 201, 209-210
Citizens 99, 113, 256
Civil 140
Civilization 1, 8, 19, 117, 178, 195, 201, 206-207, 209-211
Civilizations 8
Civilized 170
Clairvoyance 84-85, 94, 254
Clairvoyant 3, 83-85, 116, 254
Clairvoyants 85
Clement of Alexandria 281
Cleopatra 220
Cleverness 292
Climate 287
Clitoris 14
Coccygeal 50
Coccyx 57, 79, 228
Coitus 215, 243
Cold 4, 91, 122, 269, 292
Collision 117, 155, 200, 209
Collyrium 91, 281
Colombia 289
Color 63, 69, 71, 134, 203
Colors 83
Column 152, 282
Columns 23, 92, 119, 215, 220

Commandments 67, 168, 179, 181, 260, 283
Commands 21, 40, 185, 292
Companions 147
Compass 9, 282
Compassed 230
Compassion 39-41, 180, 243, 280
Compensation 205-206
Complex 287
Complexity 287
Complicate 127
Complicated 127, 196, 250
Complicates 127
Complication 196-197, 250
Compound 281-282
Compounds 270
Comprehend 75-76, 78, 98, 192, 221, 255, 269, 272-273, 275
Comprehended 255
Comprehending 255
Comprehends 264, 288
Comprehension 75, 180, 190, 222, 250
Comprehensive 76
Concentration 53, 221, 270, 284
Concept 110-111, 267
Conception 243
Conceptions 80, 160
Concepts 254, 293
Conceptual 75
Condemn 78
Condemned 41, 45, 218
Condemning 185
Condensations 77, 287
Connubial 59
Conscience 205
Conscious 167, 276, 279, 282
Conscious Will 276
Consciously 70, 78, 221, 237, 253-257, 275
Consciousness 45, 47, 54-55, 59, 64, 110, 122-123, 127-128, 152, 191, 195-196, 255-256, 279, 282, 284-285, 287, 293, 295
Consequence 17, 133-134, 268, 294
Consequences 156, 290
Conserving 95

Constellation 9, 110, 193, 263
Constellations 121, 251, 259
Contagious 271-272
Contemplate 51, 59, 119, 161, 256
Contemplating 83
Contemplation 54, 73
Contentment 293
Continent 1, 5, 11, 13, 113, 185
Continents 1, 10, 15, 269
Copper 1-2, 18, 266
Copto 217-218
Copulation 50
Cords 79, 107, 152, 191
Core 199
Coronary 88
Coronation 220
Corpse 4
Cosmic 9, 16, 23, 40, 68-69, 75, 77, 80, 87, 104, 110, 116, 122, 127, 134, 152, 156, 167, 171, 191, 193, 199-201, 207, 209-210, 251, 263, 267, 279, 284-286, 290-291
Cosmic Laws 279
Cosmic Movement 40
Cosmic Night 75, 77, 267, 291
Cosmic Scale 167
Cosmically 9
Cosmocreator 284
Cosmos 33, 81, 279, 290-291
Count Fenix 220
Count of St. Germain 218-219
Countries 9, 133, 183, 186, 217
Country 7, 16, 26, 42, 180, 219, 279, 287
Courage 284
Covenant 50
Covet 99
Cowards 236
Craftsman 211
Craniums 73
Create 3-4, 14, 58, 76, 162, 274, 276, 286, 295
Created 1, 14, 76, 106, 125, 145, 215, 274-277, 286
Creates 77, 123
Creating 15

Creation 41, 79, 91, 134, 248, 281, 287, 290-291
Creative 76-77, 79, 151, 155, 165, 190, 198, 222-223, 237, 277
Creator 196, 282, 295
Creature 109
Creatures 3, 17, 133, 247-248, 281-282, 294
Cricket 237
Cried 5, 115, 120, 126, 145, 158-161, 182, 207, 210, 223
Cries 58
Crime 41, 58, 207, 217
Crimes 189
Criminology 282
Critical 270
Criticisms 292
Criticize 67
Crookedness 294
Cross 28, 51, 58, 69, 72, 80, 89, 124-125, 137, 159, 190, 215, 229, 236, 241, 243, 246, 270, 289, 293
Crossbred 17
Crosses 28
Crosspiece 241
Crow 264
Crowded 143
Crowds 133, 143, 192-193
Crown 34-35, 46, 60-62, 73, 85, 87-90, 106, 113, 158-159, 181, 183
Crown of Life 34-35, 60-62
Crowned 160-161, 167
Crowns 89, 92, 100, 103, 106, 140, 160, 169, 214, 288
Cruce 31
Crucified 69, 72, 80, 89, 119, 153, 163, 229
Crucifies 58
Crucifixion 229
Crude 16, 125, 275, 293
Cruel 29, 73, 107
Cruelly 129, 131
Cruelty 292
Crushing 7
Cry 49, 84, 107, 146, 182

Crying 122, 181, 200, 235
Crypto 280
Crystal 103, 116, 238, 256, 288
Crystallize 4, 121
Cteis 78-79, 282-283
Cubic 103
Cubits 98, 248
Culminated 186
Cult 20, 286
Cultivate 67, 99
Cultivates 99
Cults 4
Culture 13, 179
Cultures 8, 287
Cup 49-50, 147, 157, 178, 201, 203, 209
Cup of Omer 157
Cupid 39
Cupidity 294
Cupola 45
Cups 119, 149
Cure 24, 193
Curse 146, 257
Cursed 49
Cusco 8
Custom 273, 289
Cut 16, 126, 220, 248, 290
Cuts 68
Cutting 292
Cycle 270
Cylinders 290
Cymbals 68
Cynics 179, 200
Dag Dugpas 283
Dagger 217
Daily 81, 114, 165, 198, 216, 270
Dainty 210
Dakini 283
Dalai Lama 282
Damage 42, 79, 265, 290
Damn 123
Damned 201
Dancing 293
Danger 28, 39, 123
Dangerous 90, 241, 271-272
Dangers 51
Daniel 18, 34, 64

Dante 152, 248
Dares 228
Dark 2, 7, 114
Darkened 134, 137
Darkness 4, 62, 65, 115, 125, 143, 153, 160-162, 173, 175, 194, 206, 266-267, 294
Darknesss 294
Data 291, 293
Date 9, 155, 263
Dathan 199
Daughter 295
Daughters 186, 295
David 84, 108, 260
Dawn 21, 34, 41, 77, 99, 260
Dawning 250
Dead 12, 39-43, 60, 77, 94, 117, 153-154, 157, 179, 192, 198, 218-219, 229-230, 289
Dean of Linguistics 289
Death 20, 27-29, 35, 39-40, 43, 45-46, 60-62, 69, 71, 73, 78, 114-116, 119, 131, 139, 153, 163, 165, 169, 189, 192, 209, 217-220, 223, 225, 230-231, 235-237, 257, 274, 284-285, 288, 293, 296
Debemos 101
Debir 281
Debts 132, 140
Decalogue 157, 283
Decapitate 45, 72-73, 78, 85, 104, 127-128, 191, 250, 285
Decapitated 72, 191, 285
Decapitates 179, 191
Decapitation 54
Decay 186, 284
Decoctions 281
Deeds 58, 62, 70-71, 76, 78, 171, 181, 183, 189, 194-196, 209, 230
Defeat 51, 73
Defeated 73, 92, 113, 163, 168
Defeating 105
Defects 20, 78, 197
Defends 167
Defiance 292
Defiled 78, 177

Defileth 252
Deformed 275
Degenerate 3, 13
Degenerated 4, 14, 16
Degeneration 189
Degradation 294
Degree 10, 160-162, 241, 282
Degrees 9, 46, 53-54, 67, 88, 91, 98, 220-221, 225, 241, 250, 279
Deities 294
Deity 290
Deka 283
Deliriums 272
Delphi 286
Deluge 7
Delusion 294
Demon 45, 161, 181, 195, 199, 225, 229
Demon of Desire 45, 199
Demon of Evil Will 45, 199
Demons 23, 62, 64, 66, 123, 139, 143, 185, 195-196, 199, 215, 223, 225-228, 259, 282
Demoralization 189
Dense 77, 125, 139, 196, 287
Deny 14, 51, 89, 264
Denyest 146
Denying 51
Descend 9, 49, 98, 116, 123, 126-127, 152, 154, 205, 243, 248, 282, 288
Descended 81, 113, 126, 185, 248, 283, 286
Descending 228, 237
Descends 58, 93, 125, 153, 228
Descent 197, 248
Describe 186, 293
Described 16, 53, 238, 280-281, 289
Descriptive 281, 284
Desert 17, 50
Deserve 148, 154
Deserved 120
Desire 45, 49, 64, 70, 75, 90, 110, 117, 122, 132, 139, 147-148, 179, 196-197, 199, 216, 221-222, 224, 249, 254, 292-294
Desired 63, 216

Desires 148, 178-179, 196, 250
Despise 68, 171-172
Despising 51
Destinies 3-4, 12
Destiny 5, 155, 160, 169, 185
Destroy 154, 157, 288
Destroyed 4-5, 16, 19, 113, 116, 120, 133, 135, 195, 209, 211, 267, 295
Destroying 15
Destruction 5, 11, 265, 295
Destructive 128
Detached 55
Detaching 237
Determinate 249
Determined 14
Devarajas 120, 141
Devas 279, 291
Devastating 17
Develop 64, 66-67, 70, 75, 81, 94, 97, 282
Developed 2-3, 14, 39, 88, 99, 124, 216, 284, 289
Developing 97
Development 50, 75, 83, 97, 244, 271, 273-274, 284, 290
Developmental 221
Develops 64, 83-84, 89, 215, 293
Devi 50
Deviation 268-269
Devices 4
Devil 60, 105, 162-163, 216-217, 229-230
Devils 143, 182, 198, 207-208
Devolution 284
Devolving 288
Devoted 288, 292
Devotee 73, 91, 105
Devotees 95, 97-98, 122-123
Devotion 293
Devotional 285
Devour 4, 18, 160-161
Devoured 11, 13, 15, 18, 230
Devoureth 152
Dew 64
Dexterity 292
Dharmasayas 76

Dhyan Chohans 279, 291
Dialectic 199, 211
Diameter 87
Diamond 76, 88, 127
Diamonds 217, 219
Diapason 69
Dictates 272
Dictatorships 192
Die 40, 49, 51, 78, 90, 99, 110, 127, 139, 156, 179-181, 225, 236, 270, 284
Died 40, 45, 65, 133, 192
Dies 78, 179
Digerere 79, 283
Dignity 152, 248
Diligent 282
Dimension 3, 15, 146
Dimensional 291
Dimensions 264, 291
Diminished 2
Dinner 40
Diplomacy 70
Diplomatic 140
Diplomats 139-140
Direct 5, 147, 237, 285
Directed 132, 140, 279, 290
Direction 16
Disappear 269
Disappeared 15, 218-219
Disappointed 222, 247
Disaster 226
Disastrous 290
Disbeliever 257
Disc 53
Disciple 53, 80, 159, 180, 217, 220, 237, 241, 253
Disciples 30, 40, 180, 218, 258, 283, 285
Disciplines 241
Discrimination 294
Discs 47, 81
Diseases 189, 193, 281
Disintegrate 62, 199, 236, 265, 275
Disintegrated 75, 78, 231
Disintegrates 265
Disintegration 25, 157
Dissolution 197

Dissolve 45, 72-73, 78, 81, 90, 127-128, 191, 197, 248, 250, 285
Dissolved 72, 127, 191, 196, 250, 285
Dissolves 179, 196-197, 250
Dissolving 196

Distractions 89
Diverse 18, 274, 292-293
Diversity 295
Divinae 101
Divine Being 245, 288
Divine Spouse 54, 129
Divinities 283
Divinity 23
Divorced 43, 61
Divorces 189
Doctor 289
Doctor of Medicine 289
Doctors 4, 79, 281
Doctrine 20, 23, 29-30, 65, 72, 111, 120-122, 128, 181, 258, 280, 291, 295
Doctrines 285
Dogs 260
Dominance 283
Dominate 94, 202, 242
Domini 31
Dominion 18
Doom 20, 201, 209-210
Doomed 287, 290
Door 45, 63, 84, 88, 92, 103, 131, 148, 151, 171, 222, 226
Doors 45, 55, 107, 119, 151, 156, 171
Dorje 283
Dorsal 190-191, 244, 249
Double 21, 68, 105, 173, 209, 286
Doubt 8, 16, 257, 271
Doubts 292
Dove 89
Downwards 124, 228-229, 241, 290
Dragon 34, 43, 45, 100, 159-163, 165, 167-170, 172-173, 192, 198-199, 229, 235, 245, 250
Dream 256
Dreamed 119
Dreamer 255

Dreaming 54
Dreams 7, 255
Drowsiness 53
Drukpas 162
Drum 68
Drunk 203, 207, 222
Drunkard 66, 290
Drunken 203
Drunkenness 65, 70
Dugpa 283
Dumas 217
Duties 295
Duty 29, 69, 226
Dynasties 2
Eagle 104, 165, 246
Eagles 18, 23, 167, 259
Ear 61, 66, 72, 75, 78, 85, 92, 94, 171, 220
Ears 217, 220
Earth 1-4, 9-11, 15-19, 23-25, 33, 39, 42, 46, 53, 57-58, 71, 73, 81, 85, 93, 103, 106-109, 113-117, 120, 124-125, 131, 134-135, 137, 139-141, 143, 145-146, 152-154, 156-157, 160, 162-163, 165, 167-168, 170, 172-173, 177-178, 180-182, 184-186, 189-190, 192-195, 198, 200-203, 206-207, 209-211, 213, 221, 224, 226-227, 230, 235, 238, 242, 246-247, 250-252, 256, 259, 266-269, 277, 280, 282-283, 288, 295
Earthquake 115, 117, 131, 155, 157, 200
Earthquakes 4-5, 11-12, 15-16, 19, 24, 45, 115, 134, 242
East 26, 37, 79, 99, 114, 120, 140, 152, 163, 198, 239, 267, 279
Easter 11, 62
Easter Island 11
Eclipse 9
Eclipses 263
Ecstasy 53-54, 67, 69, 83, 88, 104, 119, 220, 256, 293
Ecstatic 293

Eden 43, 49, 59, 63-64, 76, 82, 110, 131, 165, 171, 198, 226, 228, 286
Effigies 123
Effort 284
Egg 14, 243, 292
Eggs 292
Ego 20, 25, 45, 51, 69, 71, 135, 160, 179, 199, 283, 285-286, 288, 290, 292
Egos 127, 283
Egregores 185-186, 284
Egypt 7, 59, 153, 220, 237, 242
Egyptian 242
Egyptians 37, 286
Ehecatl 40
Eight 83, 93-94, 97-98, 190-191, 205, 284, 288
Eighteen 63, 127, 174, 185
Eighteenth Arcanum 175
Eightfold Path 190-192, 284
Eighth 68, 167, 181, 190, 215, 224, 249
Eighth Arcanum 167
Ejaculate 125, 257
Ejaculation 148, 177, 216, 287
Ejeculatium 125, 181, 238
Elder 34, 39, 61, 275-276
Elder of Days 34, 61, 275-276
Elderly 127, 221
Elders 87, 89, 103, 105-109, 126, 157, 177, 213
Electromagnetic 137
Electron 265
Electronic 272, 286, 290
Electrons 265
Element 19, 198, 265
Elemental 3
Elementals 3, 246
Elements 19, 117, 135, 141, 198, 246-247, 270-271, 287
Eleusis 242
Eleven 40
Eleventh 249
Elias 201
Eliminate 20, 271
Elimination 290

Eliphas Levi 131, 185-186, 217
Elixir 39-40, 185, 217, 219, 284
Elixir of Long Life 185, 284
Elixir of Longevity 39-40, 217, 219
Eloah 284
Elohim 279, 284, 291
Elohim Sabbaoth 279
Emanate 98, 163
Emanated 34, 106, 245
Emanates 33, 35, 54, 68, 106
Emerald 103, 125, 249
Emerald Tablet 125
Emotion 143, 271, 274-275, 283, 285
Emotional 295
Emotions 265, 270-276
Emperor 61
Empty 46, 51, 172, 254-255
Enchant 94
Enchanted 58, 76, 105
Enchantment 33
Enchantments 50, 57, 83
Endocrine 4, 47
Endurance 292
Endure 160, 238, 266, 268
Endured 3
Endures 1
Enemies 110, 116, 123, 131, 152, 154, 162, 181
Enemy 110, 123, 160
Eneregy 265
Energetic 79, 239, 251
Energies 165, 237, 241, 274, 276
Energy 3, 16-17, 81, 151, 155, 171-172, 186, 196-197, 223, 237, 239, 265-266, 274-275
Engendered 243
England 198, 218
English 7, 289
Engraving 6, 22, 44, 158, 176
Enjoy 99, 149, 258
Enjoys 90, 258
Enlightenment 280
Enoch 185-186, 280-281
Enoichion 280
Enos 280
Ens Seminis 46, 78-80, 103-105, 179-180, 284

Ens Virtutis 79, 284
Envy 2, 197, 205, 271-272, 283
Eon 288
Ephesus 57
Epidemics 134
Epiphyses 88
Epistle 135
Epoch 12, 14-15, 154, 185-186, 192, 220, 226, 259, 277
Epochs 160, 270
Equal 218, 245
Equalled 218
Equally 180
Equals 147, 152, 245
Equator 4, 10
Equatorial 269
Equilibriating 285
Equivilent 293
Era 1, 9, 19, 25, 181, 263, 281
Erin 279
Erotic 123
Error 160, 226, 243, 286
Errors 186, 192, 221
Erudite 241
Erudites 199
Eruptions 11
Escape 5, 15, 209-210, 219
Escaped 5, 14, 217
Escapes 89, 256, 293
Esculapius 132
Esoteric 13, 25, 88, 162, 187, 264, 280, 282, 289, 291, 293
Esotericism 289
Esoterism 26, 75
Esoterists 264
Essence 167, 179-180, 186, 280, 283, 293, 295
Essenes 242
Eternal 34-35, 39, 55, 58, 61, 69, 71, 76, 98-99, 115-116, 121, 131-132, 148, 187, 246, 248, 256-257, 281, 287
Eternal Beloved 34-35, 58
Eternal One 69, 71, 98-99, 115-116, 131, 187, 246, 248, 257
Eternally 45, 230
Eternities 62

Eternity 55, 172
Ether 75
Ethereal 195, 205, 254
Ethereal Body 205, 254
Ethnological 279, 281
Etymology 280
Euclid 265
Euphrates 141, 198
Europe 41, 220
Evaporate 247
Eve 49, 131, 167
Event 5, 7, 9-10, 16, 65, 73, 106, 116, 133, 156, 227, 263, 268-269, 271
Events 19-20, 23-24, 129, 134, 209, 263-264, 281, 295
Evil 3-4, 45, 57, 62-64, 71, 76, 78, 110, 127, 148, 160, 171, 182-183, 189, 196, 199, 209, 215, 229, 250, 257, 260, 288, 290
Evilness 127, 160, 170, 294
Evolution 14, 127-128, 174, 182, 193, 196-197, 221, 244, 250-251, 280, 284
Evolved 291
Evolves 127, 215, 227, 287
Evolving 127
Executioner 68, 122, 256
Exertion 292
Exhalation 104
Exhaled 81, 104
Exhausted 147
Exodus 157
Exotic 68
Experience 25, 29, 54, 61, 220, 287
Experienced 69, 81, 269
Experiences 127, 196, 250, 293
Experiencing 274
Expiate 160, 183
Expiation 155, 293
Expired 230
Eye 17, 33, 88, 91, 156, 281
Eyebrows 83, 87
Eyes 27-28, 43, 63, 70, 91, 104-105, 108, 126, 149, 214, 216, 218, 235, 281, 288
Eyesalve 91

Face 2, 5, 35, 58, 104, 118, 134-135,
    145, 149, 165, 167, 237, 257,
    266, 277
Faces 126, 140, 157
Factors 17, 285
Facts 263, 269-270
Factual 237, 263
Faculties 167, 239, 251, 257, 288
Faculty 53, 85
Fail 171-172
Failed 28, 174, 182, 195
Failing 135
Fails 179, 247
Failure 193-194
Failures 200
Fainted 28, 57
Fairies 3
Faith 65-66, 70, 97, 171, 179, 257,
    294
Faithful 35, 39, 60-62, 65-66, 73, 91,
    206, 214, 235, 258, 288
Fakir 285
Fall 19, 27, 90, 95, 105, 117-118,
    135, 137, 155, 160, 165, 210,
    226, 237, 253-255, 281, 290
Fallen 58, 133, 137, 160, 170, 178,
    186, 194, 205, 207-209, 211,
    229, 280-281
Fallen Angels 280-281
Falling 2, 39, 117, 170, 255
Falls 169, 186, 205, 257
False 20, 131, 140, 171, 179, 196,
    198-200, 222, 224, 230, 244,
    250, 260, 292, 295
Falsehood 146
Falsely 185
Falseness 275
Falsity 222
Familiar 28
Families 133, 183, 186, 286
Family 165, 183, 288-289
Famine 115, 134, 143, 209
Famous 46, 216-218, 243, 267, 294
Fanatic 244
Farmer 28
Fascinating 264
Fast 65, 72, 78, 85, 90

Fasting 152
Fatal 135, 163, 205-206, 230, 257,
    290
Fate 146
Father-mother 14
Fault 15, 58, 177
Faults 15, 292, 294
Fear 28, 43-44, 60, 64, 135, 154, 157,
    178, 187, 209-210, 213, 294
Fearful 192, 236
Feast 35
Feasts 70, 85, 91
Feather 94
Features 218, 281
February 9, 25, 161, 263, 266, 270
Fecundate 236, 247, 286
Fecundated 14, 77, 104, 125, 247
Fecundates 59, 68
Fecundity 133
Feel 29, 55, 214, 226, 272
Feeling 28, 55, 95, 97, 253, 271
Feelings 167, 180, 283
Female 14, 59, 77, 132, 167, 222,
    243, 279, 282-283
Feminae 125, 181, 238
Feminine 120-121, 286
Field 49, 87, 89, 180, 264, 270
Fields 27, 180
Fifteen 69
Fifth 3, 7, 12, 15, 54, 68, 89, 108,
    115, 122, 137-139, 169, 181,
    185, 190, 194-195, 198, 214,
    221, 223, 225, 227, 229, 249,
    279-281, 295-296
Fifth Angel 137-139, 185, 194
Fifth Initiation of Fire 280
Fifth Path 89
Fifth Race 296
Fifth Races 281
Fifth Root-race 295
Fig 63, 117
Filthiness 203
Filthy 259
Filtrate 134
Fire 3, 5, 11-12, 15, 19-20, 28, 42-43,
    45-46, 49-50, 53, 58-59,
    63-64, 67, 69-70, 75-81, 83,

Index   313

85, 87-89, 91-92, 95, 98-99, 103-104, 114-115, 117, 123, 125-126, 131-132, 135, 141, 143, 145-146, 152-153, 162, 167, 173, 178, 182, 187, 190, 193, 197-198, 201, 206, 209, 214-215, 218, 220-221, 223-226, 228, 230, 236, 242-243, 246-249, 251, 280, 288, 290
Firecrackers 266
Firmament 42, 103, 117
First Begotten 39, 41-42
First Heaven 235, 256, 274
First Logos 290
First Truth 191, 285
Fish 7, 12, 15-16, 134
Fissiparous 279
Five 1, 80-81, 87, 89, 108, 139-140, 159, 167, 205, 251, 290-291
Flame 43, 64, 70, 110, 214, 288
Flamel 242
Flames 5, 79, 247
Flaming 42-43, 65, 73, 81, 104, 126, 152, 167, 192, 215, 248, 250
Flood 1, 6, 9, 11, 165, 167, 295
Flores 23
Flower 57, 59, 63, 68, 71, 83, 87, 245
Flowers 42, 46, 99
Flute 57, 59, 68, 237, 253
Fly 125, 165, 167, 178, 201, 223
Flying 104, 135, 200
Fontanel 89
Food 4, 63, 282
Foods 149
Forehead 85, 123, 174, 178, 203, 215, 220, 223-224, 230, 249, 257
Foreheads 120-122, 124, 137, 139, 147, 174, 177, 194, 231, 257
Forest 94, 99
Forests 16
Forge 126, 192, 215, 248, 250
Forgery 281
Forget 29, 99
Forgetting 243
Forgive 68
Formula 125

Formulae 270
Fornicate 70, 123, 153
Fornicates 153
Fornicating 153, 169, 222
Fornication 51, 58, 65-66, 70, 123, 132, 134, 143, 153-154, 170-171, 178, 181, 191, 203, 206-207, 209, 213, 285
Fornications 189
Fornicator 66, 153, 191, 285
Fornicators 57, 71, 122, 151, 193, 226, 260
Forty 16, 98, 122-123, 128, 151, 170, 177, 248
Fortyeight 271
Fortyfour 177
Foundation 69, 131, 170-171, 180, 197, 205, 225, 239, 249
Foundations 239, 243, 249
Fountain 54, 148, 216, 235-236
Fountains 127, 133, 178, 193
Four 1, 13, 18, 57, 85, 98, 103-106, 108-109, 112-114, 119-123, 125-128, 141-142, 157, 169, 172, 177, 188, 191-192, 195, 213, 230, 245-248, 254, 284-285, 295-296
Four Angels 119-121, 123, 125, 127-128, 141-142
Four Horses 112
Four Noble Truths 284-285
Four Truths 192, 284
Four Winds 18, 120, 128, 141, 246
Fourteen 291
Fourteenth 182-183
Fourth 3, 7, 9, 12, 15, 18-19, 54, 68, 104, 114, 134, 146, 162, 167, 181, 190-191, 193, 198, 221, 225, 249, 281, 285, 288, 295
Fourth Path 162, 285
Fourth Truth 191, 285
Fowl 18, 147
Fowls 223, 225
France 28, 198
Francis 94
Francisco A. Propato 182, 190
Frankincense 210

Fraternatis Rosicruciana Antiqua 289
Fraternity 264, 289
Fratricide 170
Free 39, 61, 117, 174, 224
Freedom 284
French 7, 27, 41, 198, 216-217, 219
French Revolution 41, 219
Friend 27, 29, 220, 273
Friends 84
Frogs 198
Fruit 63, 147, 257
Fruits 17, 117, 132, 147, 149, 189, 209-210, 257
Funeral 39
Furnace 43, 137
Future 5, 12, 23, 25, 55, 75, 93, 97-99, 117-118, 186, 222, 235, 238, 251, 256, 258, 277
Gabriel 129, 131, 185, 189
Gad 124
Galen 132
Galilee 40-41, 97
Gambling 293
Ganges 94
Garden 39, 83, 99, 146, 148-149, 221
Garden of Delights 146, 148-149
Gardener 99
Gardens 33, 68, 147, 149
Garima 94-95
Gate 148, 172, 222, 245, 251
Gates 98, 238-239, 244, 251-252, 260
Gelatinous 13
Gemmation 285
Gemmiparity 285
Gemmulation 285
Generating 105
Generation 133, 283
Generative 282-283
Genesis 14, 49, 63, 68, 77
Genie 145, 190, 229
Genika 279
Genitalia 286
Geniuses 117
Gentiles 151
Gentleness 29
Geographic Poles 10

Geographical 268
Geological 15, 207, 281
George Casay 27
George Coston 218
Germain 41, 217-220, 269
German 27-28, 215
Germans 7, 28
Germany 218, 289
Germs 268
Gestapos 192
Giant 11
Giants 58, 186
Gibbet 241
Gift 39
Gifts 154, 292-294
Girdle 43
Girdles 187
Glaciation 269
Gland 75, 83, 87-88, 91-92, 103
Glands 4, 14, 47, 86-88, 91
Glandular 88
Glass 103, 187, 249, 251, 281
Glasses 76
Gloriari 31
Glorified 126, 209, 214, 236
Glorify 47, 187
Glorious 45-46, 75, 250
Gloriously 214, 238, 251
Glory 34-35, 37, 39, 42, 47, 57, 62, 68, 98, 105-106, 109-111, 119, 126, 155, 163, 178, 183, 186, 188, 193, 207, 213, 237, 252
Glutton 66
Gluttony 65, 70, 205, 283
Gnomes 3, 57, 247
Gnosis 24, 26
Gnostic 24, 26, 53, 171, 253, 263, 286, 289, 293, 295
Gnostic Church 289
Gnostic Movement 24, 26, 253, 263
Gnostic Psychology 293, 295
Gnostic Unction 53
Gnosticism 279-280, 282-284, 287, 290-291
Gnostics 78, 131, 273
Gnothi 286

Goats 137
Goblets 147
God 3, 14, 19, 21, 33, 35, 39, 51, 53-54, 58, 66, 68, 70, 77-78, 80, 85, 90-91, 98-99, 103-105, 108-110, 115-117, 120-124, 126, 129, 137, 139, 141, 145-147, 149, 151-152, 154-155, 157, 161, 163, 168, 170, 172, 177-179, 181-182, 185, 187-189, 193-195, 198, 201-202, 206-207, 209-210, 213-215, 222-223, 230-231, 235-237, 242, 245, 251-252, 255-261, 274, 276-277, 279-282, 284-285, 287-290, 292
God Almighty 104, 157, 187, 193, 198, 251
God of War 279
God of Winter 287
Goddess 58, 63, 189, 284
Goddesses 279, 284
Gods 12, 33-34, 49, 59, 68, 76-77, 87-88, 98, 123, 148, 151-152, 157, 171, 175, 182, 213, 222, 231, 248, 279, 284
Goethe 168
Gold 1, 18, 39, 45-46, 50, 71, 79-80, 91, 103, 114, 139-140, 143, 167, 194, 203, 209-210, 217, 219, 241, 243, 247, 249, 251, 286
Golden Age 2, 18, 21, 288
Golgotha 69, 73, 89, 92, 106
Gomorrah 135
Good 20, 23, 63, 171, 180, 182, 197, 215, 226, 265, 271, 281-282, 293-294
Good of Mankind 281
Gorgon 287
Gorilla 169
Gospel 80, 131, 178, 181
Gospels 172
Grace 39, 62, 261, 281
Grapes 182
Gratitude 282
Gravitate 264

Gravitating 266
Gravitational 264
Gravity 286
Great Arcanum 80, 104, 113-114, 125-126, 155-156, 177, 191, 216-218, 220-223, 226-227
Great Cosmic Day 291
Great Day 118, 198, 243
Great Work 64-65, 69, 79, 91, 105, 125, 171-172, 178, 241, 246-248, 277
Greece 286-287
Greed 2, 179, 197, 205
Greek 140, 186, 242, 279, 283-284, 286-287, 290-291, 294
Greeks 7, 280, 286
Green 76, 131-132, 139
Guadalajara 21
Guardian Wall 39, 41
Guardians 41
Guardianship 280
Guillotine 41
Gunas 292-293
Guru 244-245
Guru-deva 94
Gurus 283
H-bomb 265
Habitation 207-208
Hailstones 107
Hair 115, 134, 140
Hairs 43
Halo 87
Hanasmuss 285-286
Happiness 28, 63, 83, 111, 148-149, 163, 180, 185, 195-197, 256
Happy 147, 247
Harlot 70, 107-108, 151, 153, 155-157, 170, 175, 200-201
Harlots 19, 116, 135, 153, 200, 203, 206, 211
Harmonies 69, 216
Harmonious 76, 271
Harmoniously 275-276
Harmonize 55
Harmony 290-291
Harp 81
Harpers 177, 211

Harping 177
Harpocrates 95
Harps 108, 177, 187
Harvest 117, 132, 182, 189, 209
Harvests 145
Hasha 7
Hashim 267
Hate 23, 58, 65, 67, 123, 206, 228
Hated 131, 173, 272
Hateful 207-208
Hates 122, 192
Hatha Yoga 285
Hatred 2, 17, 24-25, 134, 179, 193-194, 207, 271, 274
Head 40-41, 43, 49, 67, 105, 120, 124, 126, 132, 145, 158-159, 168-169, 181, 183, 214, 229, 239, 248, 288, 291
Headache 147
Heal 216
Healed 169-170, 172
Healing 257, 289
Health 216, 281
Healthy 216
Heart Temple 246-247
Hearts 2, 28, 69, 71, 135, 206
Heaven 19, 53, 80-81, 85, 93, 102-103, 105-106, 108-109, 116-117, 125, 129, 133, 135, 137, 145-146, 153-163, 170, 173, 177-179, 181-182, 185, 187, 194-195, 200-202, 207, 210, 213-214, 223, 229-230, 235, 237, 256, 270, 274-276, 283, 286, 288
Heavenly 9, 93-94, 97-98, 131, 146, 237, 239, 241, 243, 245, 247, 251, 256, 263, 268
Heavens 18-19, 21, 117, 135, 146, 156, 163, 281
Hebraic 275
Hebrew 140, 199, 241, 246, 279-280, 284, 290, 293
Hebrews 267
Hegel 13
Heindel 227
Heliakon 286

Heliogabalus 131
Hell 43, 45, 114-116, 230, 288
Hemlock 200
Hemp 107
Henchmen 162
Heracles 287
Hercolubus 10-11, 17, 19, 269
Hermaphrodite 286
Hermaphrodites 13-14, 295
Hermaphroditic 14
Hermes 124-126, 152, 248
Hermetic 241, 282
Hermetically 247
Hess 266
Hierarch 26, 99
Hierarchies 279
Hieratic 242
Hieroglyphics 242
Hierophant 152, 154, 248
Hierophants 39, 280
Hilarion IX 121, 152, 190, 248
Himalayas 2-3, 246
Hindu 291
Hindustani 37, 114, 162, 295
Hiram 45, 199, 286
History 15, 242, 280-281
Hod 265, 274-276
Holy Beings 5
Holy Collyrium 91
Holy Eight 98, 190
Holy Four 245-247
Holy Ladder 133
Holy Land 29
Holy Man 34
Holy Sepulchre 40, 154
Home 80, 133, 149, 159
Homes 134
Homo Nosce Te Ipsum 286
Honduras 8
Honest 114
Honey 146, 200
Honor 109-110, 132, 149, 213, 252
Honorable 229, 279
Hope 242-243
Horns 18, 100, 108, 141, 160, 169, 172-174, 203, 205-206, 224, 230

Horse 113-116, 183, 214, 224, 288
Horsemen 141
Horses 112, 140, 143, 210, 214, 223, 288
Hour 23-24, 69, 78, 80-81, 85, 129, 141, 143, 155, 157, 159, 165, 178, 190, 201, 205, 209-210, 238, 256, 263
Hours 64, 216, 255, 266
Huiracocha 181, 216, 236, 238, 289
Human Beings 2-3, 17, 21, 23, 49, 54, 64, 70, 82, 98, 106, 109, 114-117, 123, 132-133, 137, 139, 145, 152, 156, 169, 173-174, 183, 185, 189, 193-194, 199, 202, 207, 209, 227, 230, 236, 248, 255, 286, 288
Humanities 116, 156, 200-202
Humanity 2, 5, 7, 14, 16, 18-19, 23, 25-26, 30, 39, 41, 67, 89, 97, 107-108, 110, 117, 119-124, 128-129, 132, 137, 145-147, 153-157; 169-170, 173, 182-183, 186, 192-195, 203, 206, 226-227, 239, 251, 256, 277, 280, 284, 289-290, 295
Humble 30, 51, 53, 66, 83, 110, 133, 161, 259, 280
Humbleness 29, 51, 90, 99, 110, 165
Humbly 89, 149
Hunger 114, 126
Hurricane 113, 201, 250
Hurricanes 11, 13, 69
Husband 63, 85, 235
Hydrogen 139-141, 143, 173, 199, 224, 287
Hydrogens 287
Hyperborean 13, 270
Hyperboreans 7, 13, 287
I. 1, 3, 8, 10, 15-16, 18-20, 25, 27-29, 33-35, 39, 43-45, 49, 54, 57-58, 60, 62, 64-66, 68-73, 75-78, 80-81, 83-85, 90-92, 99-100, 103-104, 106-111, 113-115, 120, 122-123, 125-129, 131, 135, 137, 139-141, 143, 145-146, 151, 154, 159-160, 163, 169-172, 177-179, 181, 185, 187, 189, 191, 193, 195-199, 201, 203, 207, 209, 213-214, 218, 220-224, 226, 229-231, 235-236, 248, 250-251, 254, 256, 258-261, 263-265, 267, 269, 273-274, 279-281, 283-286, 288, 290-293
I. A. O. 236
I. E. O. U. A. 81
Ice 218, 269
Iced 132
Ida 46, 51, 79, 152, 191, 295
Idolaters 236, 260
Idolatry 211
Idols 65, 70, 143
Iglesia Gnostica 289
Igneous 49-50, 79, 87, 267
Ignis 236
Ignite 51
Ignorance 244, 294
Ignorant 180, 222, 241, 268
Ignore 14, 172, 258, 264
Ignored 3, 108
Ignores 173
Ila 295
Iliaster 267, 287
Illuminate 171, 267
Illuminated 73, 84-85, 93, 107, 116, 122, 220
Illuminates 98, 291
Illumination 53-54, 73, 220
Imagination 108, 253-254, 256-258
Imaginative 253-254
Imagine 290
Immaculate 50, 61, 71, 73, 76, 80, 83, 88-89, 98, 107, 160
Immaculate Conceptions 80, 160
Immolated 4, 53, 61, 67, 76, 85, 93, 95, 99, 111, 128, 191
Immortal 3, 42, 219
Immortalize 42, 90
Impatience 51
Incarnate 53, 73, 77, 79, 90, 126, 128, 159, 187, 191-192, 220,

222-223, 236, 248-249, 285, 288
Incarnated 35, 37, 61-62, 108, 133, 191-192, 196, 227, 242, 248, 251, 258, 292
Incarnates 72, 78, 81, 280
Incarnating 220
Incarnation 33, 54, 161, 220, 288
Incas 8
Incense 34, 129
Incurable 189
India 7, 46, 94, 288-289
Indian Lingam 283
Indians 289
Individual 276, 280, 285-286
Individuality 35, 110-111, 179
Indo-European 279
Indo-Germanic 279
Infancy 71
Infantile 253-254
Infect 272-273
Infected 273
Infecting 273
Infects 272-273
Inferior Manas 265, 295
Inferius 233, 238
Infernal 287
Infernos 45, 58, 84, 118, 224, 236, 290
Infinite 23, 34, 41, 75, 81, 120, 132, 190-191, 221, 251, 282
Infinity 98, 190
Inhabitant 251
Inhabitants 71, 115, 135, 256
Inhabited 1, 15, 135, 156
Inhabiters 163, 203
Inhalation 236
Inhale 87
Inhaled 81, 104
Iniquities 19, 207
Iniquity 222, 288
Initiate 39, 66, 88-89, 93, 106, 175, 217, 238, 242, 244, 250, 256-258
Initiated 207, 217, 223, 227, 230, 270, 280

Initiates 69, 88, 90, 114-115, 170, 180, 191, 217-218, 226, 242, 250, 252
Initiatic 218, 289
Initiation 49, 54, 60, 62, 67, 72-73, 88-89, 92, 98, 123, 126, 151-152, 159, 175, 180, 237, 242-243, 246-248, 253, 258, 260, 280-281
Inmisio Membri Virili In Vagina Feminae Sine Ejeculatium Seminis 125, 181, 238
Inner Name 289
Innermost 33-34, 51, 88, 91-92, 106, 194-195, 205, 221, 225, 235, 249-250, 286, 295
Innocence 2-3, 54, 76, 110, 286
Innocent 119, 127, 196, 253-254
Inquisition 218
INRI 92, 131, 246
Instinctive 167, 196, 295
Intellect 178-179, 285, 287, 293
Intellectual 25, 70, 117, 179, 265, 286-288, 295
Intellectual Animal 265, 286-287
Intellectual Animals 288
Intellectualism 70, 178-179, 224
Intellectuals 71
Intelligence 169, 279, 287, 295
Intelligent 3, 287
Intelligent Principle 287
Intention 284
Intentions 190, 226
Internal God 58, 66, 68, 77, 90, 99, 109-110, 152, 181, 213-214, 235, 245, 255, 259, 280
Internal Meditation 53-55, 67, 70, 83, 89, 94, 97
Interplanetary 116, 207
Introspective 281
Introversion 51
Intuition 75, 94, 253, 256-258
Intuitional 295
Intuitive 88, 253, 256
Invisible 3, 219
Invoke 95
Invoking 40

Involution 197
Iod 141, 246, 248
Iod-Heve 292
Iran 279
Ireland 279
Iron 1-2, 18, 71-72, 140, 160-161, 169, 194, 210, 215, 266, 288-289
Iron Age 18, 288
Ironic 123
Isaac 222
Isis 77
Island 11, 117, 201
Islands 11
Isolate 272
Isolated 272-273
Isolation 271
Israel 65, 121-123, 125, 128, 177, 239, 271
Issachar 124
Itababo 229
Ivory 194, 210
Jacinth 143, 249
Jacob 58, 121, 222, 282
Jam 263
Japan 24, 113
Jasper 103, 238, 249
Javhe 120-121, 229-230
Jealousy 274, 292
Jehovah 49, 119-120, 292
Jewish 229
Jews 60, 84, 119
Jezebel 3-4, 70-72, 84-85, 90, 97
Jinn 27, 40-42, 70, 93, 95, 97-99, 120, 146-148, 219
Jinn States 93, 95, 97, 99, 120
Jivan-Atman 37
Jnana Yoga 285
Job 165
Jochai 276
John 40, 62, 77, 80-81, 111, 114, 131, 159, 172, 235-237, 258-259, 288
Jonah 154
Jordan 62
Joseph 124
Joshua 281

Journalism 70
Joy 39, 54-55, 68, 97, 115, 147-148, 180, 216
Joyful 149
Joyfully 247
Juan Bautista Maíno 32
Juda 108
Judah 84, 124
Judas 45
Judge 18, 76, 115, 157, 214, 288
Judged 76, 99, 157, 175, 193, 213, 218, 230
Judgement 18, 83, 157, 178, 203, 209, 224, 229, 231
Judgements 187, 193, 213, 270
Judges 76
Judgeth 209
Judging 185
Judgment 76, 223, 294
Julian 61
Jungle 80, 196
Jupiter 10
Justice 104, 116, 118, 135, 148, 167, 171, 210, 249
Juvenal 286
Kabbalah 36, 162, 275, 292
Kabbalist 182, 276
Kabbalist Schimeon Ben Jochai 276
Kabbalistic 143, 151, 162, 174, 177, 183, 195, 245, 274
Kabbalistically 246
Kabbalisticaly 122, 141
Kabbalists 34, 151, 286
Kagyug-pa 283
Kali Yuga 3, 11, 19, 169-170, 288, 296
Kalki 30, 214, 280, 288
Kalki Avatar 214, 288
Kalpa 291
Kamas 294
Karma 60-61, 120-121, 128, 133, 155, 178, 185, 192, 196, 210, 229-230, 275
Karmapa 283
Karmic 132, 140, 279
Kasyapa 180
Kether 36, 61, 163, 290

Key 26, 29, 49, 79, 84, 125, 137, 157,
    180-181, 216, 229, 236, 286
Keys 30, 43, 45
Kharishnanda 181
Kidnapping 189
Kidney 71
Kidneys 2, 71
Kill 49, 64, 70-71, 110, 113-114, 139,
    152-153, 209, 249
Killed 7, 45, 115, 143, 152-153, 171,
    173, 200, 292
Killeth 171
Killing 119, 293
Kills 27, 29
Kind 180, 294
Kindred 109, 178
Kindreds 33, 125, 154, 170
Kinds 193
King 63, 109, 140, 186-187, 206,
    215, 220, 223, 286, 289
King of Fire 63
King of Kings 206, 215, 289
King of Nature 286
King-Sun 61
Kingdom 18, 80, 131, 147, 163, 182,
    194-195, 198, 205-206, 222,
    274-275, 287
Kingdoms 16, 156, 287
Kings 33, 39, 59, 63-64, 107, 109,
    117, 146, 198, 203, 205-207,
    209, 215, 219, 223-224, 231,
    249, 252, 289
Kirjath-Sepher 281
Kiss 67-68, 110, 122-123, 256
Kisses 243
Kissing 214
Klipoth 162-163, 228
Knowledge 3, 15, 89, 180, 186, 215,
    220-221, 225, 253-256, 264,
    270, 282, 286, 289, 294
Koran 146-149, 170
Krishna 152, 248, 280, 287, 295-296
Krishnamurti 264
Krita Age 288
Kriya 220, 241
Kriyas 244
Kriyasakti 295

Krumm-Heller 215, 289
Krupto 280
Kuan Yin 37
Kundabuffer Organ 289-290
Kundalini 50, 77, 104, 148, 152-153,
    215-216, 221, 223, 228, 242,
    244, 246, 249
La Ra 237
Labor 114, 150
Laboratories 271
Laboratory 4, 116, 246
Ladder 110, 133, 282, 290
Ladder of Jacob 282
Laghima 94-95
Lake 172, 224, 230, 236
Lakes 16
Lama 282
Lambs 106
Lamed 284
Lament 209
Lamentable 286
Lamp 65, 133, 248
Lamps 3, 46, 103
Lance of Longinus 73
Land 7-9, 13, 29, 73, 134, 287
Lands 7, 21, 146, 192
Language 76-77, 80, 94, 187, 214,
    242
Languages 79-80, 219
Laodicea 45-46, 87, 89, 91, 163
Laodiceans 91
Lapidum 184, 238
Lapis Philosophorum 167
Large 17, 106, 245, 247, 283, 290
Laryngeal 75
Larynx 45, 75-77, 79, 81, 187, 223
Latin 8, 125, 181, 279, 281, 283-284,
    286, 289-290, 292
Latin America 8, 289
Law 50, 67, 93, 108, 116-117, 120,
    134, 139, 156-157, 168, 171,
    179-180, 183, 185, 189, 192,
    196, 200-201, 209, 221, 270,
    288
Lawgiver 291
Laws 3, 77, 95, 271, 279, 288, 291
Laziness 143, 205, 258, 283

Lead 5, 91, 126, 217, 219, 243, 245, 247
Leadbeter 291
Leaders 5
Lefthand 162
Legend 284
Legion 283
Legions 162, 195, 224, 229
Legs 28, 105, 124, 241
Lemon 70, 249
Lemuria 11, 14, 185
Lemurian 11, 13-14, 185, 242, 270
Lemurians 13-15
Length 245, 247
Leo 251
Leone 218
Leopard 18, 100, 169
Leper 68, 110
Leto 287
Letter 26, 236, 241, 293
Letters 246, 248, 277, 281, 284, 286
Letting 274
Level 53, 282, 287, 290
Level of Being 282, 290
Levels 45, 64, 122-123, 282, 287, 290, 293
Levi 124, 131, 185-186, 217
Liar 275
Liars 57, 236, 257, 275-276
Liberate 85, 97, 265
Liberated 94, 107, 196, 253
Liberates 265
Liberating 242
Liberation 24, 26, 83
Liberty 260
Libraries 280
License 6
Lie 84, 95, 153, 252, 260, 275
Lies 182, 223, 225, 276
Lieth 245, 247
Light 25, 35, 38-39, 41, 50, 53, 55, 59, 62, 68, 73, 79, 87-89, 96, 98, 115, 126, 133-134, 147-148, 153, 162, 167, 172, 186, 211, 214, 223, 230, 238, 243, 245, 247-248, 251-252, 258, 266-267, 282

Lightning 33, 35, 45, 50, 54, 59, 63, 69, 104, 107, 122, 189, 209, 219, 273
Lightnings 103, 131, 157, 200
Lights 266
Lilliputians 15
Linen 71, 187, 194, 210, 213-214, 288
Linga-Sarira 294
Lingam 57, 105, 283
Lingam Yoni 57
Lion 18, 84, 100, 104, 108, 145, 169, 246
Lioncolored 107
Lions 140, 143, 249
Lips 123, 216-217, 220
Liquefaction 54
Liquid 15, 19, 187, 238, 249, 251
Liquor 53
Liver 63
Locusts 139-140
Lodge 120-121, 160, 162-163, 182, 214, 224, 229, 245, 250, 254, 256
Lodges 23, 241, 244
Loedere 79, 290
Logical 17, 134, 186
Logoic 106, 197
Logoic Ray 106
Logos 35-36, 171, 191, 195, 215, 236-237, 248, 277, 283, 290
Logos Mantra Magic 236
London 178
Lord of Anguish 119
Lord of Lords 206, 215, 289
Lords 5, 77, 117, 139, 206, 209, 211, 215, 289
Lords of Nature 215
Lotus 46, 57, 59-60, 63-64, 69, 71, 83, 87, 89, 99, 163, 195
Lotusborn 60
Louis 186, 219
Love 2, 23, 26, 34, 39, 41-42, 50-51, 57-59, 61, 64, 67-68, 71, 83-84, 89, 91, 97, 99, 104-105, 107, 114, 116, 121-123, 149, 163, 167, 181, 185, 192-193,

243, 246, 256-257, 271-273, 279, 281
Loved 39, 62, 84, 114, 159
Lovely 59, 76, 147
Lover 151
Lovers 26
Loves 167, 170
Loveth 260
Loving 129, 147, 216-217
Loving Devil 216-217
Loyal 122
Loyalty 66
Lucifer 162
Luciferic 289-290
Luciferic Organ 290
Luke 40, 69, 106, 135, 172, 222
Lukewarm 91
Lully 242
Luminaries 117
Luminous 34
Luna 27, 29
Lunacy 293
Lunar 9, 49, 79, 163, 226, 251, 285-286, 290
Lungs 81
Lust 179, 205, 249, 271-273, 283
Lusted 210
Lustful 272
Lute 68
Luxury 219
Lying 147, 255, 275
Lyre 2, 82, 187, 191
Ma Ma 253-254
Machine 290
Macro 290
Macrocosm 93, 103, 105
Macrocosmos 43, 45, 290
Magazines 123
Magic 57, 59, 68, 70, 123-124, 131, 148, 159, 171, 177, 211, 216-219, 236-237, 241-244, 253, 272, 291
Magic Flute 57, 59, 68, 237, 253
Magic Key 216
Magical 3-4, 49, 66, 79, 87, 90
Magician 84, 186, 217, 219, 257
Magicians 3, 190, 216, 267

Magisterium 53, 221
Magisterium of Fire 53, 221
Magistery of Fire 221
Magma 15, 19
Magnetic 9-10, 47, 81, 87, 89, 216, 268, 272
Magnetism 19, 216
Magnetization 216
Magnetize 216
Magnetizer 216
Magnitude 58, 202
Magnum Opus 171
Magog 230
Maha 42, 290
Maha Avatar 42
Mahaban 69
Mahabarata 292-293
Mahachoan 215, 223, 290
Mahamanvantara 80, 291
Mahapralaya 291
Mahayana Buddhists 288
Mahima 94-95
Maiden 289
Maidens 147, 161
Maids 165
Mail 292
Main 281
Maitreya 23, 30, 212-215, 217, 219, 221, 223, 225, 227, 288
Maitreya Bodhisattva 212
Maitreya Buddha 30, 213-215, 217, 219, 221, 223, 225, 227
Majestic 45
Major 83, 89, 93, 220, 249, 277
Major Arcana 277
Maladies 189
Male 14, 59, 77, 132, 167, 222, 243, 279, 282-283
Maledictions 146
Malefemale 14
Malice 292
Maliciousness 127
Malignant 169-170
Malkuth 275
Malleable 187, 238, 249, 251
Mammary 14

Man 14, 18, 25, 27-28, 31, 33-35, 37, 43, 45, 48, 50, 54, 57, 64-66, 68, 72-73, 77, 80-81, 84-85, 90, 92, 98, 103-105, 108, 117, 125, 128, 139, 141, 149, 152, 155-156, 159-162, 165-169, 171, 174, 177-178, 181-183, 188, 192, 209, 214-217, 221-222, 226, 241, 243, 246, 248, 257-260, 273, 281, 283, 286, 288-291
Man-Sun 61
Manas 265, 295
Manasic 265
Manasses 124
Mane 113
Manger 161
Manifesation 284
Manifest 180, 187
Manifestation 134, 287
Manifestations 283
Manifested 290
Mankind 181, 279, 281, 295
Manliness 284
Manly 182
Manly P. Hall 182
Manna 50-51, 66, 157
Manner 125, 152, 194, 210, 231, 249-250, 257, 268
Mansion 147
Mansion of Delights 147
Manteia 293
Mantle 249
Mantra 236
Mantras 80
Mantua 21
Manu 5, 7, 20, 291-292, 295-296
Manuel S. Sanches 23
Manus 291, 295-296
Manushyas 295
Marble 71, 194, 210
March 28, 69
Marie Antoinette 219
Mario Roso de Luna 27, 29
Mark 29, 122, 174, 178, 187, 189, 194, 224, 230-231
Marpa 283

Marriage 5, 49, 115, 213
Married 153, 186
Marrow 271
Marrying 5, 115
Mars 2, 139, 156, 279-280, 289
Martyr 39, 51, 65
Martyrdom 73
Martyrdoms 54
Martyrs 203
Marut 286
Mary 80
Masculine 14, 121, 286
Masochists 196
Masonic 286
Mass 11, 117, 134, 201, 209
Massive 50
Mast 283
Master Atom 89, 291
Master Key 286
Master Masons 286
Master of Samadhi 220
Masters 3, 11-12, 26, 39, 41, 75-76, 84, 103, 125, 132, 170, 213-214, 219, 255, 289
Masters of Medicine 170
Materia 167
Material 77
Materialism 199, 211
Materialist 291
Materialistic 2, 70, 116-117, 131, 139, 173, 194, 199, 224, 293
Materials 265
Maternal 243, 248
Mathematical 13, 132-133, 245, 270
Matrimony 284
Matter 9, 15-16, 64-65, 69, 79, 91, 104, 129, 178, 197, 220, 237, 243, 247, 251, 266-267, 270, 273, 275, 287
Matters 20
Matthew 76, 118, 131, 154
Max Heindel 227
Maximum 152, 248
May 27, 60, 64, 131, 179, 186, 216, 223, 225, 260, 281-284
Mayans 8
Mayas 242

Maíno 32
Measure 76, 98, 114, 125, 151, 244, 248
Measured 76, 98, 151, 244-246, 248
Measures 114
Meat 281
Mechanical 2-3, 199
Mechanics 19
Medical 2, 24
Medici 220
Medicine 170, 199, 270, 272, 281, 289
Medieval 187, 294
Meditate 53, 59, 63-64, 69, 76, 82, 254
Meditated 123
Meditates 57
Meditating 75, 254
Meditation 53-55, 67, 70, 83, 89, 94-95, 97, 220-221, 254, 275, 285, 291
Medium 54
Medulla 43, 45-46, 49-50, 88, 98, 151-152, 182, 190-191, 225, 242, 246, 277
Medullar 46, 50, 104-105, 151, 168, 223, 228, 244
Medusa 248
Melchizedek 63
Melodies 2, 33, 39, 55, 68, 75
Melodious 59
Melody 33, 76, 83
Melt 19, 117, 135, 269
Melting 268-269
Mem 284
Member 216
Members 220
Membri 125, 181, 238
Memories 57, 76, 219, 250, 263
Memorize 285
Memory 18, 250, 273, 294
Men 12, 15, 20, 27-28, 33, 62, 116-118, 133, 135, 139-141, 143, 155, 173, 177, 189, 193, 200, 202, 207, 209-211, 219, 223-224, 230, 235, 264, 266-268, 281, 286, 288, 292, 294

Menstruum Universale 167
Mental 4, 123, 179, 195, 199, 221, 224, 276, 282, 291, 295
Mental Body 199, 221, 276, 291, 295
Mental Plane 123
Mental World 123, 276
Mental Worlds 224
Mentally 237, 253-254
Mercabah 286
Merchandise 194, 209-210, 287
Merchants 71, 119, 139, 207, 209-211
Merciful 181
Mercury 2, 104, 125, 132-133, 156, 190-191, 243, 246
Mercy 28, 107, 120
Merits 244, 293
Mermaid 59
Mermaids 59
Mesmer 217
Message 20, 25, 30-31, 101, 214, 233, 258, 261, 263, 280, 285
Messengers 279
Messiah 119
Metal 46, 49-51, 289
Metallic 247
Metamorphosis 6
Metaphysics 290
Meteor 266
Meteoric 265
Method 285
Methods 289
Mexican 8, 186, 289
Mexican Army 289
Mexico 8, 13, 21, 24, 289
Mexico City 24, 289
Michael 129, 134, 162, 185, 193, 275
Micro 291
Microcosm 93, 103, 105
Microcosmic 93, 97
Microcosmical 87-88
Microcosmos 43, 45, 291-292
Microscope 272
Middle Ages 17, 73
Midrashim 281

Might 5, 9, 126, 165, 174, 178, 198, 263, 268, 270-271, 282, 288, 292
Miguel de Molinos 51
Milarepa 283
Mild 53
Milissa 217
Military 140
Milky Way 259
Millenium 231
Millennial 63
Millennium 229
Millimetres 87
Million 13, 63, 127, 185
Millions 4, 26, 39, 41-42, 89, 114, 123, 127, 131, 139, 161, 174, 185, 189, 194-196, 200, 230, 241, 283, 287
Millstone 210-211
Minature 292
Mind 45, 47, 52-54, 64, 70-72, 76, 83, 95, 122-123, 135, 173, 196, 199, 205, 215, 220, 222-223, 254-255, 265, 275-276, 291, 293-295
Mindfulness 284
Minds 272, 288
Mineness 292
Mineral 16, 196, 287
Mingled 131-132, 186-187, 200
Ministers 219
Ministrations 292
Minor 83, 249
Miracle 122, 157
Miracles 20, 173, 198-199, 224
Miraculous 57, 59, 81-82
Mirage 196
Mirror 59
Miserable 91, 99, 259, 280, 282
Misery 90, 110, 127, 134
Missiles 173, 199
Mission 17, 23, 219, 279
Mist 88
Mitosis 13
Mix 67, 180
Mixed 7-8, 88, 92, 117, 148, 186, 243
Mixture 8-9, 34-35, 58, 178

Mocked 5
Modalities 16
Mode 282
Model 97
Modern 2, 11, 14, 206, 209-211, 267, 270, 295
Modest 83
Modified 266, 268
Mohammed 148-149, 152, 287
Mohammedans 171
Molecules 266-267
Molinos 51
Moment 9, 15-16, 18, 27-28, 49, 57, 165, 216, 266, 269-272, 274
Moments 19-20, 29, 97
Momentum 266, 269, 271
Monad 35, 106, 286-287, 292
Monas 292
Monasteries 283
Money 209
Monistic 290
Monk 285
Monkeys 11, 182
Monster 4, 194
Monstrosity 275
Monstrous 11, 116, 134
Month 141, 257
Months 94-95, 97, 139-140, 151, 170, 248, 287
Moon 2, 75, 94-95, 98, 115-116, 132, 134-135, 158-161, 167, 189, 226-227, 241, 246, 252, 263, 283
Moonlight 83
Morbid 272
Moreover 64, 265
Morning 19, 27, 33, 67, 72-73, 260
Mortal 295
Mortally 131, 170, 192
Mortals 282
Mortified 51
Mortifying 51
Moses 35, 48-49, 80, 104-105, 118, 187, 287
Mother 19, 33, 58, 63, 80-81, 116, 133, 135, 153, 159-161, 167,

203, 206, 211, 227-228, 243, 246, 286-287, 289
Mother Goddess 58, 63
Mothers 107, 162, 165, 189
Motionless 28
Motivation 284
Motor 295
Motto 79
Mount 35, 177, 185
Mount Armon 185
Mount Nebo 35
Mountain 94, 117, 132, 237, 246-247
Mountains 8, 117-118, 126, 146, 180, 192, 201, 205, 246, 268, 279, 287, 289
Mountaintops 6
Mounts 108
Mourn 209
Mourning 15, 113, 209
Mouth 18, 43, 65, 81, 91, 100, 143, 146, 152, 165, 167, 169-170, 177, 198, 215, 224-225, 288
Mouths 143
Move 27, 54, 89, 116, 146, 247, 257
Moved 34, 117
Movement 1, 15, 24, 26, 28, 40, 245, 253, 263
Movements 26, 134, 165
Moves 256-257
Movie 123
Movies 123
Moving 59, 75, 248
Mozart 57, 59, 237, 253
Mridanga 68
Mu 5, 11
Mud 68, 99, 170, 200, 259, 280
Multiple 35, 106, 279
Multiplicity 283
Multiply 110, 131, 191
Multitude 4-5, 125, 213
Multitudes 4-5, 7, 89, 156, 173, 206, 230, 244
Murdered 286
Murderers 236, 260
Murders 143
Murmur 33
Murmurs 59
Music 285, 293
Musical 216
Musician 219
Musicians 211
Muslim 286
Mutual 149
Myrrh 34
Myself 20, 25, 45, 69, 71-72, 135, 160, 170, 179, 199, 236
Mysteries 14, 39, 55, 57-58, 89, 207, 221, 223, 237, 242, 248-249, 274, 281, 283, 293
Mysteries of Initiation 281
Mystery 33, 35, 121, 143, 145-146, 203, 295
Mystic 53, 83, 93-95, 179, 220, 247, 283
Mystical 20, 45, 53, 55, 57, 68-69, 83, 89, 97-98, 226, 237, 241
Mysticism 196, 242
Mystics 289
Myth 280
Mythical 286
Mythologies 295
Mythology 287, 291
Myths 242
N-rays 266
Nadi 46
Nadi Chitra 46
Nahuas 8, 11-13, 15
Naked 63-64, 91, 199-200, 206
Nakedness 91
Named 5, 13, 23, 131
Names 78, 170, 187, 203, 217, 239, 241, 287
Nancy 27
Naples 41
Naropa 283
Narrow 53, 148, 172, 222, 226, 245
Nasal 81, 87
Nation 109, 178, 287, 290
Nations 15, 72, 125, 131, 135, 140, 143, 145-146, 154, 156-157, 161, 170, 178, 187, 192-194, 201, 206-207, 211, 215, 229-230, 252, 257, 261, 283, 289

Native 289
Natives 15, 113
Natural 17, 243, 265
Nature 3-4, 17, 51, 58-59, 63, 82, 84, 89, 91, 97, 118, 133, 141, 143, 145, 162, 180, 189, 196, 199, 215, 224, 231, 242, 267, 269, 282-283, 285-288, 291
Navel 63-65
Nebo 35
Necessity 281
Necklace 217
Nectar 55, 64
Needed 4, 9, 14, 27-28, 57, 97
Needle 9
Needs 67, 168, 180, 220, 292
Negation 121
Negative 270-276, 289
Neglect 282
Neighbor 67-68, 85, 181, 197, 271
Neighbors 84-85
Neighbour 68, 281
Nemesis 178, 192, 205
Nemo 51
Nepthalim 124
Neptune 3
Nerves 27, 46
Nervous 14, 46-47, 244
Netzach 265, 276
New Age 24, 214, 221, 231, 258
New Jerusalem 25, 85, 93, 99, 232-235, 237-239, 241, 243, 245-247, 249, 251, 257, 260
Newborn 89, 125
News 27
Newspapers 123
Next 5, 7, 269-270, 289
Nicholas 242
Nicholas Flamel 242
Nicolaitans 58, 65-66, 162
Nigh 147, 288
Night 5, 15, 18-19, 27-28, 33, 38-39, 54, 75, 77-78, 83, 104, 107, 126, 134-135, 163, 178, 230, 252, 258, 267, 291
Nightfall 28
Nights 161

Nile 59
Nimiam 281
Nine 122, 151, 175, 177, 248-249
Nineteen 263
Nineteenth 182
Ninth 49-50, 68-69, 98, 122-123, 127, 151-152, 162, 175, 177, 181, 190, 248-249
Ninth Arcanum 175
Ninth Sphere 49-50, 98, 122-123, 127, 151-152, 162, 175, 177, 190, 248
Nipples 14
Nirvana 33-34, 39, 68-69, 75-76, 83, 88, 160-161, 167, 179-180, 192, 214, 280, 284
Nirvanic 165
Nirvanis 69
Nist 51
Nitrogen 266
Noah 5, 115, 292
Noble 113, 281, 284-285
Noble Truth of Suffering 285
Nordics 7
North 1, 9, 20, 113, 182, 239, 269, 279, 287
North Pole 9, 287
North Wind 287
Nos 31
Nose 87, 89
Nostradamus 17
Nostram 101
Nostri 31
Nothing 14, 20, 27, 41, 68, 72, 90-91, 99, 104, 109-110, 116, 196, 241, 258-259, 267-269, 271, 275-276, 293
Nothingness 52-54, 90, 110
Nourished 14, 110, 165, 186
Nourishes 104, 114
Nourishment 78
Nous 89
N rays 266
Nuclear 11, 16, 65, 115, 199, 267
Nucleus 291
Numbers 48, 122, 141, 151, 277
Numerous 147, 193, 230, 290

Nuns 165
Nuptial 54, 147, 149
Nurse 27, 246
Ob 281
Obedience 66, 89, 292
Obedient 66
Obelisk 282
Oberkirch 218
Object 282, 293-294
Objective 292
Objectivity 274
Observe 116, 271, 276
Observed 275
Obsolete 270
Obstacle 99, 255, 274
Occult 141, 182, 184, 238, 272, 291
Occultism 241
Occultists 186
Ocean 4-5, 7, 10-11, 15-16, 20, 33, 59, 134, 268
Oceanic 5
Oceans 4, 15-16
Octagonal 69
Ocultum 184, 238
Offence 148
Offended 271
Officiant 46
Offspring 113, 260
Oil 34, 46, 65, 114, 171-172, 209-210
Oiments 210
Olive 46, 50, 152, 172
Olympian 119
Omega 33-34, 235, 259
Omer 50, 157
Omnibus Debemos Subjicere 101
Omnipotence 248
Omnipotent 59, 213, 281
Omniscience 163
Opera 39, 59, 237, 253
Operas 39
Oportet 31
Opposite 14, 221, 273
Opus 171
Orbit 268-269
Orbits 264
Orchard 63, 180
Orchards 180

Ordeal 152, 248
Ordeals 39, 190, 244
Orders 23, 231, 244
Organ 14, 77, 289-290
Organic 16-17, 294
Organism 2, 13-14, 17, 39, 82, 89, 167, 193, 239
Organisms 17, 268
Organization 264
Organized 264, 283, 295
Organs 14, 50, 57, 79, 216, 238, 279
Orgasm 79, 125, 153, 155, 177, 191, 215-216, 285
Orgies 70
Orient 26, 294
Oriental 40, 42, 186, 286, 294
Orifiel 129, 145, 185, 200
Origen 281
Origin 27, 49-50, 123, 148, 152, 235, 248, 282, 284-285
Origin of Suffering 285
Original 1, 8-10, 264
Originate 7, 271
Origo 236
Oriphiel 144
Ormus 34
Orphan 107, 129
Orphans 189
Orpheus 82, 187
Ortelut 45, 199
Osculation 54
Osirified 37, 39
Osirified One 37
Osiris 34, 37, 292
Ovaries 14, 79, 172
Ovid 6
Oviparous 13-14, 292
Oviparus 292
Ovulated 14
Ovum 14, 286, 292
Pa Pa 253-254
Pacific 11, 15, 20
Pacific Ocean 11, 20
Padmasambhava 60
Paganini 219

Pain 15, 28-29, 58, 60, 69, 71, 80, 107, 119, 143, 183, 191-192, 194, 196, 235, 285, 292
Pained 158-161
Painful 129, 197, 220, 293
Painfully 73
Pains 194-195
Palms 85, 125
Panama 8
Pancreas 2
Pandemonium 141
Paracelsus 242, 284
Paradise 54, 75-76
Paradises 146-148
Paradisiacal 33, 40, 82
Parasites 91
Parents 292
Parere 292
Paris 178
Paropamisan Mountains 279
Particles 87, 115, 200, 267
Pascal 34-35, 37
Passion 105, 132, 143, 224, 236, 292-293
Passionate 71, 167, 247
Passions 51, 65, 89, 178, 247
Passive 282
Passports 2
Past 2, 12, 14, 17, 55, 75, 79, 121, 136, 140, 156, 201, 235, 256, 275
Pastures 180
Path 25-26, 41-42, 51, 53-54, 71, 89, 91, 94, 120, 123, 162-163, 190-192, 221, 280, 284-285
Pathogenic 271
Pathology 47
Paths 133, 172, 222, 285
Patience 57, 70, 85, 97, 171, 179, 190
Patient 97, 171, 179, 181
Patiently 25
Paul Otto Hess 266
Pay 19, 140, 171, 178, 275
Paying 192, 229
Peace 30, 34, 53, 113-114, 147, 180, 196, 256, 292
Pearl 251

Pearls 23, 147, 194, 203, 210, 251
Pedestal 282
Pellegrini 217
Pellucid 288
Penance 90, 152
Pendulum 270
Penis 215
Penny 114
Pentagonal 88
Pentecost 49, 153, 251
Pentecostal 49, 75, 246, 249, 251
Perceive 275, 291
Percent 26, 243, 264
Perception 76, 282, 291
Perceptions 293
Perdition 90, 203, 205
Perfect 35, 51, 53, 68, 78, 80, 88, 98, 106, 109, 133, 149, 154, 214, 226, 246, 250, 259, 276, 279, 284, 287-288, 290-291
Perfect Matrimony 284
Perfection 51, 68, 286
Perfections 183
Perfectly 9, 264, 275
Perfects 250, 287
Perfumed 42, 81, 83
Perfumes 139
Pergamos 63-66
Persecute 131
Persecuted 129, 131, 165, 218, 280
Persecution 272
Persecutions 192
Perseus 126, 287
Persevere 97
Persia 7
Persian 279
Personalities 286
Personality 35, 91, 110-111, 243, 247, 250, 286
Personification 283
Persons 14, 216, 260, 290
Peru 8, 289
Perverse 7, 19, 66, 73, 127-128, 169, 195, 206-207, 210, 225-226, 229, 250
Petals 46, 57, 59, 63-64, 69, 75, 83, 87, 89, 163, 195

Peter 19, 96-97, 131, 135
Petra 131
Phallus 14, 49-50, 78-79, 148, 157, 243, 248, 282-283, 289
Phases 127
Phemonoe 286
Phenomena 9, 13, 263-266, 268, 282
Philadelphia 83-85
Philosophers 111, 131
Philosophical 66, 69, 104, 131, 167, 210, 218, 238, 241-243, 246, 249
Philosophical Stone 66, 69, 104, 131, 210, 218, 238, 249
Philosophorum 167
Philosophy 104, 125, 131, 241-242
Phlegethon 190
Phoenix Bird 82
Phosphorus 266
Physical 14, 20, 29, 34, 40-42, 54, 75, 93-95, 133, 139, 167, 178, 185, 193-195, 198, 205, 218-221, 224-225, 237, 252-253, 255-256, 258, 267, 269-271, 275, 285, 294-295
Physical Body 14, 29, 34, 40-42, 54, 75, 93-95, 185, 193, 205, 218-221, 225, 237, 253, 255, 258, 294
Physically 117, 225, 250, 286, 291, 293, 296
Physicians 4, 132
Physicists 267
Physics 199, 267, 270
Physiological 125, 241
Physiology 47
Piano 76, 83
Pig 70
Pilate 45
Pillar 85
Pillars 145
Pindar 287
Pineal 87-88, 91-92, 103
Pingala 46, 51, 79, 152, 191
Pipers 211
Pipes 46, 172
Pistis Sophia 281

Pit 137, 140, 153, 203, 229
Pitakas 181
Pitch 113
Pituitary 83, 87-88
Pity 28, 84, 243
Plague 193, 202
Plagues 115, 143, 153, 185, 187-188, 193, 207, 209, 236, 260-261
Plain 9, 20
Plan 195
Plane 9, 123, 139, 178, 255
Planes 5, 110, 127, 205, 239
Planetary 25, 99, 117, 137, 155, 157, 186, 200-202, 209, 291
Planetary Spirits 186
Planets 2, 156, 200-202, 221, 263-264
Plant 16, 196, 287
Plantations 134
Plants 180, 268
Plastic 95
Plateau 7
Plato 152
Play 2, 187
Playful 247
Plays 173, 290
Pleasant 63
Pleasure 17, 55, 106, 292
Pleiades 264, 268
Plenitude 180
Plex 81, 83
Plexus 46-47, 238
Pluralized I 286, 290
Plus 152, 220, 245
Pm 25, 161
Pocket 199
Poem 75, 83
Poet 21, 216-217, 283
Poetess 286
Point 1-2, 9, 13, 87, 94-95, 245, 269, 273, 282-283
Pointed 219
Pointing 124, 241, 292
Points 4, 121, 141
Poisoned 163
Poisoning 173
Poisonous 94, 132

Polar 270
Polarities 279, 286
Pole 9-10, 48, 229, 268, 287
Poles 4, 9-10, 20, 268-269
Police 192
Policy 292
Politics 70, 139, 219
Pollution 16
Polyvoyance 88, 91
Popluation 279
Populate 123, 277
Populates 1
Pornographic 123
Portico 286
Position 27, 238
Positive 109, 272
Possess 34, 294
Possessed 3
Possesses 41
Possession 3, 5
Possessions 292
Postchristian 281
Postpone 128, 222
Potable 243, 249
Potencies 4, 145, 197, 256
Potency 87, 91, 281
Potentates 71, 139, 209
Potential 282
Pots 281
Potter 72
Pour 189
Poured 104, 178, 189, 191-195, 197-201, 281
Pours 180
Poverty 51, 60
Power of Tongues 80, 219
Practical 26, 272
Practical Magic 272
Practice 26, 30, 95, 97, 177, 181, 216, 218, 221, 226, 241, 244, 254-255, 283, 285, 289
Practices 97, 220, 253, 255, 258, 280, 285, 288
Practicing 95, 124, 159, 190, 241-242, 291
Praise 110, 213, 282, 292
Praised 258

Praises 85, 259, 280
Praising 250
Prakamya 94-95
Pralaya 75, 292
Prana 81, 104
Prapti 94
Pray 53, 59, 82, 90
Prayed 29
Prayer 67, 285
Prayers 108, 129
Praying 29, 129
Preach 178
Preached 131
Preachers 172
Preaching 65
Precept 286
Preceptors 292
Precepts 125
Precipice 169
Precipitate 163
Precipitated 269
Precise 9, 19, 28, 236-237, 259, 293
Precisely 19, 28, 132, 162, 263-264
Predict 25, 219, 269
Presence 83, 85, 178, 222, 282, 284
Pride 116, 205, 250, 271, 274, 283, 292
Priest 5, 58, 77, 104-105, 109, 182, 186, 236
Priestess 77, 141, 236
Priestesses 231
Priesthood 98
Priests 33, 63, 107, 109, 119, 231, 280, 294
Priests of Nature 63
Primary 291
Primeval 264
Primitive 196, 279
Primogenitary 187
Primordial 13, 79, 287, 292-293
Prince 39, 45, 73, 126, 135, 160, 191, 281, 285
Prince Courst 281
Princes 73
Principal 216, 264
Principates 2

Principle 205, 236, 283, 287, 290, 294
Principles 17, 79, 205, 225, 242, 282
Printing 23
Prison 60, 96-97, 218, 230
Prittvi 57
Prittwi 198
Problem 154
Problems 25, 135
Procedures 242
Proceeded 103, 224
Proceedeth 152
Proceeding 256
Process 9-10, 14, 25, 79, 105, 157, 196-197, 250, 255, 267-268, 285, 288
Processed 272
Proclaiming 108
Procreation 198, 287
Procured 286
Prodigies 90, 199, 224
Prodigious 216
Produce 17, 152, 193, 237, 271
Produced 141, 271, 275, 291
Produces 53-54, 275, 286, 295
Producing 282, 292
Production 283, 291
Productive 283
Profane 116, 151, 241, 259, 280
Profaned 119-120, 132
Profundities 33, 43, 111, 213, 235, 245, 274
Progenitor 291
Progeny 21
Project 16
Projected 227
Projections 72, 274
Propato 182, 190
Prophecies 17, 217, 225, 281
Prophecy 12, 94, 154, 211, 214, 259-261
Prophesied 12, 153, 217
Prophesies 288
Prophesy 33, 85, 107-108, 146, 151-153, 214, 258
Prophesying 19
Prophet 18, 34, 120, 154, 198, 224, 230, 237, 239, 244
Prophetess 70-72, 84, 90, 97
Prophetic 281
Prophets 115, 145-147, 153-154, 157, 163, 192-193, 200, 210-211, 222, 258-260
Proportion 200
Proposals 122
Prostate 59
Prostitute 290
Protoplasm 13, 292
Protoplasmatic 292
Protoplasmic 13, 286
Proud 68, 73
Prout 287
Provided 294
Prudent 249
Pseudo-esoteric 294
Pseudo-occult 294
Psyche 137
Psychic 281
Psychological 20, 133, 139-140, 160, 195, 198-199, 248, 250, 258, 271, 273-276, 283
Psychology 270, 290, 293, 295
Psychometry 94
Psychophysical 275
Public 15, 287, 293
Publicly 42, 218
Punish 288
Punished 136, 201
Punishes 189
Punishing 183
Punishment 120, 155, 210
Purana 288
Puranic 295
Purely 3
Purest 35, 45, 215
Purge 122
Purifications 35, 73
Purified 93
Purity 216, 288
Purple 70, 73, 107-108, 119, 194, 203, 210
Purânic 295
Pygmies 57, 247

Pythagoras 152, 242, 248, 286
Qualifying 185
Qualities 292-294
Quality 218, 292-294
Quantity 125, 151, 162, 177, 183, 198
Quarrel 292
Quarrels 283
Quarters 230
Quaternaries 225
Queen 3-4, 87, 160, 209, 217
Queen of Heaven 160
Queen of Woeful Destinies 3
Queens 59, 64, 215, 231
Quench 148
Question 172, 226
Quiet 53, 90, 94, 254-255
Quietly 57
Quietude 51, 95
Quite 281
Quod Nemo Nocet Nist Qui Accipit 51
Ra 237
Ra-mu 5
Rabbi 40-41
Rabbi of Galilee 40-41
Race 1-2, 5, 7-9, 13, 15, 17, 108, 113-114, 117-118, 135, 155, 169-170, 183, 205, 207, 227, 235, 238, 251, 254, 277, 279, 287-288, 290-291, 295-296
Races 8-9, 12, 108, 242, 279, 281, 291, 296
Radiant 2, 137
Radiate 88
Radiation 265-270
Radiations 267
Radically 20
Radio 173
Radioactive 115, 200, 265, 270
Radioactivity 134, 193
Ragon 217
Rags 289
Raiment 78, 91, 103
Rain 107, 153, 180
Rainbow 21, 103, 145
Raise 49, 88, 168, 221, 223

Raised 18, 28, 49, 96, 105, 221, 284
Raises 244
Rajas 143, 292-293
Rama 152, 248, 280
Ramon Flores Derma 23
Ramu 5
Range 282
Rank 220, 289
Raped 132
Rapes 189
Raphael 129, 132-133, 185, 192
Rapture 54
Rationalize 75
Raw 64-65, 69, 79, 91, 247
Ray 33-35, 37, 61, 68, 106, 116, 135, 162, 195-197, 210, 219, 289
Ray of Medicine 289
Ray of Strength 162
Raymond Lully 242
Rays 63, 115, 121, 134, 173, 249, 266, 283
Razor 25-26, 51, 190
Ready 78, 160, 213, 256
Real 51, 289, 293, 295
Reality 3, 9, 16, 20, 34, 40, 109, 146, 245, 251, 264, 266-268, 274, 293
Realize 29
Realized 28, 124, 282
Realizing 284
Reap 181-182
Reason 131, 135, 137, 179, 187, 196, 210, 219, 251
Reasoning 75, 287, 294
Rebel 199
Rebellion 282, 293
Rebels 45, 199
Rebirths 285
Receive 3, 40, 62, 72-73, 81, 104, 106, 109, 111, 123-124, 152, 174, 177-178, 180, 205, 207, 215, 247, 250, 253, 257, 284
Received 27, 40, 78, 85, 122, 205, 217, 219, 224, 231, 237, 244, 246, 260
Receives 60-62, 72, 88, 91, 180, 220, 244, 249-250, 257, 260, 287

Receiveth 66, 72, 178
Receiving 51, 64, 94, 216, 241
Receptacle 79, 247, 282, 295
Receptive 283
Recognize 110, 127
Recognized 29, 283
Recognizes 295
Reconquer 76, 254
Reconquered 286
Recorded 217, 263
Records 242, 281
Rectifictur 184, 238
Rectifying 184, 238
Red 59, 73, 76, 113, 160, 283
Red Sea 59
Reddish 134
Redeemed 109, 177
Redeemer 137, 215
Redemption 91
Red-skinned 113
Reduce 13, 94, 285
Reduced 19, 95
Reduces 79
Reed 98, 151, 244-246
Regenerator 104, 125
Regent 132-133, 189, 275
Reincarnate 231
Reincarnated 120, 161, 186
Reincarnates 179, 250
Reincarnating 25, 161, 196, 250
Reincarnation 60-61, 121, 185, 222, 250, 258
Reincarnations 245
Reins 71
Religare 284
Religion 23, 67, 131, 226, 280, 283, 285
Religions 23, 251, 285, 288
Religious 4, 215
Remain 2, 19, 24, 26, 29-30, 51, 53, 65, 78, 90, 117, 165, 229, 241, 248, 255, 271, 288, 290
Remained 28, 40-41, 154, 185, 196, 290
Remaining 64
Remains 13, 15, 39, 41, 119, 122

Remember 3, 9, 19, 27-28, 51, 58, 64, 67-68, 73, 78, 89-90, 92, 99, 104-105, 110, 123, 201, 217, 226, 238, 265
Remembered 19, 207
Remembering 253
Remembrance 201
Reminds 4, 113, 245
Remnant 155, 168, 224, 227
Remnants 11, 295
Remorse 58
Renal 71
Renounce 111, 192
Renounces 39, 284
Renouncing 280
Renunciation 123, 180-181
Repent 58, 65, 70-71, 78, 91, 195, 229
Repentance 185
Repented 70, 143, 185, 193-194
Representation 13, 282, 291
Representations 283
Reproduce 260-261
Reproduced 13
Reproducing 279
Reproduction 13, 279, 285
Reptiles 23, 259
Resentment 68, 271
Resentments 68, 127
Respect 27, 67, 268, 293-294
Respiratory 243
Resurrect 12, 45, 62, 82, 88, 94, 154-155, 171
Resurrected 26, 40-41
Resurrecting 81
Resurrection 29, 40-41, 62, 154-155, 229, 231
Resurrects 92
Retrospective 281
Return 25, 63, 110, 148, 171, 195, 197, 207, 223, 225-227, 230, 245, 264, 282
Returned 9, 185, 196, 220, 289
Returning 54, 280
Returns 1, 110, 197-198, 223
Reuben 124
Revealed 53, 284

Revelation 25, 30, 33, 35, 39, 43, 57, 60, 62, 64, 70, 77, 84, 91, 100, 103, 108, 113, 120, 124, 129, 137, 141, 145, 151, 159, 169, 177, 182, 185, 189, 203, 207, 213, 229, 235, 256
Revelations 288
Revenge 49, 68
Revolution 11, 41, 127-128, 135, 192, 196-197, 219-220, 250, 291
Revolutionary 263-264, 290, 295
Revolutions 197
Reward 146-147, 157, 209, 259
Rewarded 209
Rhythms 69, 77
Ribs 18
Rich 60, 91, 117, 174, 207, 210
Riches 109, 111, 139, 210
Richest 34
Riding 288
Rifles 28
Right 9, 39, 43, 46, 50, 57, 92, 108, 145, 147-148, 174, 246, 260, 281, 284
Righteous 193, 213, 259
Righteousness 120, 213-214, 288
Rigor 139
Rigorous 73, 241, 250
Rind 282
Ring 269
Rings 105, 250, 265-266, 268-271, 277
Ripe 117, 182
Ripened 132
Rise 40, 50, 79, 89, 95, 98, 100, 110, 133, 151-152, 169, 186, 225, 256
Risen 97, 222, 257-258
Rises 46, 50, 60, 64, 79, 89, 169, 228, 251, 291
Rishis 295
Rising 73, 80, 104, 187, 226
Rite 3
Rites 293
Rituals 46, 77
Rival 219

River 34, 62, 80, 94, 141, 198, 253, 255-257, 259, 261
Rivers 16, 133, 192-193, 198
Roads 28
Roareth 145
Roaring 27, 135
Robes 115, 125-126
Robot 3
Robots 3
Rock 84, 118, 131, 148, 159, 220
Rocket 156
Rockets 2, 20, 116, 140, 143, 199
Rocks 117-118, 265, 268
Rod 72, 151, 157, 161, 215, 289
Rod of Aaron 151, 157
Rogues 293
Rohan 218
Rolled 117
Roman 229
Romans 7
Romantic 83
Rome 178, 242
Roof 20
Room 281
Rooster 105
Root Manu 291
Root Races 108
Rooted 83, 180, 281
Root-race 295
Roots 249, 289
Ropes 107
Rose 39, 64, 170, 213, 289
Rose Cross 289
Rosecrucian 289
Roses 33
Rosicrucianism 241
Rudolf Steiner 186, 227
Ruins 7, 134, 209
Rush 9
Rya 279
Sabbaoth 279
Sackcloth 90, 115, 134, 151-152
Sacrament 14
Sacred Individuals 289
Sacred Order 190
Sacrifice 67, 89, 177, 181, 190, 241, 280, 282, 285

Sacrificed 4, 65, 70
Sacrifices 293
Sacrificing 256
Sacrilege 58, 110, 120
Sage 215, 238, 291, 295
Sahu 286
Sailors 210
Saint 41, 62, 80, 94, 269
Saint Francis of Assisi 94
Saint Germain 41, 269
Saintliness 65
Saintly 51
Saints 18, 34, 41, 46, 61, 87-88, 97-98, 108, 120, 123, 129, 157, 163, 170-171, 173, 179, 187, 193, 200-201, 203, 211, 213, 230, 286
Saith 33, 57, 60-61, 64, 66, 70, 72, 77-78, 84-85, 91-92, 108, 159, 179, 206, 209, 213, 258-259, 261
Sake 57, 107, 110
Sakyamuni 180
Salamanders 3, 247
Salt 13, 104, 125, 243
Salutations 217, 293
Salvation 23, 26, 126, 157, 163, 213
Samadhi 220, 293
Samael 21, 30, 129, 137, 185, 194, 214, 221, 280, 283, 285, 287, 289-290, 293, 295
Samael Aun Weor 21, 30, 221, 280, 283, 285, 287, 289-290, 293, 295
Sambhala 288
Samsara 205
Sanctification 244
Sanctity 123
Sanctorum 50, 119
Sanctuary 23, 33, 64, 67, 73, 119-120, 132, 220
Sanctuary of Barquisimeto 23
Sanctum 50, 119, 248
Sand 100, 169, 230, 265, 267
Sandals 67
Sandlike 87
Sands 118, 156

Sanskrit 265, 279-280, 288, 290-293, 295
Sapphire 249-250
Sardine 103
Sardis 45, 75-79, 81
Sardius 249
Sardonynx 249
Sariputra 180
Satanic 65, 71, 179, 196, 280
Satellites 264
Sathapatha Brahmana 295
Satisfy 179, 196, 250
Satori 293
Sattva 280
Saturated 63, 266
Saturn 145, 200, 263-265
Save 5, 50, 121, 129, 171, 174, 193-194, 196, 231, 274
Saved 7, 118, 122, 125, 135, 155, 171, 177, 190-191, 195, 197, 201, 218, 252, 257, 295
Saves 274
Saving 66
Savior 23, 26-27, 62, 81, 129, 131, 154, 159, 161, 172, 181, 222, 229, 258, 296
Scaffold 217
Scale 167, 171, 226
Scandal 293
Scarlet 70-71, 107-108, 194, 203, 210
Sceptre 215
Schimeon 276
School 23, 53, 67, 221, 226, 242-243, 245, 254, 293
Schools 23, 25, 200, 223, 241, 244-245, 260, 283, 285, 294
Schrader of Germany 218
Science 2, 4, 9, 11, 20, 24, 42, 63, 70, 84, 89, 91, 95, 104, 116-117, 119, 124, 131-132, 141, 151, 157, 171, 173, 193, 199, 218, 224, 241-242, 264, 266-268, 289
Sciences 291
Scientific 9, 79, 129, 155, 241, 268
Scientist 265, 269, 287

Scientists 3, 9, 11, 16, 116, 139, 143, 157, 265, 267
Scoria 64
Scorpions 139-140, 200
Scripture 19
Scriptures 40, 181, 264, 291, 294
Scroll 117, 219
Sculptures 13
Scythe 145, 200
Sea of Galilee 97
Seabeds 11
Seal 69, 71, 110, 113-115, 120-122, 124, 129, 131, 133, 135, 139, 145, 148, 186, 229, 259
Seal of Solomon 120-121
Sealed 25, 83, 101, 107-109, 111, 120-125, 128, 148, 242
Sealed Book 25, 101, 107, 109, 111
Sealing 211
Seals 30, 83, 108-109, 111, 113, 115, 117
Seaquakes 115, 134
Search 7, 33, 53, 64, 72, 110, 238, 281-282
Searched 104
Searches 53-54
Searcheth 71
Searching 242, 245
Season 115, 229
Seasons 1, 269
Seat 18, 65, 68, 100, 169, 194, 198
Seated 145, 183, 205, 224
Seats 68, 103, 157
Seauton 286
Sebal 45, 199
Second 7, 11, 13, 17-18, 25, 27, 45, 53, 60-62, 68, 76, 104, 113, 132, 135, 141, 156, 167, 181, 190-192, 198-199, 216, 220-221, 230-231, 235-236, 244-245, 249, 253, 257, 266, 274-275, 281, 285, 288, 290, 294
Second Arcanum 141
Second Epistle 135
Second Logos 290
Second Truth 191, 285

Secrecy 180
Secret 15, 23, 26, 29-30, 41-42, 53, 68, 71, 79, 91, 104, 110, 125, 159-160, 181, 216, 218, 220, 224, 229, 242, 255, 257-259, 280-281, 291-292, 295
Secret Doctrine 23, 29, 181, 258, 280, 291, 295
Secret Order 220
Secretion 4
Secretly 118, 129, 135-136, 195, 201, 207
Secrets 30, 260
Sect 67, 245, 283
Sects 23, 251, 286
Securities 135
Security 25
Seduce 70
Seed 49, 118, 168, 277, 287, 291, 295-296
Seed Manu 291
Seed of Life 296
Seeds 288
Seer 83, 258-259, 280
Sees 76, 85, 273
Segregate 134
Select 5, 20, 118
Selection 277
Self 67, 89-90, 181, 196, 282, 286
Self-control 294
Self-explore 276
Self-realization 220, 242
Self-realize 292
Self-realize Himself 292
Self-realized 218, 239, 242
Selfish 67, 127
Selfishness 2, 127
Self-praise 258
Self-realizing 292
Semen 58, 64, 80, 125, 148-149, 153, 155-156, 171, 177, 180, 187, 191, 211, 216, 238, 242-243, 249, 251, 256-257, 284-285
Seminal 79, 89, 104, 148, 172, 213, 291
Seminis 46, 78-80, 103-105, 125, 179-181, 238, 284

Sensation 95, 97, 216, 238, 282
Sensations 282
Sense 3, 85, 131, 275, 279, 292
Senseless 146
Senselessness 294
Senses 3, 20, 47, 64, 167, 291, 293
Sensitive 51
Sensory 291, 293
Sensual 25, 67, 293
Sephira 257, 273-275
Sephiroth 205, 250, 257, 260, 273, 275, 277, 290
Sephirothic 265, 273-275
Sephirotic 34, 274
Sephirotic Crown 34
September 122
Septenary 35, 106, 251, 294
Sepulcher 40
Sepulchers 39
Sepulchre 40, 154, 217-219
Sepulchres 69
Seraching 287
Seraphic 197
Seraphim 197, 256
Serene 53
Serpent of Metal 46, 49-51
Serpentine 67, 75
Serpents 46, 94, 143, 190, 220-221
Set 17, 84, 92, 103, 145, 229, 289
Seth 186
Seven 7-8, 29, 43, 45-47, 49-51, 53, 56-57, 67, 69, 77, 81, 83, 88, 90, 92, 97-98, 100, 103-106, 108, 113, 115, 117, 129, 131, 145, 155, 160, 167, 169, 184-185, 187-189, 191, 193-195, 197-199, 201, 203, 205, 214, 220-221, 223, 225, 229, 236, 242, 249, 251, 264, 280, 283-284, 290-291, 294-296
Seven Angels 129, 131, 184-185, 187-189, 203, 236
Seven Bodies 221, 294
Seven Churches 43, 45-47, 49-50, 53, 56, 77, 88, 90, 97-98, 104-106, 167, 242
Seven Seals 83, 108, 113, 115, 117

Seven Spirits 43, 77, 88, 103, 108, 145, 280, 284
Seven Subraces 7-8
Seven Vials 185, 187, 189, 191, 193, 195, 197, 199, 201, 203, 236
Seventh 3, 9, 12, 54, 68-69, 129, 131, 133, 135, 145-147, 149, 155-156, 181, 190, 200, 205, 220-221, 249, 264, 268, 295
Seventh Arcanum 155
Seventh Seal 129, 131, 133, 135
Seventh Trumpet 145, 147, 149
Sex 49, 63, 66, 84, 98, 103, 118, 122, 126-127, 131, 148, 151-152, 157, 162, 171-172, 175, 177, 182, 190, 192, 215, 220-221, 223, 226, 238, 243, 245, 248-249, 251, 260, 273, 295
Sexes 14
Sexless 279
Sexual 14, 50, 57, 65, 77, 87, 89, 91, 104, 109, 121, 124-125, 131, 148, 154-155, 159, 171-172, 175, 177, 190-191, 193, 197, 213, 217-219, 221, 223, 226, 235-239, 241-244, 249-251, 273, 279, 284, 286, 289-291, 295
Sexual Alchemy 65, 89, 104, 109, 121, 124, 213, 239, 241-242
Sexual Center 289
Sexual Magic 124, 131, 148, 159, 171, 177, 217-219, 241-242, 244, 291
Sexuality 215
Sexually 165, 167, 215, 236
Shade 147
Shadow 49, 73, 90-91, 99, 110, 163, 205, 222, 241, 259
Shadows 64, 109, 111, 186
Shakyamuni 284
Shamballa 26, 40-42
Shame 91, 199-200
Shameful 189
Sharks 7
Sheep 137, 210
Shell 282

Shelter 110
Shephards 32
Shepherd 127
Ship 192
Shipmaster 210
Ships 2, 116, 133, 156, 200-201, 207, 210
Shoes 214
Shushumna 46, 182
Shy 42
Sick 4, 132, 221, 292
Sickle 181-183
Sicknesses 24, 115, 134, 143, 193, 271
Sicut Superius Sicut Quot Inferius 233, 238
Sidereal 1, 40
Sides 50, 131
Sidon 58
Sighing 242, 245
Sight 11, 88, 103, 173, 218, 281
Sign 21, 98, 122-123, 137, 185, 190-191, 201
Signed 119, 223
Significance 264
Significant 264
Signifies 25, 70, 83, 123, 135, 169, 226, 266, 268
Signify 203, 220, 251
Signs 135, 239
Silence 129, 255
Silenced 255
Silent 41, 51, 53
Silk 71, 194, 210
Silver 1-2, 18, 71, 113, 119, 139, 143, 194, 209-210, 241
Silver Ages 2
Simeon 124
Sin 67, 85, 90, 127, 153, 167, 195, 275
Sincere 53, 122, 242
Sincerity 201, 242
Sinful 147, 294
Sing 34, 59, 187, 231, 237, 253
Singing 69, 253
Single 26, 49, 104, 155, 269, 284
Sings 59

Sink 122, 155, 157, 160, 172, 223, 226, 230, 244
Sinking 171, 182
Sinned 99, 110, 189
Sinner 68, 91, 180, 185
Sinners 136, 180, 201
Sinning 90, 99, 109-111, 259
Sins 19, 39, 129, 153, 203, 205, 207, 256, 283
Sion 176-177, 179, 181, 183
Sister 68
Sisters 5, 23, 26, 64, 95, 107, 119, 159, 162, 168-169, 172, 192, 226, 263
Sivananda 24, 26, 94
Sivananda Aryabarta Ahsrama 24, 26
Six 10, 59, 94-95, 104-105, 121, 151, 174, 183, 241, 291
Sixteen 75, 289
Sixth 3, 8, 12, 54, 68, 85, 104-105, 115, 117-118, 141, 143, 150-151, 181, 190, 198, 205, 207, 221, 235, 238, 249, 251, 277, 295
Sixth Arcanum 104-105, 150-151
Sixth Trumpet 141, 143
Sixty-six 174
Skeptic 257
Skepticism 211
Skeptics 179, 200
Slander 181
Slandered 195
Slanderers 275
Slandering 217
Slanders 217
Slave 39, 73
Slavery 114
Slaves 5, 210
Slavonic 279
Sleep 54, 95, 237, 255, 294
Sleeping 255-256
Sleeps 54, 57
Slug 68, 99, 259, 280
Sly 127, 140
Smiled 27, 197
Smiling 195

Smog 16
Smyrna 59-61
Snare 51
Snow 43
Social 189, 216
Society 3
Sodom 135, 153
Soft 42, 53
Soil 16, 41, 217-219
Soissons 27
Solar 1-4, 7, 9-12, 19-20, 35-36, 49, 53, 77, 79, 81, 93, 105, 115, 238-239, 251, 264, 266, 268-270, 274, 286
Solar Dynasties 2
Solar Logos 35-36
Solar Man 286
Solar Stone 11
Soldier 27, 29
Soldiers 27, 229
Solid 225
Solomon 50, 120-121, 186, 286
Solution 281
Solvent 167
Soma 286
Son 25, 31, 33-35, 37, 43, 45, 54, 57-58, 61, 64, 66, 68, 70, 72-73, 80-81, 84, 87, 90, 92, 98, 103, 107, 126, 128, 133, 156, 159-163, 167, 181, 183, 214, 236, 243, 248, 260, 290-291, 296
Son of God 70
Song 109, 177, 187
Songs 99, 293
Sons 121
Soph 163, 195, 197, 245, 257
Sophia 281
Sophism 110, 222
Sorcerers 236, 257, 260
Sorceries 143, 211
Sorcery 211
Sore 189
Sores 194-195
Sorrow 209, 235
Sosiosh 288
Soul 34-35, 45, 47, 51-55, 58, 64, 68, 90, 92-93, 110-111, 114, 126-128, 185-186, 192, 205, 213, 220, 225, 235, 259-260, 280, 286, 293
Souls 41, 51, 62, 93, 115, 137, 139, 174, 186, 194, 198, 210-211, 223, 231, 260, 267, 275
Sound 43, 68-69, 82, 116, 131, 134-135, 140, 145, 159, 211, 223, 236-237
Sounded 80-81, 131-134, 137, 141, 156
Sounds 43, 68-69, 82, 99, 216, 277
South 1, 8, 15, 20, 24, 239, 269, 289
South America 8, 15, 289
Sow 182
Sows 189, 209
Space 5, 34, 63, 69-70, 116, 120, 129, 156, 163, 173, 183, 195-196, 199, 202, 205, 227, 239, 245, 251, 257, 267, 273-274
Spaceships 7
Spaniards 8
Spanish 23
Spark 110, 287
Spasm 148, 241
Speak 12, 29, 72, 79-81, 90, 98, 173, 268, 271, 281
Speaking 9, 23, 170, 239, 292
Speaks 33, 143, 173, 201, 214, 219
Spear 69
Special 67, 87, 266
Specialist 95, 120
Species 17, 268, 279
Specter 73
Speech 284, 290, 292
Sperm 247, 286
Sperms 286
Sphere 49-50, 98, 122-123, 127, 151-152, 162, 175, 177, 190, 224, 248
Spheres 227, 239, 251
Spikes 117, 132
Spill 49, 65, 79, 105, 148
Spilled 58, 79, 148
Spilling 155-156, 247
Spills 58, 153, 191, 285

Spinal 43, 45-46, 49-50, 88, 98, 151-152, 182, 190-191, 225, 242, 244, 246, 277
Spine 190-191, 244
Spiral 280
Spiral Path 280
Spirit of Life 154, 196
Spirits 43, 77, 88, 103, 108, 145, 186, 198-199, 207, 280, 284
Spirits of God 77, 103, 108
Spiritual 54, 133, 167, 171, 177, 185, 199, 225, 241, 270, 285, 288
Spirituality 116, 178-179, 215
Spiritually 60, 91, 153, 296
Spirituous 125
Splendid 7
Splendorous 88
Splendors 2, 83, 186
Sportsmen 119
Spouse 54, 129, 181, 236
Spring 1-2, 104, 127, 269
Square 131, 245-246, 282
St. Germain 217-220
Stables 113, 126
Staff 49-50, 92, 118, 151, 225, 244, 248
Staff of Aaron 50
Star 11, 67, 72-73, 88, 133, 137, 163, 195-197, 260, 264
Star of Dawn 260
Starch 266
Starry 33, 83, 87-88, 116, 239
Stars 43, 57, 77, 117, 134-135, 158-161, 167, 264, 266
Starts 123, 248, 251
Starvation 6
Statistics 198
Stature 1, 13, 15
Staurus 78, 293
Steam 15, 104
Steel 28
Steeples 119
Steering 169
Steiner 186, 227
Step 202, 225, 256
Steps 39, 73, 133, 190-191, 221, 225, 256-258, 284

Sterile 198
Sterilizing 16
Stigmatas 73
Stigmatized 89, 98
Stings 140
Stock 270, 279
Stokin 45, 199
Stolidity 294
Stomach 63, 65
Stoned 163
Stones 84, 103, 132, 194, 203, 210, 249-250, 265
Straight 222, 245, 280
Straight Path 280
Strait 148, 172, 222
Strasbourg 218
Strength 37, 43, 84, 109, 111, 125, 162-163, 205, 284
Strengthen 78, 97, 127
Strengthened 127
Strengthening 97
Struggle 20, 49, 105, 190, 255, 283
Struggles 190
Struggling 133
Stubborn 218, 270
Stula-Sarira 294
Stupid 294
Style 73, 217
Subconsciousness 254
Subject 216, 241
Subjective 274
Sublimated 243
Sublime 33, 39, 45, 59, 77, 83, 145, 216, 220
Sublunar 162, 227
Submarines 173
Submerge 10, 94-95, 195, 254
Submerged 4-5, 40-41, 52, 54, 58, 61, 94-95, 118, 185, 194, 224
Submergence 7, 269
Submerges 64
Submerging 66, 185
Submersion 295
Subrace 7-9
Substance 267, 292
Substances 79
Subterranean 39, 57

Subtle 4, 77, 87, 237
Subtlest 51
Subtypes 16
Suffer 60, 84, 146, 154, 165, 265, 272, 281
Suffered 107, 154, 185, 194, 197, 218, 269
Sufferest 70
Suffering 23, 26, 30, 39, 57, 67, 107, 110, 122, 193, 196, 256, 280, 284-285
Sufferings 35, 190
Suffers 58
Suffocated 5
Sufism 53
Suicide 217
Sulphur 125, 243, 246
Summa Materia 167
Summer 1, 269
Sun 1, 9, 11-13, 15, 34, 37, 43, 73, 94-95, 98-99, 110, 115, 126, 131, 134-135, 137, 145, 158-161, 165, 167, 193, 223, 241, 246, 252, 258, 263-264, 266-268, 282, 284, 287, 296
Sun-Man 35
Sung 34, 109, 177
Suns 17, 61, 264, 268
Super 245-246
Superdivine 163, 195, 197
Superficial 116
Superhuman 288
Superior Manas 265
Superior Worlds 25, 45-46, 54-55, 85, 93, 95, 116, 119, 177, 237-238, 241-243, 250, 256-257
Superius 233, 238
Superlative Consciousness 295
Supernal Triangle 61
Supernatural 218
Supersonic 5
Suprasensible 40-41, 54-55, 95, 214
Survive 20
Survived 250
Survivors 7-8, 129
Surya 296

Sutras 293
Swadha 293
Swaha 293
Swami Trillinga of Benares 94
Swan 59
Sware 145
Swayambhuva 291
Swear 221
Sweet 33, 59, 99, 146, 178, 215-216, 237
Sweetness 54, 140, 197, 271
Swift 10
Swim 7
Switzerland 27
Swollen 180
Sword 43, 64-65, 71, 73, 104, 113-114, 126, 152, 166-167, 171, 173, 215, 224-225, 249-250, 288
Syllable 237, 253-254
Syllables 237, 253-254
Sylphs 3, 247
Symbiosis 128
Symbol 50, 137, 151, 157, 160, 167, 169, 193, 239, 282-283
Symbolic 125, 139, 177
Symbolize 104, 121, 154, 246, 251
Symbolized 70, 190, 203, 246, 283
Symbolizes 190, 249, 282
Symbols 165, 187, 242
Sympathetic 46, 50, 79, 152, 155, 191
Symphonies 75
Symphony 33, 69
Synagogue 60, 65, 84
Synthesis 121, 163, 172, 286
Synthetism 75
Systems 264
Syyin 171
Séra 283
Tabernacle 34, 98, 170, 187, 235
Table 7, 35, 68, 76, 145
Tablecloth 61
Tablet 125
Tablets 50, 157
Tail 58, 105, 160, 228, 290
Tails 140, 143

Talk 13, 156
Talked 203, 236, 244
Talking 43, 103
Tamas 143, 293-294
Tame 49, 168
Taming 105
Tantras 293
Tantric 162
Tantrism 65, 283, 285
Tapas 285
Target 28
Tarot 104, 124, 141, 151, 155, 239, 292
Tartarean 41
Task 271
Tasnim 148
Taste 51, 55, 199
Tathagata 180
Tattva 57, 59, 63, 69, 75, 198
Tattvas 4
Tau 105, 241
Tav 293
Te 286
Teach 26, 42, 57, 70, 89, 108, 156, 159, 168, 283
Teaches 25, 53, 70
Teaching 43, 67, 77, 226, 237, 283-284, 289, 293
Teachings 186, 242, 264, 280, 285, 289
Tears 15, 49, 110, 113, 122, 126, 161, 189, 235
Teeth 18, 140, 222
Tejas 198
Teleelectronically 140, 143
Telepathically 3
Telepathy 94
Telescopes 9
Television 173
Tempest 33, 113, 122, 242, 250
Tempests 45, 107, 189, 209
Temple 2, 4, 23, 26, 42, 46, 50, 58, 64-65, 76, 82, 84-85, 92, 95, 103, 105, 107, 119, 126, 132, 151, 154, 157, 159, 168-169, 172, 181-182, 187-189, 200, 215, 220, 226, 244, 246-247, 251, 259, 280, 286
Temple of Solomon 50
Temples 14, 55, 70, 73, 75, 77, 88, 123, 133, 242, 251
Temptation 51, 85
Temptations 175
Tempted 168, 229
Tempting 105, 123, 165, 167-168, 228
Tempts 165
Ten Commandments 181, 283
Tenth 69, 155, 181, 249, 288
Tenth Arcanum 155
Terminate 210, 224
Termination 291
Ternary 133, 245-246
Terra 184, 238
Terrestrial 1, 104, 115, 117, 125, 134-135, 137, 226, 265
Test 271
Testament 157, 249
Testicles 79, 172
Testifieth 261
Testify 81, 260
Testimony 14-15, 40, 81, 115, 153, 157, 163, 168, 187, 214, 224
Tetradimensional 294
Tetragrammaton 245-246
Teutonic 279
Teutons 7
The Book That Kills Death 27, 29
The Metamorphosis 6
Theaters 123
Theft 293
Thefts 143
Thelema 79
Theogony 281
Theories 118, 173, 223, 226, 242-244, 285
Theorize 26
Theory 13, 15, 199, 226, 243, 245
Theosophical 27, 35, 106, 186, 294
Theosophical Septenary 35, 106, 294
Theosophist 218, 251
Theosophists 289, 294-295
Theosophy 241, 245

Thief 19, 78, 135, 199
Thieves 84, 288
Thigh 215, 289
Thing 65, 127, 139, 220, 252-253, 265, 273, 282
Think 67, 254-255, 271-273
Thinking 255
Thinks 254
Third 3, 7, 11, 13, 15, 17, 25-26, 40, 45, 53, 68, 76, 80, 104, 114, 131-134, 141, 143, 154, 156, 160, 167, 171, 178, 181, 190-191, 193, 198-199, 215, 221, 235, 237, 244-245, 248-249, 253, 256, 281, 284-285, 290-291, 294-295
Third Logos 171, 215, 237, 248, 290
Third Race 295
Third Truth 191, 285
Third World War 17
Thirst 26, 59, 76, 126-127, 148, 260, 292
Thirsty 236, 260
Thirteenth 38-39
Thirteenth Arcanum 38-39
Thirty-six 83
Thirty-three 225, 244, 246
Thirty-two 133
Thornless 147
Thorns 73, 88, 159
Thorny 180
Thought 28, 59, 124, 179, 181, 221, 247, 253, 283, 290
Thoughts 95, 179, 283, 292
Three 1, 5, 9, 18, 25-26, 45, 61, 76, 86, 114, 133, 135, 143, 151, 154, 183, 191, 198-199, 201, 220, 233, 235, 239, 244-245, 253, 256-258, 263, 266, 270, 279, 283, 285-286, 289-290, 292-293, 295
Three Atoms 86
Three Brains 283, 295
Three Factors 285
Three-brained 295
Threescore 151-152, 161-162, 174
Threw 4, 215

Thrice-Spirit 154
Throat 76
Throne 43, 51, 87-88, 92, 102-106, 108-109, 118, 125-126, 129, 145, 161, 177, 200, 213, 235, 256-257, 280, 284
Throne of God 126, 177, 256-257, 280
Thrones 2, 147, 197, 231, 249, 256
Thunder 6, 45, 59, 68-69, 107, 113, 177
Thunderbolt 283
Thundering 273
Thunderings 103, 131, 157, 213
Thunders 69, 145, 200
Thyatira 67, 69-73
Thyine 194, 210
Thyroid 75
Tibet 7, 26, 40, 190, 220, 280, 283
Tibetan 42, 242, 293
Tidal 116, 134
Tigers 11, 13
Tiphereth 265, 280
Tis-chio 217
Titular 281
To Soma Heliakon 286
Toltecs 8
Tomb 40
Tongue 109, 140, 178, 199, 221
Tongues 80, 116, 125, 133, 143, 146, 154, 156, 170, 192-194, 206, 219
Topaz 249
Tower 116-117, 224
Tower of Babel 116-117, 224
Traitor 45
Traitors 45, 199, 286
Tranquil 67-68, 70-71
Tranquility 95, 237
Tranquilly 255
Transform 15-16, 20, 35, 67, 80, 84, 275
Transformation 54, 207
Transformations 270
Transformative 80
Transformed 11, 13, 16-17, 35, 93, 104, 231

Transforms 16, 34, 92, 128, 250, 275
Transmutation 171
Transmutations 247
Transmute 49, 82, 91, 125, 148, 165, 167, 197, 239, 241, 243, 247
Transmuted 79, 104, 172, 196-197, 217, 219, 243, 247
Transmutes 167
Transubstantiation 35
Treason 116
Treasure 34, 95, 218
Tree 17, 36, 61, 63-64, 117, 120, 139, 152, 215, 221, 257, 260, 273, 277
Tree of Life 36, 61, 63, 152, 221, 257, 260, 273, 277
Trees 16-17, 46, 50, 63, 120, 131, 152, 180, 241
Triad 34, 225, 292
Trials 218
Triangle 24, 26, 61, 124-125, 133-134, 239, 241, 243
Triangles 121
Triangular 63
Tribe 84, 108, 124, 186
Tribes 121-125, 128, 186, 239, 286
Tribulation 60, 70, 107, 113, 115, 126, 134
Tribunals 192
Tridimensional 265
Trillinga 94
Trinity 154
Triple 133-134
Triumph 23, 137
Triveni 50
Tropical 287
Troy 242
Trumpet 103, 132-133, 135, 141, 143, 145, 147, 149
Trumpeters 211
Trumpets 129-131
Truth 5, 23, 26, 53, 62, 72-73, 111, 121, 179-180, 191, 199, 213, 220, 275-276, 281, 285, 289, 293
Truths 14, 72, 191-192, 284-285
Tubes 271

Tula 13
Tunic 213
Tunics 76, 125
Turkey 70
Twelfth 124, 239, 241, 249
Twelfth Arcanum 124, 239, 241
Twelve 121, 124-125, 158-161, 167, 238-239, 243, 245-246, 251, 257, 287
Twenties 289
Twentieth 113, 120, 140
Twenty 103, 105-106, 108-109, 157, 185, 213, 263
Twenty-four 87-89
Twenty-seven 286
Twenty-two 277
Twice 186, 285
Two 9, 13, 17, 20, 27, 46, 50, 63-64, 79, 83, 98, 101, 107, 110, 121, 131, 139-141, 151-157, 161-162, 165, 167, 169-175, 190-191, 215, 220, 237-238, 241, 253, 263, 267-268, 270, 275, 282, 286
Two Beasts 169, 171, 173, 175
Two Witnesses 46, 79, 98, 151-157, 172, 190
Tyana 94
Tylo 10
Tyre 58, 286
Uncle Sam 113
Unclean 198-199, 207-208
Uncreated 41
Unction 53
Understand 1, 15, 169, 180, 217, 273, 282
Understanding 51, 94, 174, 284, 291
Understood 4, 7, 29, 121, 133, 283
Undines 247
Union 49, 124-125, 157, 243, 282-283, 285, 293
Unisexual 14
United States 9, 113, 178, 269
Unity 35, 106, 292
Universal 1, 6, 9, 11, 67, 104, 167, 196, 247, 257, 276, 279, 281-284, 287, 290-291, 295

Universal Flood 1, 6, 9, 11, 295
Universal Gnosticism 279, 282-284, 287, 290-291
Universal Solvent 167
Universe 2, 45, 69, 75, 77, 104-105, 238, 277, 287, 290, 292
University 289
University of Berlin 289
University of Mexico City 289
Unveiled 132
Urania 160, 167
Urania-Venus 166-168
Uranus 263-264
Uriel 129, 133, 185, 193
Uterine 59
Uterus 49-50, 59, 76, 124, 148, 157, 243
Uxoricides 189
Vagina 125, 181, 215, 238, 283
Vaivasvata 5, 20, 292, 295-296
Vaivasvata Manu 5, 20, 292, 295-296
Vajra 283
Vajradhara 283
Valentine 281
Valley 89, 119, 122, 153, 191, 281
Valleys 180
Valour 292
Value 259, 280
Values 179
Vanity 294
Vapor 209
Vashat 293
Vasitvan 94
Vatican 209
Vau 141, 246, 248
Vayu 69, 198
Vedas 288
Vegetable 285
Vehicle 221, 223, 295
Vehicles 54, 88-89, 98, 238, 246, 249, 251, 257
Veil 23, 29, 58, 119, 242
Veins 113
Velocity 268
Velvet 33
Venerable 39, 241, 281, 289
Venerable Masters 289
Venom 217
Venus 2, 133, 156, 160, 167
Venus-Eve 167
Venus-Urania 161, 167
Venustic 54, 60, 62, 72-73, 126, 159, 260
Verb 43, 62, 80, 192, 214-215, 223, 280, 285, 290
Vertebra 244
Vertebrae 58, 244, 246
Vessel 210
Vessels 72, 172, 194, 210
Vesture 64, 214-215, 288-289
Vestures 80
Vial 189, 192-194, 198, 200
Vials 108, 185, 187-189, 191, 193, 195, 197, 199, 201, 203, 236
Vibrate 81, 237
Vibrated 82
Vibrating 64, 237
Vibration 68, 266
Vibrations 4
Vices 89, 189
Victims 146, 272, 276
Victorious 75, 163, 187
Victoriously 145, 187, 228
Victory 125, 187
View 273, 284
Vigil 256
Vigilance 110
Vigilant 91, 122, 202
Village 288
Villains 179, 200
Vine 182
Violence 123, 211, 255, 274
Violent 27, 290
Violently 11, 146
Violet 39
Vipers 19, 210
Virgil 21
Virgin 159-162, 165, 227-228, 241, 290
Virgin Mother 160-161, 228
Virgin Mothers 162, 165
Virginal 68
Virgins 34, 80, 147, 149, 161, 167, 177

Virile 216
Virili 125, 181, 238
Virtue 57, 180, 272, 284, 288
Virtues 57, 66, 70, 97, 244, 249, 256
Virtuous 180
Virtutis 79, 284
Virus 271-272
Viruses 271-272
Visceras 2
Vishnu 34, 37, 280, 288
Vishnu Purana 288
Vision 18, 143, 147
Visions 18, 83, 90, 281
Vital 17, 39, 104, 221, 282, 294
Vital Body 221, 294
VITRIOL 184, 187, 238
Vivified 268
Vivifies 180
Vivify 247
Vivifying 219, 267
Vocalization 237
Vocalize 82, 237
Vocalized 81, 236, 253
Vocalizes 237
Vocalizing 81, 237
Vocation 284
Voice 33, 35, 37, 39-40, 43, 59, 68-69, 74, 76-77, 92, 103, 108-109, 114-115, 120, 126, 135, 141, 145-146, 154, 163, 177-179, 181, 189, 200, 207, 211, 213, 223, 235, 237, 253, 279
Voices 27, 69, 103, 131, 135, 145, 156-157, 200
Volcanic 11
Volcanoes 19, 135
Voluntary 51
Voluptuousness 149
Vow 180
Vowel 81-82
Vowels 80-82, 159, 191, 236
Vows 293
Vulcan 58, 126, 192, 215, 248, 250
Vulgar 65
Vultures 71, 115, 139-140, 143, 157, 207, 209
Vulva 216, 248

Wailing 119, 210
Wailing Wall 119
Wakefulness 293
Walls 45
War 17, 24-25, 27, 29, 71, 113-115, 139-140, 143, 153, 157, 162-163, 168, 170, 173, 199, 206-207, 209-210, 214, 220, 224, 279, 288, 292
Warmed 247
Warn 23
Warned 5, 250
Warning 116, 223, 226
Warnings 226
Warrior 105
Warriorlike 113
Warriors 8, 113
Wars 2, 4, 17, 27, 114, 116, 143, 165, 193-194, 202, 224
Wash 123, 180-181, 256, 281
Washed 39, 126
Waste 16, 50, 65, 85, 274
Wasted 274
Wasting 104, 274
Watch 78, 105, 122, 284
Watched 279
Watcher 186, 195
Watcheth 199
Watchful 78
Watching 195, 200-201
Water 3, 5-6, 9, 15, 20, 29, 49-50, 58, 69, 73, 80-81, 98, 123, 127, 135, 141, 147-149, 152, 162, 165, 171-172, 180, 190, 198, 201, 221, 235-236, 242, 246-248, 256, 260, 263, 282
Water Carrier 9, 263
Waters of Life 42, 59, 104-105, 127, 148, 171-172, 192, 253, 255-257, 259-261
Weddings 34
Weed 110
Weeks 29
Weep 108, 209
Weeping 192, 210, 222
Weighed 171
Weighs 120, 128

Weight 94-95, 202, 287
Weor 21, 30, 221, 280, 283, 285, 287, 289-290, 293, 295
Wept 108
West 26, 114, 140, 163, 239, 293
Whale 154
Wheat 114, 210
Wheel 53, 60-61, 121, 155, 160, 169, 185, 205-206
Wheels 47, 81
Whip 122, 256
Whips 67-68, 123
White 27-28, 43, 49, 61, 66, 78, 80, 89, 91, 98, 103, 113, 115, 120-121, 123, 125-126, 152, 162, 181-182, 187, 213-214, 248, 250, 256, 264, 285-286, 288
White Fraternity 264
White Lodge 120-121, 162, 182, 250, 256
White Tantrism 285
Whiten 126
Whiteness 59, 71, 88
Whore 203-206, 209, 213
Whoremongers 236, 260
Widow 209
Wife 213, 236, 250, 295
Willpower 4, 47, 50, 79, 197, 221, 253, 285-286, 294
Wind 117, 120, 246, 287
Window 88
Winds 18, 69, 120, 128, 141, 246
Wine 49-50, 58, 65, 69, 78-79, 85, 104-105, 114, 147-148, 178, 201, 203, 207, 210
Winepress 182-183, 215, 289
Wings 18, 50, 104-105, 129, 140, 165, 167
Winter 1-2, 161, 287
Wisdom 11, 13, 34, 43, 66, 71, 85, 88-89, 92, 103, 109, 111, 116, 126, 174, 186, 197, 205, 217, 220, 235, 242, 244-245, 249-250, 272, 277, 280-281, 291, 295

Wise 12, 61, 63, 73, 116, 180, 182, 185, 198, 219, 252, 264, 267, 282, 286
Witchcraft 186, 211
Witness 39, 81, 91, 131, 231
Witnesses 19, 46, 79, 98, 151-157, 172, 190
Wives 189
Wolf 200
Woman 28, 41, 49-50, 59, 63, 70, 77, 80-81, 84, 105, 107-108, 141, 149, 155, 158-163, 165-168, 182, 185, 203, 205-206, 215-216, 221-222, 226, 241, 248, 254, 283, 295
Womb 14, 63, 124, 129, 159, 243, 248, 251
Women 4-5, 15, 20, 40, 59, 69, 132, 140, 165, 167, 177, 189, 195, 198, 241, 292-293, 295
Wood 71, 143, 194, 210, 215
Wool 43
Word of God 115, 214, 231, 288
World Wars 17, 27
Worldly 23, 174, 292
Worldly Salvation Army 23
Worm 282
Worms 99, 282
Wormwood 133-134
Worship 12, 84, 106, 110, 143, 151, 170, 172-173, 178, 187, 189, 214, 229-230, 258-259, 283, 295
Worshipers 282
Worshipped 61, 109, 126, 131, 157, 170, 189, 213, 224, 231
Worshipping 20
Worships 170
Wrath 118, 134, 146, 157, 163, 178, 182, 185, 188-189, 201, 207, 215, 227, 289, 292, 294
Yankees 113
Yellow 114
Yesod 103
Yin 37
Yod 284
Yoga 220-221, 241, 245, 285

Yogi 95, 181, 220-221, 244, 285
Yogi of Benares 95
Yoke 53
Yoni 57
Youth 29, 39, 222
Youthful 41
Youths 147
Yucatan 8
Yuga 3, 11, 19, 169-170, 288, 296
Zabulon 124
Zachariah 172
Zacharias 46
Zachariel 129, 141, 185, 198
Zanoni 41, 216-217
Zapotecs 8
Zealous 91
Zodiac 87, 103, 124, 213
Zodiacal 1, 4, 7, 9-10, 19, 87, 106, 121, 124, 191, 215, 238-239, 251
Zodiacal Course 215
Zoroaster 152
Zoroastrians 288

To learn more about Gnosis, visit gnosticteachings.org

Glorian Publishing (formerly Thelema Press) is a non-profit publisher dedicated to spreading the sacred universal doctrine to suffering humanity. All of our works are made possible by the kindness and generosity of sponsors. If you would like to make a tax-deductible donation, you may send it to the address below, or visit our website for other alternatives. If you would like to sponsor the publication of a book, please contact us at 212-501-6106 or help@gnosticteachings.org.

Glorian Publishing
PMB 192, 18645 SW Farmington Rd., Aloha OR 97007 USA
Phone: 212-501-6106 · Fax: 212-501-1676

VISIT US ONLINE AT:

gnosticbooks.org
gnosticteachings.org
gnosticradio.org
gnosticschool.org
gnosticstore.org
gnosticvideos.org

If you enjoyed this book, you may also be interested in:

THE DOOMED ARYAN RACE
GNOSIS, THE GLOBAL CRISIS, AND THE NEED TO AWAKEN CONSCIOUSNESS

> "It is impossible to deny that we presently live in moments of global crisis..."

Samael Aun Weor analzyes the wide range of catastrophic problems now afflicting our planet, then proceeds to explain the cause and effect relationship these problems have with the psyche of this humanity. Far from a "doom and gloom" speech, this book instead presents a radical solution that any person can apply to their own life in order to initiate powerful change. The solution is the long sought after mystery of Tantra and its ability to transform the consciousness.

> "Only on the path (based on tremendous, intimate super-efforts within ourselves) is it possible to develop all the marvelous, hidden potentialities of the human being."

Pages: 268
ISBN: 978-1-934206-30-0
Price: $17 (US)

Books by Samael Aun Weor

Aquarian Message
Aztec Christic Magic
Beyond Death
Book of the Dead
Book of the Virgin of Carmen
Christ Consciousness
Christ Will
Christmas Message 1964-1965 (aka The Elimination of Satan's Tail/The Dissolution of the I)
Christmas Message 1966-1967 (aka The Buddha's Necklace)
Christmas Message 1967-1968 (aka The Doomed Aryan Race / The Solar Bodies)
Christmas Message 1968-1969 (aka The Gnostic Magic of the Runes)
Christmas Message 1969-1970 (aka My Return to Tibet / Cosmic Teachings of a Lama)
Christmas Message 1971-1972 (Parsifal Unveiled)
Christmas Message 1971-1972 (The Mystery of the Golden Blossom)
Christmas Message 1972-1973 (The Three Mountains)
Christmas Message 1973-1974 (Yes, There is a Hell, a Devil, and Karma)
Christmas Message 1977-1978 (Treatise of Occult Medicine and Practical Magic, revised)
Cosmic Ships
Didactic Self-knowledge (Collected Lectures)
Dream Yoga - Writings on Astral Travel and Dreams
Esoteric Course of Alchemical Kabbalah
Esoteric Course of Theurgy
Esoteric Treatise of Hermetic Astrology
Esoteric Treatise of Theurgy
Flying Saucers
For the Few
Fundamental Notions of Endocrinology and Criminology
Fundamentals of Gnostic Education
Gazing at the Mystery
Gnosis in the Twentieth Century
Gnostic Anthropology
Gnostic Catechism
Grand Gnostic Manifesto 1972
Grand Gnostic Manifesto of the Third Year of Aquarius
Great Rebellion
Great Supreme Universal Manifesto of the Gnostic Movement
Igneous Rose
Initiatic Path in the Arcana of Tarot and Kabbalah
Introduction to Gnosis
Kabbalah of the Mayan Mysteries
Logos, Mantra, Theurgy
Magnum Opus
Major Mysteries
Manual of Practical Magic
Matrimony, Divorce and Tantrism
Metallic Planets of Alchemy
Mountain of Juratena
Mysteries of Christic Esoterism
Mysteries of Life and Death
Mysteries of the Fire: Kundalini Yoga
Perfect Matrimony, or The Door to Enter into Initiation
Perfect Matrimony - Kindergarten
Pistis Sophia Unveiled
Platform of POSCLA
Power is in the Cross
Revolution of Beelzebub
Revolution of the Dialectic
Revolutionary Psychology
Secret Doctrine of Anahuac
Secret Notes of a Guru
Seven Words
Social Christ
Social Transformation of Humanity
Supreme Christmas Message 1965-1966 (The Science of Music)
Supreme Christmas Message 1967-1968
Treatise of Occult Medicine and Practical Magic
Treatise of Sexual Alchemy
Universal Charity
We'll Reach the One Thousand, But Not the Two Thousand
Yellow Book
Zodiacal Course

Visit gnosticbooks.org for more information.